THE STRUGGLE FOR THE AMERICAN CURRICULUM 1893–1958

THE STRUGGLE FOR THE AMERICAN CURRICULUM 1893–1958

HERBERT M. KLIEBARD
Professor of Education
University of Wisconsin-Madison

Routledge & Kegan Paul
New York and London

Published in 1987 by
Routledge & Kegan Paul
29 West 35 Street
New York, NY 10001

11 New Fetter Lane
London EC4P 4EE

First published in 1986 by Routledge & Kegan Paul

Printed in the USA

Library of Congress Cataloging in Publication Data

Kliebard, Herbert M.

The struggle for the American curriculum, 1893-1958.
Bibliography: p.
Includes index.
1. Education—United States—Curricula—History—
20th century.   2. Curriculum planning—United States—
History—20th century.   3. Education—United States—
Curricula—History—19th century.   4. Curriculum
planning—United States—History—19th century.
5. Dewey, John, 1859-1952.   I. Title.
LB1570.K585   1986   375′.00973   85-11744

ISBN 0-7102-0055-2
ISBN 0-7102-1363-8

British Library CIP data also available

To Bernice

CONTENTS

ILLUSTRATIONS

between pages 270 and 271

PREFACE

In a recent review of two historical studies in education, Carl Kaestle (in press), commenting on one of them, remarked that it "moves beyond the two competing models of interpretation that have shaped debates for the past fifteen years." He went on to describe these two competing schools of thought as to the course of education in the United States:

> School systems exemplify democratic evolution, said the traditionalists. No, responded the radical revisionists, school systems illustrate the bureaucratic imposition of social control on the working class. Recently, some historians have emphasized that public school systems are the result of contests between conflicting class and interest groups.

Although I did not chance on the review until I had substantially completed this book, I realized that Kaestle expressed in that last school of thought almost precisely what I had been attempting. I had been actively following the development of the competing schools of thought in the twentieth century and invariably came away with the feeling that they were both faulty. They were both right as well, but simply saying that the main thrust of American education in the twentieth century lay between the two was hardly persuasive. What I sought was a way of expressing the nature of the forces that eventually determined the result of the conflict.

Actually, I had seriously entertained the idea of writing a history of the modern curriculum in the United States for several years and had published perhaps a couple of dozen articles on the subject. I think I can reconstruct pretty accurately what prompted my initial interest in this subject. First, I was bothered by the imbalance in historical studies in education. A great deal of attention has been lavished on the question of who went to school but relatively little on the question of what happened once all those children and youth walked inside the schoolhouse doors. In a sense, reluctance to tackle that kind of question is understandable; it would be a formidable task to try to answer it in the contemporary context. Trying to address that question, even in the recent past, means drawing interpretations from grossly incomplete evidence. Regrettably, it often means making inferences from the statements of leading figures in the educational world rather than from classroom documents and reports of participants.

On the other hand, it is not inconceivable, to say the least, that certain major statements on key subjects reflected what was actually going on. Throughout my writing of this volume, I tried to treat those documents, usually issued by major leaders in education or by national committees, not as influencing the course of events, but as artifacts of a period from which one might be able to reconstruct what was actually happening in the teaching of school subjects. Apart from the question of whether any of the ideas presented were worthwhile (and in a few cases I think they were), those statements represented for me a kind of weather vane by which one could gauge which way the curriculum winds were blowing. One important rule of thumb I tried to follow in this matter, however, was to assume from the outset that statements by leading proponents of curriculum reform movements were invariably far more ambitious and grandiose than one could possibly expect in practice. For example, most statements issuing from the leaders of the activity movement argued for their version of the curriculum as the major part or even the whole of what children would study in school. We all know that that did not happen except in the case of isolated experimental schools. But this does not mean that the impact of the activity movement was not felt in school practice. To the extent that those ideas were incorporated in the public schools generally, they tended to appear within the existing framework of the curriculum. Something like the activity curriculum, in other words, became visible within the context, say, of social studies or English. The subject organization of the curriculum, by and large, persisted, but within that framework there were internal changes reflecting the influence of the major reform movements. In some cases, this may have led certain historians to underestimate the impact of curriculum reform in the twentieth century. The labels that we give to the school subjects do not tell the whole story since those labels do not nearly reflect the diversity that actually exists in terms of curriculum practice.

Secondly, I was frankly puzzled by what was meant by the innumerable references I had seen to progressive education. The more I studied this the more it seemed to me that the term encompassed such a broad range, not just of different, but of contradictory, ideas on education as to be meaningless. In the end, I came to believe that the term was not only vacuous but mischievous. It was not just the word "progressive" that I thought was inappropriate but the implication that something deserving a single name existed and that something could be identified and defined if we only tried. My initial puzzlement turned to skepticism, my skepticism to indignation and finally to bemusement. As I hope readers of this book will discover, I came to the conclusion that there was not one but several reform movements in education during the twentieth century each with a distinct agenda for action. Delineating the main ideological positions of the various interest groups and the way they balanced as well as contradicted one another became my main task. In other words, I felt that the evolution of the modern American curriculum could be interpreted in terms of the interplay among the predominant interest groups that saw in the course of study the vehicle for the expression of their ideas and the accomplishment of their purposes.

The main actors in this story, then, are the leaders of the

various interest groups, but their ideas must be seen against the backdrop of the hard realities, not only of school practice and the bureaucratic structure of schooling in this country, but the political and social conditions of the time. All of this cannot be given equal weight, of course, and center stage is given over to the battle among competing ideas about the curriculum of American schools. In making this decision, I was hoping that, if nothing else, the book would serve to clarify those ideas and their implications and thereby help identify and explicate the curricular options that we have inherited from our professional forebears.

One issue that presented itself almost immediately was how to treat the towering figure of John Dewey. Although I had been a student of Dewey's work for almost all my professional life, I found myself puzzled as to where he belonged in the context of the interest groups I had identified. I decided in the end that he did not belong in any of them and that he should appear in the book as somehow hovering over the struggle rather than as belonging to any particular side. I suppose I should also confess to using Dewey's voice in some of the chapters as a way of commenting myself on how the battle was proceeding.

Before undertaking a major work, my dear friend and colleague, the late Edward A. Krug, liked to write an essay covering the major themes just to see if it would all hang together. I decided to try that this time. Once it was completed, however, it occurred to me that the essay might serve both as a first chapter and as a way of foreshadowing later developments in the story. Therefore, Chapter 1 of the present volume is both a beginning chapter and an introduction (or at least I intended it as such). It begins at the beginning (for my purposes the 1890s), but it also touches on themes and developments that are treated much more elaborately in subsequent chapters. All four of the central interest groups along with some of their major leaders and certain of their key ideas, for example, are introduced in Chapter 1, but a fuller treatment of the ways in which their ideas functioned to affect the evolution of the curriculum in American schools is discussed in later chapters.

Another problem that continually presented itself in the organization of this volume was that so many things were happening at once. In my attempt to deal with that, I decided against attempting a strict chronological rendering of the story. Thus, in the 1920s, scientific curriculum-making was at its zenith, but the movement that supported the activity curriculum was also rising to the fore. Rather than trying to tell both stories at once, I thought it best first to tell one story and then the other, hoping thereby to be reasonably coherent in telling each of them. That approach, however, was not without its cost, since I found it necessary to backtrack constantly into time periods that had already been treated in order to pick up another thread.

The 65-year span that is covered in the book encompasses a period of intense activity in curriculum matters – actually when curriculum reform emerged from somewhat tentative beginnings to become a national preoccupation. The seedbed for the period of intense interest in the curriculum was the 1890s with the Report of the Committee of Ten, published in 1893, being the single most significant event. But it was also the decade when the main lines of curriculum change were being drawn up and recognizable features of the various interest groups that were to do battle over the curriculum were becoming visible. Over the course of that period, each of the interest groups won its victories, but there were no unconditional surrenders or overwhelming triumphs. It is this ambiguous outcome of the struggle that accounts for much of the diversity in interpretation that has surrounded the course of American education in the twentieth century. The book ends with the passage of the National Defense Education Act of 1958, a massive entry by the federal government into curriculum matters that dramatically changed the political balance and the nature of the interplay among the protagonists in the struggle. The way in which the curriculum of American schools was determined was never quite the same after that.

ACKNOWLEDGMENTS

Of the conscious and conspicuous debts that I owe in the writing of this book, I should start with one that is over twenty years old. When I was a graduate student, very few people identified with the curriculum field exhibited any interest in history. The mood was one of "sweeping away the cobwebs of the past" as the basis for a total reconstruction of the course of study. Arno Bellack, my graduate advisor, was very much an exception. He not only encouraged my historical interests but possessed an astonishing knowledge of the roots of the American curriculum. His incredible insights into a wide variety of areas, even snatches of actual conversation, recur to me to this day. Over the years, Arno has continued to be not only my friend but my most important sounding board.

When I arrived at the University of Wisconsin, it was my great good fortune that there was a space shortage. (The School of Education was undergoing growing pains.) As a result, I was plunked into Edward Krug's basement office. I was, therefore, in daily interaction with a man whose sheer brilliance was, at that time, evident only to a happy few. Out of the corner of my eye, I was privileged to watch his monumental *Shaping of the American High School* in the making. It isn't often these days that one has the opportunity to learn a craft while sitting, literally, at the elbow of a master. Beyond the brilliance of his mind, Ed Krug's kindness is legendary, and I shall always be thankful to him for his readiness to provide gentle but astute criticism of my youthful endeavours and, of course, for his encouragement.

I am also deeply grateful to a great number of people for their assistance in the preparation of this manuscript. For their invaluable help in locating source documents, I would like to express my thanks to Dianne Bowcock, JoAnn Brown, Hsiao Chin-Hsieh, Sharon Keller, and George Stanic. Maria Dalupan deserves special commendation for her skill and dedication in accomplishing the tedious task of checking the accuracy of the numerous references, tracking down gaps that appeared in my original manuscript, and reviewing the final draft for errors.

Actual preparation of the final draft required assistance from more people than I can possibly acknowledge here. I owe special thanks to Joanne Foss and Sally Lanz for faithfully correcting the many errors that appeared in my original drafts. Other members of the office staff in both the Department of Curriculum and Instruction and the Department of Educational Policy Studies stood ready at short notice to provide whatever assistance I needed. Donna Schleicher supervised the preparation of the manuscript with her usual aplomb and good humor, thereby helping to preserve what sanity I had left. Colleagues such as Michael Apple, Carl Kaestle, and Gary Wehlage stood by in times of trial and offered support and encouragement.

I am grateful to the Graduate School of the University of Wisconsin, Madison, for granting me a semester's research leave, which permitted me to do the bulk of the research required to undertake the writing of this book. Research support from the John Dewey Society is also warmly appreciated.

The task of including a set of photographic plates turned out to be a much more formidable one than I ever imagined. For their assistance in obtaining some of the photographs that appear here, I would like to express my appreciation to Louisa Brown, Morris Library, Southern Illinois University; Stuart Campbell, Robert Hutchins Goddard Library, Clark University; Kenneth C. Cramer, Dartmouth College Library, Ruth Jones, University Archives, The Ohio State University Library; Robin McElheny University Archives, Harvard University Library; David M. Ment, Special Collections, Milbank Memorial Library, Teachers College, Columbia University; Warren E. Phillips, President, Dunwoodie Industrial Institute; Richard L. Popp, University of Chicago Library; and Myrna Williamson, State Historical Library of Wisconsin. Professor Craig Kridel of the University of South Carolina was especially helpful in providing me with leads in locating certain of the photographs that were included.

An abridged version of the first chapter was published earlier in *Educational Researcher.* Short segments of the manuscript were incorporated in articles I wrote for the 1984 and 1985 Yearbooks of the National Society for the Study of Education and the *Journal of Early Adolescence.*

CHAPTER 1

CURRICULUM FERMENT IN THE 1890S

i

At the heart of America's educational system in the nineteenth century was the teacher. It was the teacher, ill-trained, harassed and underpaid, often immature, who was expected to embody the standard virtues and community values and, at the same time, to mete out stern discipline to the unruly and dull-witted. But, by the 1890s, nineteenth-century society with its reliance on the face-to-face community was clearly in decline, and with the recognition of social change came a radically altered vision of the role of schooling. As cities grew, the schools were no longer the direct instruments of a visible and unified community. Rather, they became an ever-more critical mediating institution between the family and a puzzling and impersonal social order, an institution through which the norms and ways of surviving in the new industrial society would be conveyed. Traditional family life was not only in decline; even when it remained stable, it was no longer deemed sufficient to initiate the young into a complex and technological world.

With the change in the social role of the school came a change in the educational center of gravity; it shifted from the tangible presence of the teacher to the remote knowledge and values incarnate in the curriculum. By the 1890s, the forces that were to struggle for control of the American curriculum were in place, and the early part of the twentieth century became the battleground for that struggle.

Preoccupation with the curriculum did not, of course, appear suddenly full-blown. There had been signs earlier in the nineteenth century of a growing attention to what had become the course of study in American schools. From about 1800 to 1830, the monitorial method, an English export, had enjoyed a short-lived favor in cities like New York and Philadelphia, and the Lancastrian system, as it was sometimes called, required a careful breakdown of the course of study into standard units of work (Kaestle, 1973). Perhaps the most profound standardizing influence on the curriculum of nineteenth-century schools was the widespread use of popular textbooks such as the McGuffy reading series and the famous blueback spellers. Insofar as poorly educated teachers had to rely on such textbooks as the standard for what to teach, these books contributed to a growing nationalization of the curriculum. In Chicago, between 1856 and 1864, the superintendent of schools, William Harvey Wells, divided all students in the city into grades and established a distinct course of study for each subject at each grade level (Tyack, 1974, pp. 45–6). This early attention to curriculum was a portent of what, in the twentieth century, became a national preoccupation.

Although changes in American society were being wrought throughout most of the nineteenth century, public awareness of those changes seemed to reach crisis proportions in the 1890s. An acute public awareness of the social changes that had been taking place for some time were tied to such developments as a tremendous growth in popular journalism in the late nineteenth century, including both magazines and newspapers, and also the powerful influence created by the rapid advance of railroads as a means of relatively cheap and reliable transportation. Both these developments, in addition to the continued growth of cities, were significant factors in the transformation of American society from one characterized by relatively isolated self-contained communities into an urban, industrial nation. The decade of the 1870s, for example, was a period in which the sheer number of newspapers in America doubled, and by 1880 the *New York Graphic* published the first photographic reproduction in a newspaper, portending a dramatic rise in readership. Between 1882 and 1886 alone, the price of daily newspapers dropped from four cents per copy to one cent, due largely to the success enjoyed by Joseph Pulitzer's *New York World* (Mott, 1941, p. 508), and the introduction in 1890 of the first successful linotype machine promised even further growth. In 1872, only two American daily newspapers could claim a circulation of over 100,000, but, by 1892, seven more newspapers exceeded that figure (p. 507). A world beyond the immediate community was rapidly becoming visible.

But it was not newspapers alone that were bringing this new consciousness to Americans in the late nineteenth century. Magazines as we know them today began publication around 1882, and, in fact, the circulation of weekly magazines in America exceeded that of newspapers in the period that followed. By 1892, for example, the circulation of *Ladies Home Journal* had reached an astounding 700,000 (p. 507). Neither should book readership be ignored. Edward Bellamy's utopian and socialist-leaning novel, *Looking Backward*, sold over a million copies in 1888, giving rise to the growth of organizations dedicated to the realization of Bellamy's ideas. The printed word, unquestionably, was intruding on the insulation that had characterized American society in an earlier period.

Of at least equal importance to mass circulation journalism was the effect on American social life of the growth of railroads in the late nineteenth century. By 1880, the East and the Midwest had adopted four feet eight inches as the standard track gauge, but the overwhelming majority of the Southern track lines were five feet, and the Western states had lain very narrow track lines in the early 1880s. By 1883, however, leaders of the railroad industry had created the system of standardized time zones that we use today, and, by the end of that decade, most railroad track in the United States had become standardized.

In 1889, the United States already had 125,000 miles of

railroad in operation, whereas Great Britain had only about 20,000 miles and Russia 19,000. As Robert Wiebe (1967) has pointed out, "The primary significance of America's new railroad complex lay not in the dramatic connections between New York and San Francisco but in the access a Kewanee, Illinois, or an Aberdeen, South Dakota, enjoyed to the rest of the nation, and the nation to it" (p. 47). Like mass journalism, railroads were penetrating the towns and villages across the United States, creating not only new industries and new markets, but changing social attitudes and remaking our sense of what kind of world we were living in.

For a time, that social transformation seemed almost unacknowledged, or, in some cases, attributable to radical influences or other visible enemies. By the 1890s, however, the signs of change were unmistakable, although these signs were sometimes viewed with alarm and sometimes with approval. The population of the United States doubled in the last four decades of the nineteenth century due in large measure to the arrival of 14 million immigrants. Cities like Chicago grew enormously over that period, with that city reaching a million in population by 1900, a growth of about tenfold in forty years. Psychologically, the impending arrival of the twentieth century must itself have been one source of reflection and national soul-searching. Underneath the gaiety that, in popular terms, is supposed to have permeated the 1890s, there lay a profound psychic tension that made people wonder what kind of America was in the making. Surely, the panic of 1893 and the severe economic depression that followed were also occasions for deep concern and reflection. With the society in such a rapid state of flux, it should not be surprising that the matter of what we teach our children in school should also come under scrutiny.

The curriculum status quo in the 1890s was represented by the doctrine of mental discipline and its adherents. Although the roots of mental discipline as a curriculum theory go back at least as far as Plato's notion that the study of geometry was a way to improve general intelligence, its nineteenth-century version was derived most directly from the eighteenth-century German psychologist, Christian Wolff (1740), who laid out a carefully detailed hierarchy of faculties that was presumed to comprise the human mind. Mental disciplinarians built on that psychological theory by alleging that certain subjects had the power to strengthen faculties such as memory, reasoning, will and imagination. Moreover, mental disciplinarians argued, certain ways of teaching these subjects could further invigorate the mind and develop these powers. Just as the muscles of the body could be strengthened through vigorous exercise, so the mental muscles, the faculties, could be trained through properly conceived mental gymnastics. Thus, they were able to elaborate a rather coherent and seemingly plausible way of addressing the persistent problems that had perplexed educators and philosophers for centuries. Such puzzling questions as what we should teach, what rules we should apply to the teaching of subjects, and even questions of balance and integration in the curriculum could be addressed simply, but effectively, through the analogy of mind and body. There was even assumed to be a natural order for the emergence of faculties, and if this order were followed, a defensible sequence in the curriculum could be enunciated. Moreover, the range of faculties presented a basis for defining the scope of the curriculum. Since neglect of any faculty meant atrophy, it became incumbent on educators to see to it that no imbalances were created in the curriculum by emphasizing subjects that developed some faculties and not others. An ideal education meant all-round mental fitness, not just the development of one or two mental muscles.

The most famous document of nineteenth-century mental disciplinarianism was the report of the Yale faculty in 1828, essentially an impassioned defense of traditional education and humanistic values in the face of possible intrusions by the natural sciences and practical subjects. The report recognized two main functions of education, "the *discipline* and the *furniture* of the mind" ("Original Papers," 1829, p. 300), that is, strengthening the powers of the mind (what we would today call developing the ability to think) and filling the mind with content (what we would today call the acquisition of knowledge and skills). The authors of the report, Yale President Jeremiah Day and Professor James K. Kingsley, a leading classical scholar, had no doubt that the former was by far the more significant function of education (as we would probably assert today), and, to them, this meant a reaffirmation of the curriculum they had been teaching all along ("Original Papers"). Greek, Latin and mathematics as well as belles lettres had, after all, in their experience, established their value, whereas some of the newer subjects, such as modern foreign languages, were unproven quantities. Thus, there was firm resistance to any tinkering with what appeared to be a sound and proven program of studies. By the end of the nineteenth century, the textbooks being written for the growing number of normal schools in the United States overwhelmingly adopted the mind-as-a-muscle metaphor as the basis for explaining to future teachers what they ought to teach and how they ought to go about it. As that metaphor became firmly established, the implicit injunction to think of the mind *as if* it were a muscle, began to lose its "as if" quality, and, to many teachers, the mind became quite literally a muscle (Turbayne, 1962).

To a large extent, the belief that the mind was in fact, or at least like, a muscle provided the backdrop for a regime in school of monotonous drill, harsh discipline and mindless verbatim recitation. This may very well have gone on anyway, since the poorly trained and often very young teachers undoubtedly were at a loss to do anything else, but mental discipline provided them with an authoritative justification for continuing to do it. Anecdotal accounts of school life in the nineteenth and early twentieth centuries attest to the fact that, with few exceptions, schools were joyless and dreary places. In 1913, for example, a factory inspector, Helen M. Todd, decided to find out from the child laborers themselves whether they would prefer to go back to school rather than remain in the squalor of the factories. Todd systematically asked 500 children in these factories whether they would choose to work or go to school if their families were reasonably well-off and they did not have to work. Of the 500, 412 told her, sometimes in graphic terms, that they preferred factory labor to the monotony, humiliation and even sheer cruelty that they experienced in school. These children, it would seem, did not choose the sweatshops of Chicago strictly out of economic necessity. To some extent, the schools around the turn of the century drove them there. With a reevaluation of America's social institutions in the air, it was no wonder that the doctrine that had become identified with existing conditions in the public schools should come under critical scrutiny.

By the 1890s visible cracks were becoming apparent in the walls of mental discipline. As a theory of curriculum, after all, it represented a curious and not very stable compromise. If, indeed, the mind were really like a muscle and could be strengthened by exercise, why could not we exercise it on a wide variety of different subjects rather than the restricted set that was customarily prescribed? Why even could not a faculty like memory be developed through exercise with nonsense syllables? The theory of faculty psychology had merged with the nineteenth-century version of the liberal arts, forming a shaky coalition that served to perpetuate a time-honored literary curriculum. The question emerging in many people's minds was whether a curriculum that has its origins in the courtly life of Renaissance Europe was appropriate to the demands of the new industrial society. Although the demise of mental discipline is often associated with its failure to survive the test of empirical verification, first by William James (1890, pp. 666–7) and later by several experiments conducted by Edward L. Thorndike (Thorndike and Woodworth, 1901; Thorndike, 1924), the collapse of mental discipline and the effort to restructure the schooling that was associated with it was most directly a consequence of a changing social order which brought with it a different conception of what knowledge is of most worth.

Although lags between what knowledge a society values and what knowledge gets embodied in the curriculum of its schools are not uncommon, it is hard to imagine a culture in which the knowledge deemed to be valuable for whatever reason does not find its way into what is taught deliberately to the young of that society. This holds true whether it be knowledge of how to hunt in a society sustained by hunting animals or the study of Latin as a rite of initiation into a special class or sex education in a society where unwanted pregnancies have become a source of national concern. The route between the knowledge a society values and its incorporation into the curriculum becomes infinitely more tortuous, however, where we take into account the fact that different segments in any society will emphasize different forms of knowledge as most valuable for that society. Rarely is there universal agreement as to which resources of a culture are the most worthwhile. The practical knowledge of how to hunt animals must somehow be reconciled with a knowledge of the myths of the tribe; a knowledge of Latin declensions must be weighed against linguistic competence and literary traditions indigenous to the culture; and sex education must be seen against a backdrop of conflicting moral and religious values. Hence, at any given time, we do not find a monolithic supremacy exercised by one interest group; rather we find different interest groups competing for dominance over the curriculum and, at different times, achieving some measure of control depending on local as well as general social conditions. Each of these interest groups, then, represents a force for a different selection of knowledge and values from the culture and hence a kind of lobby for a different curriculum.

In the 1890s, not only do we see the theory of mental discipline starting to unravel as a consequence of increased awareness of a social transformation, but we see beginning to gel the interest groups that were to become the controlling factors in the struggle for the American curriculum in the twentieth century. One immediate impetus for change came as a consequence of a massive new influx of students into secondary schools beginning around 1890. In 1890, only between 6 and 7 percent of the population of youth fourteen to seventeen years old was attending secondary school. By 1900, it was already over 11 percent, and in 1920, about a third of that age-group was enrolled in secondary schools. By

1930, the number had reached almost four and a half million, over 51 percent of that population. It is difficult to establish precisely what created this sudden interest in secondary education on the part of American youth. To some extent, it may have been related to the growth of the American common school in the three or four decades preceding 1890 which created a new population whose children were ready to enter upon a secondary education. In addition, technological changes, such as the use of the telephone, affected the ability of early adolescents to find employment. (A ready source of jobs, for example, has been as a messenger.) A technological unemployment among teenagers, in a sense, left them with nothing better to do than to go to high school (Troen, 1976). To a large extent, also, clerical jobs requiring higher levels of training were consistently better paying than manual labor in this period, making attendance in high school a worthwhile investment. In addition, the clustering of a larger segment of the American population into cities made attendance in high schools simply more convenient. Evidently, the social changes that were becoming increasingly visible in the 1890s were serving to focus new attention on the institution of schooling. Certainly, the dramatic rise in secondary school enrollments could not long go unnoticed. In particular, it raised the question as to whether the curriculum that had been so ardently defended in the Yale report and had remained essentially intact ever since could continue to serve a new population of students and, for all intents and purposes, a new society.

ii

Although the National Education Association's Committee of Ten was appointed in 1892 originally to deal with another issue, the rather mundane problem of uniform college entrance requirements, their work and their recommendations were inevitably affected by the curricular implications of the growing demand by adolescents and their parents for a secondary school education. The immediate impetus for creating the Committee in the first place was that high school principals had been bewailing the fact that different colleges were prescribing different entrance requirements and, since about half of the high school graduating classes went on to college (Krug, 1962), it became exceedingly difficult to prepare so many students differently depending on their choice of college. While this in itself was a problem of considerable practical importance, almost inevitably it became imbedded in broader matters of principle, such as the extent to which a single curriculum, or type of curriculum, would be feasible or desirable in the face, not only of larger numbers of students, but, more importantly, of what was often perceived to be a different type of student.

When Charles W. Eliot, the patrician president of Harvard University, was appointed chairman of the National Education Association's Committee of Ten, it was recognition of the great influence he had exercised not only in higher education but in elementary and secondary schools as well. Eliot had been active in the National Education Association and was in demand as a speaker for local and regional teacher associations. His appointment also symbolically indicates his leadership, at least for this period, of one of four major interest groups that were to vie for control of the American curriculum in the twentieth century. Eliot, for a time at least, was in the forefront of the *humanist* interest group which, though largely unseen by professional educators in later periods, continued to exercise a strong measure of control over the American curriculum.

 Eliot, a humanist in his general orientation, was also a mental disciplinarian, but, although this commitment affected his thinking on curriculum matters to a large extent, Eliot was not exactly a defender of the status quo in curriculum matters. His reputation as an educational reformer extended beyond his espousal of the elective system at Harvard to his recommendations for reform at the elementary and secondary levels. In an article written in the same year that he was appointed to head the Committee of Ten, for example,

Eliot (1892b) argued that "there has been too much reliance on the principle of authority, too little on the progressive and persistent appeal to reason" (pp. 425–6) and that "no amount of *memoriter* study of languages or of the natural sciences and no attainments in arithmetic will protect a man or woman . . . from succumbing to the first plausible delusion or sophism he or she may encounter" (p. 423). Eliot, essentially, was the champion of the systematic development of reasoning power as the central function of the schools, and he recognized that much of what transpired in schools was simply unrelated to that function. Undoubtedly drawing on his own background as a scientist, Eliot saw reasoning power as a process of observing accurately, making correct records of the observations, classification and categorization, and, finally, making correct inferences from these mental operations. It was with respect to these mental habits that Eliot thought the curriculum should be directed, adding, however, that the power to express one's thoughts "clearly, concisely, and cogently" (p.419) is also a critical task of schooling.

Eliot differed from most mental disciplinarians in that he thought that any subject, so long as it were capable of being studied over a sustained period, was potentially a disciplinary subject. This meant that he was not nearly as restrictive as other mental disciplinarians in curriculum matters and was consistent, of course, with his strong commitment to the elective principle at Harvard. That commitment represented a sharp break with a tradition in higher education of rigidly prescribed curricula as exemplified in the Yale curriculum. Eliot's support for electivism in curriculum matters extended as far down as the later elementary grades. In a sense, although Eliot did not emphasize education for the purpose of direct social reform, he remained an optimist with respect to human capabilities. The right selection of subjects along with the right way of teaching them could develop citizens of all classes endowed in accordance with the humanist ideal – with the power of reason, sensitivity to beauty, and high moral character. To those skeptics who pointed to great individual variation in native endowment, Eliot's response, essentially, was that "we Americans habitually underesti- mate the capacity of pupils at almost every stage of education from the primary school through the university" and that, for example, "the proportion of grammar school children incap- able of pursuing geometry, algebra and a foreign language would turn out to be much smaller than we now imagine" (Eliot, 1892a, pp.620–1).

When the Committee of Ten published its report early in 1893, it bore Eliot's unmistakable stamp although, here and there, some compromise was evident. Eliot, for example, had to settle for a choice of four different courses of study in the high school rather than the system of electives that he would undoubtedly have preferred. Here was the measure of uni- formity in the high school curriculum that the school adminis- trators had been seeking. Colleges were expected to accept any of the four as a basis of admission. But on the question of dividing the school population according to the criterion of who was going to college and who was not, the Committee was firm and unanimous. There would be no curricular distinction between those students who were preparing for college and those who were preparing for "life," a position entirely consistent with the doctrine of mental discipline, as was the stand taken by the Committee that the subjects should not be taught differently to different population groups. All students, the Committee reasoned, regardless of destination, were entitled to the best ways of teaching the various subjects. What is more, education for life, they maintained, *is* education for college, and the colleges should accept a good education for life as the proper preparation for the rigors of college studies (National Education Association, 1893).

iii

Eliot's report was greeted with much approbation, but also some sharp criticism, mainly on the ground that the Commit- tee had not attuned itself sufficiently to the changing nature of the school population. Undoubtedly, the most powerful of the critics and surely one of the most vocal, was the person who had early on assumed unquestioned leadership of the child-study movement in the United States, G. Stanley Hall. Hall is the pivotal figure in the second of the four interest groups seeking to influence the curriculum at the turn of the century, the *developmentalists*, who proceeded basically from the assumption that the natural order of development in the child was the most significant and scientifically defensible basis for determining what should be taught. The child-study movement was one outgrowth of the new status accorded science in the latter part of the nineteenth century and consisted, to a large extent, of research that involved the careful observation and recording of children's behavior at various stages of development.

Coincidentally, it was Eliot who had invited Hall to deliver lectures on pedagogy at Harvard in 1880, and that appointment led eventually to Hall's first major research in child-study, an article entitled "The Contents of Children's Minds" (1883). As the title indicates, Hall's study consisted essentially of an inventory of the contents of children's minds. Presumably, if we knew what was already in there, we could proceed much more systematically in determining what ought to be taught in school. Reflecting his own distinctly mystical reverence for rural life (he once claimed that he liked to take off his clothes and roll naked in the fields of his native Massachusetts), Hall tried to discover what children really knew about animals and plants. Did they know what a plough was? Or a spade? Or a hoe? Did a city child really have any notion of what a pond was or the distinction between a river and a brook? Did they know the parts and organs of their own bodies? Could they identify a square or a circle? Hall concluded on the basis of his investigation that teachers assumed too much about the contents of children's minds – that a lot of Boston's schoolchildren did not know what a cow was or a hill or an island. Although Hall himself often enlivened these cold data with his distinctive penchant for myth and mysticism, his criticism of the position of the Committee of Ten was perceived by many as the voice of science and progress directed against an entrenched establishment barely courageous enough to put forward moderate reforms in the face of a monumental challenge to the efficacy of the existing curriculum.

Hall attributed to various National Education Association committees the growing tendency to count and measure everything educational. "Everything must count and so much for herein lies its educational value," he complained. "There is no more wild, free, vigorous growth of the forest, but everything is in pots or rows like a rococo garden" (Hall, 1904b, p. 509). Such uniformity, according to Hall, was at variance with the natural spontaneity that adolescents presumably exude: "The pupil is in the age of spontaneous variation which at no period of life is so great. He does not want a standardized, overpeptonized mental diet. It palls on his appetite" (p. 509).

When Hall focused specifically on the recommendations of the Committee of Ten, he asserted what he referred to as their "three extraordinary fallacies." The first was that all pupils should be taught in the same way and to the same extent, regardless of "probable destination." His charge that this was a "masterpiece of college policy" became the conventional wisdom about the Committee of Ten in the twentieth century. It was here that Hall referred to the "great army of incapables, shading down to those who should be in schools for the dullards or subnormal children" (Hall, 1904b, p. 510). The school population, presumably, was not so variable as to native endowment that a common curriculum was simply unworkable. Hall's second objection was to the assertion that all subjects were of equal educational value if taught equally well. He could "recall no fallacy that so completely evicts content and enthrones form" (p. 512). For mental disciplinarians, such as those that comprised the Committee, the form of the subject was what conveyed its disciplinary value; the content was, after all, only the "furniture." Here, Hall was rejecting that fundamental assumption. Finally, Hall saw "only mischief" in the doctrine that "fitting for college is essentially the same as fitting for life" (p. 512). In this last charge, Hall was subtly turning the Committee's recommendation on its head. They had argued that fitting for life was the same as fitting for college. They felt they had designed an appropriate curriculum for life and were asking colleges to accept that curriculum as the basis for admission. To Hall, however, this was just part of the strategy that the Committee had used to impose college domination on the high school curriculum. In responding to these charges, Eliot reiterated his optimism in the power of human intelligence and reason. He rejected, for example, the notion that there was a "great army of incapables" invading the schools of the 1890s, contending instead that the actual number of "incapables" were "but an insignificant proportion" of the school population. Also, in a statement that has a peculiarly modern ring, Eliot foresaw the possibility that a differentiated curriculum could have the effect of determining the social and occupational destinies of students, rather than reflecting their native propensities and capacities: "Thoughtful students of . . . *psychology of adolescence* will refuse to believe that the American public intends to have its children sorted before their teens into clerks, watchmakers, lithographers, telegraph operators, masons, teamsters, farm laborers, and so forth, and treated differently in their schools according to those prophecies of their appropriate life careers. Who are to make these prophecies?" (Eliot, 1905, pp. 330–1). Here again, however, Hall proved to be more prescient in terms of emerging educational policy than was Eliot. Predicting future destination as the basis for adapting the curriculum to different segments of the school population became a major feature of curriculum planning in the decades ahead.

As the twentieth century progressed, the Committee of Ten became a kind of symbol of the failure of the schools to react sufficiently to social change and the changing school population and to the crass domination exercised by the college over the high school. The academic subjects that the Committee saw as appropriate for the general education of all students were seen by many later reformers as appropriate only for that segment of the high school population that was destined to go on to college. In fact, subjects like French and algebra came to be called college-entrance subjects, a term practically unknown in the nineteenth century. Even subjects like English became differentiated with standard literary works prescribed for those destined for college, while popular works and "practical" English were provided for the majority. Many of these curriculum changes reflected Hall's perception that the new population of high school students simply were incapable of pursuing the kind of curriculum that the Committee of Ten advocated.

Actually, however, the recommendations of the Committee of Ten represented a moderate departure from the traditional curriculum of the nineteenth century. The study of Greek was restricted to the Classical course and, even there, the amount of Greek was reduced from the traditional three years to two, and two of the four courses of study, the Modern Languages and the English, had no Latin requirement at all. While the Committee expressed the view that the Classical and the Latin-Scientific curricula were in some sense superior to the Modern Languages and the English, this was because the two former programs were better developed and had more experienced teachers, not because they were intrinsically better. The Committee hoped that the effect of their doctrine of the equivalence of school studies would eventually put modern academic subjects on a par with classical ones, at least in principle if not in actual practice. Where the Committee refused to compromise was in terms of the humanist ideal of a liberal education for all.

iv

In its time the Report of the Committee of Ten engendered so much lively controversy that, by 1895, another committee, unimaginatively called the Committee of Fifteen, was ready to report on the elementary school curriculum. Wearing the mantle of the humanist position this time was America's leading Hegelian, the powerful and articulate United States

Commissioner of Education, William Torrey Harris. (Superintendent of Schools William H. Maxwell of Brooklyn, New York, the Chairman of the Committee, divided the fifteen members into three subcommittees of five, each dealing with a different aspect of elementary education. As head of the subcommittee that was to deal with the correlation of studies, Harris was responsible for the curriculum portion of the Report.) As a highly regarded superintendent of schools in St Louis between 1869 and 1880, Harris had the practical experience that lent one sort of credence to his pronouncements; but he also was the editor of the *Journal of Speculative Philosophy*, the leading organ of American Hegelianism, and his scholarly reputation was considerable as well. Although he had been a member of the Committee of Ten, Harris took pains in his subcommittee report to disassociate himself from the mental discipline position, then beginning to decline (National Education Association, 1895). Instead, Harris tried to articulate a new rationale for a humanistic curriculum, not only in the report itself, but in his many articles and speeches at National Education Association conferences. Harris, perhaps more than Eliot, was sensitive to the social changes that were occurring all around him, but he maintained that a curriculum constructed around the finest resources of Western civilization was still the most appropriate and desirable for America's schools. Whatever may have been the magnitude of the transformation in America's social institutions or the alleged changes in character of the school population, his five "windows of the soul," as he liked to call them – grammar, literature and art, mathematics, geography and history – would remain the means by which the culture of the race would be transmitted to the vast majority of Americans. Somewhat suspicious of the rise of the natural sciences, Harris emerged as the great defender of humanistic studies in the curriculum. Although he embraced certain reform causes such as women's access to higher education, Harris earned a reputation as a conservative in educational policy through his lukewarm reaction to manual training (a cause that was meeting with almost universal approbation among leaders in education), his deep reservations about the virtues of child-study as a basis for determining what to teach (once referring to it as "so much froth") and as an outright opponent of specialized vocational training. In his view, the intrusion of new values by industrial society made it even more imperative that the school become a haven for the tried and true virtues he so deeply cherished. The common school for Harris was a specialized institution with a very distinct function to perform: the passing on of the great Western cultural heritage, leaving other institutions, the family, church and industry to perform theirs.

But, by 1895, the forces of opposition to the traditional humanist curriculum had grown in numbers and organization. At the same National Education Association meeting in Saratoga Springs, New York, in 1892 where the Committee of Ten was appointed, a group of American educational leaders, many of whom had studied in Germany and who thought of themselves as scientific in outlook, formed the National Herbart Society. Among them was a shy, thirty-three-year-old faculty member from the University of Michigan, John Dewey. Despite the fact that, like Hall, Dewey disagreed with the American Herbartian position on a number of fundamental matters (although for different reasons), Dewey probably saw the group as the most promising in terms of effecting change in what had become a stagnant, often repressive, American school system. Three years after its formation, at the 1895 meeting of the National Education Association in Cleveland, Ohio, the Herbartians felt ready for direct confrontation with the person they saw as the embodiment of conservatism and reaction, the United States Commissioner of Education. Although Herbartianism as a movement with a specific identification in American education had a rather short-lived heyday, beginning to decline as early as 1905, Herbartian ideas and reactions to their ideas continued to exercise a profound influence on the American curriculum long after the movement itself faded from existence as a distinct entity.

Leading the attack on Harris was the president of the

National Herbart Society, Charles DeGarmo. The details of the rather convoluted criticism of the Committee of Fifteen Report are not as important as the daring and the symbolism of the confrontation. Actually, much of the controversy revolved around the fact that Harris, in making his subcommittee Report on the Correlation of Studies in Elementary Education, had used key Herbartian terms, such as correlation and concentration, but not in the prescribed Herbartian manner. When reporting on the five major branches of study, for example, Harris, although he avoided this time using his own standard term for these branches, "the windows of the soul," clearly was making the case for each separately as an important study and not in their interrelationship to one another, a pivotal point in Herbartian curriculum theory. Harris used the term "correlation" to mean "correlating the pupil with his spiritual and natural environment" (National Education Association, 1895, pp. 40–1), but not to mean the interrelationship among the subjects themselves. When he used the Herbartian concept, "concentration," he used it only in the everyday sense that the work of the elementary school should be "concentrated" around the five coordinate groups of study that Harris had been advocating for years. Although there were some differences among themselves in their own use of the term, Herbartians usually used "concentration" to refer to the practice of using a particular subject, such as history or literature, as a focal point for all subjects, thereby achieving the unity in the curriculum they sought. Here and there, Harris seemed to go out of his way to attack Herbartian practice, such as their frequent use of *Robinson Crusoe* as a way of unifying all the studies in the third grade, Harris referring to it as "a shallow and uninteresting kind of correlation" (p. 84).

The reaction to Harris's report on the part of his battle-ready opponents was fierce. The first to plunge into the fray was Frank McMurry who, along with his brother Charles, were central figures in the Herbartian movement. McMurry used the example of "Egypt" as a way of showing how the various branches of the elementary school curriculum could be correlated around such a concept. Colonel Francis Parker, who had by this time earned a national reputation as an educational reformer, was only a fringe member of the Herbartian group, but he unequivocally made his sympathies clear, comparing Harris's report to "the play of Hamlet with Hamlet left out" ("Discussion," 1895, pp. 165). When DeGarmo took the floor, his criticism was also sweeping. He suggested that, contrary to the charge of the Committee, the Committee had not actually dealt with the correlation of studies. Harris, a skilled platform performer, defended himself vigorously, and, in the months that followed the confrontation, the debate continued with almost the same intensity in professional journals. The meeting in Cleveland became, in a sense, the Fort Sumter of a war that was to rage for most of the twentieth century. Whatever may have been the merits of the Herbartian criticism, the clash between Harris and the Herbartians marked the beginning of a realignment of the forces that were to battle for control of the American curriculum. The atmosphere at that 1895 meeting was so tense and the sense of drama so great that, thirty-eight years later, DeGarmo, at the age of eighty-five, was moved to write his friend Nicholas Murray Butler, "No scene recurs to me more vividly than on that immortal day in Cleveland, which marked the death of the old order and the birth of the new" (Drost, 1967, p. 178).

v

Another witness to that "immortal day" and critic of Harris's report was a young pediatrician who, by 1892, had essentially given up medicine to undertake a career as an educational reformer. Joseph Mayer Rice, like Hall, Parker and Dewey, was loosely affiliated with the American Herbartians, having left the country in 1888 to study at the great university centers of pedagogy in Germany. Having observed several school systems in Europe, Rice returned to the United States with a similar purpose in mind. In a tour sponsored by an influential journal, *The Forum*, Rice undertook a survey of American elementary education that lasted from January 7 to June 26 1892. A tireless worker, he travelled through thirty-six cities in that period, making careful observations of the schools and classrooms he visited. The result was a series of nine articles, published in *The Forum* from October 1892 to June 1893. Those articles created an immediate sensation, and, in 1893, they were collected in book form and published under the title, *The Public School System of the United States*, thereby reaching an even wider audience.

Rice's sense of outrage is present on almost every page. One passage from his observation of the lowest primary grade in a New York City school conveys his tone as well as his general findings:

> Before the lesson began there was passed to each child a little flag, on which had been pasted various forms and colors, such as a square piece of green paper, a triangular piece of red paper, etc. When each child had been supplied, a signal was given by the teacher. Upon receiving the signal, the first child sprang up, gave the name of the geometrical form upon his flag, loudly and rapidly defined the form, mentioned the name of the color, and fell back into his seat to make way for the second child, thus: "A square; a square has four equal sides and four corners; green" (down). Second child (up): "A triangle; a triangle has three sides and three corners; red" (down). Third child (up): "A trapezium; a trapezium has four sides, none of which are parallel, and four corners; yellow" (down). Fourth child (up): "A rhomb; a rhomb has four sides, two sharp corners and two blunt corners; blue." This process was continued until each child in the class had recited. The rate of speed maintained during the recitation was so great that seventy children passed through the process of defining in a very few minutes. (Rice, 1893a, p. 34)

If nothing else, Rice's survey conveys the sense of urgency that many reformers felt about what had become a largely lifeless system of schooling. But beyond that, Rice found some school systems, such as the one in Indianapolis, to be better than some others, and Rice was determined to find the secrets of their success. Rice initially shared with the developmentalists the idea that in scientific data on the child lay the key to the relatively successful classroom techniques as well as to a rational curriculum. But he also attacked superintendents of schools for their lack of knowledge of pedagogy and for the superficial attention they gave to what was really going on in classrooms. School boards, he thought, were also composed of unqualified people, usually political appointees. The public also was the subject of Rice's wrath. But, at least in terms of emphasis, it was the quality of teaching that seemed to Rice to be most responsible for the catastrophic state of American education. Many teachers, he contended, whose incompetence had been generally recognized, continued to teach year after year in the public schools.

Rice's first series of *Forum* articles met with almost violent public reaction. These articles began to appear, after all, a year before the generally acknowledged beginning of muckraking journalism (Curti, 1951). Teachers and school administrators rushed to their own defense, attacking Rice with almost hysterical intensity. Some criticism focused on his own lack of classroom experience (Schneider, 1893), some on his alleged misuse of English (Author, 1895, p. 295), and there was even a hint of anti-Semitism here and there in their replies (Author, 1894, p. 149). Professional educators appeared to be simply unused to such open and unrelenting attack. Theirs had been a life of relative invulnerability within the walls of their schools and classrooms.

Unrepentant, Rice undertook a second survey of American schools in the spring of 1893. Although he expressed interest in those school systems that were in the process of experimenting with new curricula, in fact, he focused almost entirely on gathering data on the achievement of third-graders in reading and arithmetic. Rice was seeking comparative data that would indicate why some schools and teachers were more successful than others in these subjects. In this respect, Rice is the acknowledged father of comparative methodology in educational research, a fact recognized by Leonard Ayres as early as 1918 (Engelhart and Thomas,

1966, p. 141). In particular, Rice's work in the teaching of spelling, which he began in 1895, was a monumental effort, involving initially some 16,000 pupils, designed to discover superior techniques of teaching spelling. When that test failed to accomplish that intention, apparently because some teachers, in administering the test, gave away answers through their careful enunciation, Rice, indefatigably, undertook another comparative study involving 13,000 more pupils, this time supervising the administration of each test himself. After all that work, Rice could only conclude that the amount of time spent in drill on spelling appeared unrelated to achievement on the part of the students, but the secret of how spelling should be taught remained a mystery.

When Rice's new series of *Forum* articles was collected into one volume in 1912, that book was entitled, significantly, *Scientific Management in Education*. Although there were still vestiges of Rice's concern for the child in the school environs, the major thrust of Rice's work had shifted from the monotony and mindlessness of school life to the themes of standardization and efficiency in the curriculum. Rice's genuine dismay and disgust of what was going on in American schools in the 1890s had evolved into a grim determination that teachers and administrators must be *made* to do the right thing. Supervision, for example, would take the form of seeing to it that the achievement of students reached a clearly defined standard (p. xvi), and school administration, generally, ought to be governed, Rice claimed, by "a scientific system of pedagogical management [that] would demand fundamentally the measurement of results in the light of fixed standards" (p. xiv). Such an interpretation of science applied to education and curriculum represented a fundamental departure from science in the interest of discovering the developmental stages through which a child passes. "The child's capital," Rice declared, "is represented by time; and whether certain results are to be lauded or condemned depends upon the amount of time expended in obtaining them" (p. 9). It is the job of the teacher to see to it that "this capital . . . be expended on sound economical principles, *i.e.*, without waste" (p. 9). Educational reform, Rice argued, revolved around a clear articulation of definite goals (pp. 24–5) and on finding the techniques of measurement that would reveal whether those results have been realized.

In slow but perceptible stages, Rice's position had evolved from outraged humanitarian to a zealot for the elimination of waste in the curriculum through the application of the kind of scientific management techniques that, presumably, has been so successful in industry. Almost against his will, Rice became the principal forerunner of the third of the major curriculum interest groups that was to appear just before the turn of the century: the *social efficiency educators*. Although the social ideas that were to characterize that group in the twentieth century are difficult to detect in Rice, Rice unquestionably reflected the version of science and the techniques of curriculum-making that were to become the trademark of that movement. Although it was a reform movement in most senses of that term, it proceeded from fundamentally different assumptions and pointed in different directions from the developmentalist interest group. With Hall and the developmentalists, Rice and his ideological heirs found common cause against the humanistic position that Eliot and Harris, for example, tried to articulate, but the social efficiency educators and the developmentalists ultimately were as far apart from one another as they were from their common enemy. Their bitter battles would be reflected in their professional writings, in their open debates at professional meetings, and in colleges and universities as curriculum issues and problems gained academic respectability and were formalized into courses and degree programs.

vi

Far from the center of National Education Association proceedings and the hallowed halls of academe where the battle lines for the American curriculum were being drawn, there labored a relatively obscure, largely self-taught, government botantist and geologist whose ideas were to emerge as the major challenge to what was rapidly becoming the established dogma in social theory. By 1883, Lester Frank Ward had somehow found the time in the midst of his paleobotanical work for the United States Geological Survey to produce a two-volume tome, *Dynamic Sociology*. Although himself strongly influenced by Darwinian theory, Ward took almost the opposite position on its application to society from the doyen of the new sociology, Herbert Spencer. Spencer's enormously successful lecture tour in the United States in 1882 and his widely read works in such journals as *Popular Science Monthly* had spread the message of Social Darwinism, and his disciples, such as William Graham Sumner at Yale, were promoting his ideas in American universities. Basically, they argued that the laws that Darwin had enunciated in terms of natural selection had their parallel in the social realm. Survival of the fittest, in other words, was a law, not only of the jungle, but of civilization, and the unequal distribution of wealth and power was simply the evidence of that law's validity.

By contrast, Ward's position was that, in the social realm, "there is no alternative but to renounce all effort and trust to the slow laws of cosmical evolution" (Ward, 1883, p. 153). The laissez-faire position that the Social Darwinists had advocated was, in Ward's view, a corruption of Darwinian theory because human beings had developed the power to intervene intelligently in whatever were the blind forces of nature, and in that power lay the course of social progress. Civilization, he argued, was not achieved by letting cosmic natural forces take their course, but by the power of intelligent action to change things for the better. For Ward, "If any moral progress is ever too [sic] be made other than that which would naturally be brought about by the secular influnce of cosmical laws, it must be the result of an *intellectual* direction of the forces of human nature into channels of human advantage" (p. 216). In many respects, Ward foreshadowed in his 1883 work significant elements of John Dewey's educational philosophy.

Critical to social progress, in Ward's mind, was a properly constructed and fairly distributed system of education. Ward liked to use the metaphor of legacy in connection with education, and he argued in *Dynamic Sociology* that social inequality was fundamentally a product of a maldistribution of the social inheritance. Like Eliot, Ward expressed great optimism about the power of human intelligence, asserting without equivocation that native endowment was equally distributed across social class lines as well as gender, and whatever the differences that could be observed in the human condition, they were directly attributable to that maldistribution. Unlike Eliot and the other humanists generally, however, Ward saw education as a direct and potent instrument of social progress.

Dynamic Sociology did not go unnoticed. Albion Small, for example, Dewey's respected colleague at the University of Chicago, declared several years after its publication that, "All things considered, I would rather have written *Dynamic Sociology* than any other book ever published in America" (Commager, 1967, p. xxvii). Nevertheless, on the first of January 1892, Ward resolved to embark on another ambitious project, and within about three months, *The Psychic Factors of Civilization* was nearly complete. Published in 1893, *Psychic Factors* became recognized as the most significant among Ward's voluminous writings. In it, Ward reiterated his attacks on "survival of the fittest" as a doctrine that had any application to the social world and welcomed intervention, particularly by government, in human affairs. The trouble with governmental intervention as it now exists, declared Ward, was that it was controlled by the wrong groups. The right sort of intervention would be accomplished once the influence of partisan pressure groups was eliminated and practical and humanitarian approaches to social problems were substituted.

Ward's commitment to egalitarianism was unequivocal. "The denizens of the slums," he said in *Psychic Factors*, "are not inferior in talent to the graduates of Harvard College" (p. 290). "Criminals," he argued, "are the geniuses of the slums. Society has forced them into this field, and they are making the best use they can of their native abilities" (p. 290). The key to progress and the great undertaking that lay before us was the proper distribution of cultural capital through a vitalized system of education.

In his *Psychic Factors*, as well as in his other works, Ward reveals himself, not only as the prophet of the welfare state in the twentieth century, but as the principal forerunner of the fourth and last of the major interest groups that were to battle for control of the curriculum in the decades ahead, the *social meliorists*. By the 1890s, Ward had already laid down the main outlines of the arguments that were to put education at the center of any movement toward a just society. To be sure, Ward's position on education was often taken to be a particularly American obsession. Spencer, for example, when asked to comment on America's future, declared, "It is a frequent delusion that education is a universal remedy for political evils" (Commager, 1967, p. xxxvii). Whether a practical faith or a popular delusion, it was a belief that Dewey and many American educators came to share in the twentieth century. Ward himself noted that the most perceptive review of *Psychic Factors* was Dewey's, and Dewey certainly believed that in education lay the key to social progress. While the possibility exists, of course, that Americans share an inordinate faith in the power of education to correct social evils and promote social justice, inordinate or not, it became a powerful force in the shaping of curriculum policy in the years ahead.

vii

When the twentieth century finally arrived, the four major forces that were to determine the course of the new American curriculum had already emerged. First, there were the humanists, the guardians of an ancient tradition tied to the power of reason and the finest elements of the Western cultural heritage. Although, in later years, the leaders of this interest group remained, for the most part, outside the professional education community, they exerted a powerful influence through their standing in the academic world and among intellectuals generally. To them fell the task of reinterpreting and thereby preserving as best as they could their revered traditions and values in the face of rapid social change.

Arrayed against this group were three different kinds of reformers, each representing a different conception of what knowledge should be embodied in the curriculum and to what ends the curriculum should be directed. Hall and the others in the child-study movement led the drive for a curriculum reformed along the lines of a natural order of development in the child. Although frequently infused with romantic ideas about childhood, the developmentalists pursued with great dedication their sense that the curriculum riddle could be solved with ever more accurate scientific data, not only with respect to the different stages of child and adolescent development, but on the nature of learning. From such knowledge, a curriculum in harmony with the child's real interests, needs and learning patterns could be derived. The curriculum could then become the means by which the natural power within the child could be unharnessed.

The second group of reformers, the social efficiency educators, were also imbued with the power of science, but their priorities lay with creating a coolly efficient, smoothly running society. The Rice exposés, begun in 1892, and impelled by genuine humanitarian motives, turned out to be a portent of a veritable orgy of efficiency that was to dominate American thinking generally in the decades ahead. In fact, efficiency, in later years, became the overwhelming criterion of success in curriculum matters. By applying the standardized techniques of industry to the business of schooling, waste could be eliminated and the curriculum, as seen by such later exponents of social efficiency as David Snedden and Ross Finney, could be made more directly functional to the adult life-roles that America's future citizens would occupy. People had to be controlled for their own good, but especially for the good of society as a whole. Theirs was an apocalyptic vision. Society as we know it was flying apart, and the school with a scientifically constructed curriculum at its core could forestall and even prevent that calamity. That vision included a sense that the new technological society needed a far greater specialization of skills and, therefore, a far greater differentiation in the curriculum than had heretofore prevailed.

Finally, there were the social meliorists as represented by one of their great early figures, Lester Frank Ward. Ward was the forerunner of the interest group that saw the schools as a major, perhaps the principal, force for social change and social justice. The corruption and vice in the cities, the inequalities of race and gender, and the abuse of privilege and power could all be addressed by a curriculum that focused directly on those very issues, thereby raising a new generation equipped to deal effectively with those abuses. Change was not, as the Social Darwinists proclaimed, the inevitable consequence of forces beyond our control; the power to change things for the better lay in our hands and in the social institutions that we create. Times indeed had changed, but, according to the social meliorists, the new social conditions did not demand an obsessional fixation on the child and on child psychology; nor did the solution lie in simply ironing out the inefficiencies in the existing social order. The answer lay in the power of the schools to create a new social vision.

The twentieth century became the arena where these four versions of what knowledge is of most worth and of the central functions of schooling were presented and argued. No single interest group ever gained absolute supremacy, although general social and economic trends, periodic and fragile alliances between groups, the national mood, and local conditions and personalities affected the ability of these groups to influence school practice as the twentieth century progressed. In the end, what became the American curriculum was not the result of any decisive victory by any of the contending parties, but a loose, largely unarticulated, and not very tidy compromise.

CHAPTER 2

THE CURRICULUM VERSUS THE CHILD

i

As the ideological battle lines in the struggle for the American curriculum were being drawn, there hovered above the fray the man who at the same time personified and transcended what was to become American education in the twentieth century. John Dewey was not a man who chose sides easily. The positions advanced by the major curriculum interest groups emerging in the 1890s did not so much present options from which he would choose as they represented the raw material from which he would forge his own theory of curriculum. It is, in all likelihood, this feature of Dewey's approach to educational issues that most accounts for the curious role that he was to play in twentieth-century American education. He found himself using the same language as his contemporaries, but he generally meant something considerably different and, while competing interest groups eagerly looked to him for support and leadership, Dewey's own position in critical matters of theory and doctrine actually represented a considerable departure from the main line of any of the established movements. As such, he is not so much a central figure in one or another of these groups as he is someone who synthesized and reinterpreted certain of their ideas, and, consequently, he became identified in a way with all of them. In the long run, Dewey's position in curriculum matters is best seen, not as directly allied to any of the competing interest groups, but as an integration and especially a reinterpretation of the ideas they were advocating.

Given the subtlety and complexity of that reconstruction, it is not surprising that his ideas were frequently perverted when attempts were made to translate them into practice and that only during the period between 1896 and 1904, when Dewey himself undertook to test his theory by establishing the Laboratory School at the University of Chicago, do we get a fair picture of how his curriculum would work in practice. The Dewey School is without doubt a significant chapter in the annals of pedagogical history, but mainly because of the integrity of the theory that guided it and because it became a symbol of school reform in general. It cannot be said that the particular curriculum ideas Dewey tested there actually became translated, as is commonly believed, into widespread practice. As his reputation grew, Dewey's name was invoked in connection with curriculum and general school reforms of all sorts whether they reflected his ideas or not. At the same time, the educational theory Dewey so painstakingly developed during his Chicago period was either converted into a pitiful caricature, such as "learning by doing," or neglected altogether. The paradox of John Dewey is that, although he gained worldwide recognition during his own lifetime and has unquestionably earned a place in the panoply of the world's great educators, his actual influence on the schools of the nation has been seriously overestimated or grossly distorted. It was his fate to become identified with a vague, essentially undefinable, entity called progressive education, either an inchoate mixture of diverse and often contradictory reform or simply a historical fiction.

There was little in Dewey's career prior to his arrival in Chicago that would indicate that he was to become the towering figure in American educational thought in the twentieth century. When, for example, Assistant Professor James H. Tufts, in late 1893 or early 1894, wrote to President William Rainey Harper of the University of Chicago urging consideration of Dewey as Head-Professor of Philosophy, he failed to mention any qualifications that would pertain to his proposed role as head of a department that included pedagogy. Tufts cited the fact that Dewey's *Psychology* had been widely adopted as a textbook in prestigious Eastern colleges and that his *Leibnitz's New Essays* had been very favorably received in philosophical circles (cited in Brickman and Lehrer, 1961, p. 167). Tufts also reported that Dewey was "utterly devoid of any affectation or self-consciousness, and makes many friends and no enemies" (p. 168) as well as the fact that Dewey was a popular and successful teacher at the University of Michigan. Also mentioned was the fact that he was a church member and a friend of Jane Addams's Hull House (p. 168).

There had been a few signs in his earlier career, however, of Dewey's growing interest in philosophy of education. He had, after all, some teaching experience below the university level, although his two years as a high school teacher in Oil City, Pennsylvania and his subsequent brief period as a teacher in a village school in Charlotte, Vermont, were probably more reflective of a young man unsure of his direction rather than of a conscious intent to follow a career in professional education. Dewey's decision to pursue philosophy as his life's work was an outgrowth of a number of early influences including that of H. A. P. Torrey, a professor of his in his undergraduate days at the University of Vermont. But perhaps the most immediate spur to his interest in philosophy came from the editor of the *Journal of Speculative Philosophy*, William Torrey Harris, who not only accepted an article that Dewey had written while a high school teacher, but urged him to continue his philosophical pursuits. The latter apparently helped Dewey overcome his disappointment at being denied a fellowship by Johns Hopkins University, and, with money borrowed from his aunt, he left for Baltimore in 1882. In his first year of graduate study, Dewey came under the influence of George Sylvester Morris who instilled in him a commitment toward German idealism and a lifelong antipathy toward British empiricism. When Morris returned to his regular position at the University of Michigan, Dewey continued his graduate work and received his Ph.D in 1884 after presenting a dissertation on the "Psychology of Kant," a work that has not been preserved.

It was undoubtedly through Morris's intervention that Dewey was offered his first academic appointment at the University of Michigan as instructor in philosophy. As was common in the later nineteenth century, however, philosophy and psychology were joined together, and Dewey's teaching was almost exclusively in the area of psychology, while Morris taught most of the philosophy courses himself. Dewey's reputation grew rapidly both as a philosopher and psychologist of great promise and as a popular instructor with students. When he was offered the chair in philosophy at the University of Minnesota in 1888, he reluctantly accepted but returned to Michigan a year later when the chair in philosophy there became vacant upon the death of Morris.

It was during his Michigan period that Dewey took his first tentative steps in the direction of a serious involvement in educational matters. Firstly, his marriage to Alice Chipman and the subsequent births of their children seemed to arouse in him a natural curiosity about children's mental growth and how they gain increasing intellectual command of their world. Secondly, Dewey's work in psychology led him to direct some attention to its practical applications in the classroom. He is listed in later editions as the coauthor of *Applied Psychology* with James A. McClellan, a book directed to normal schools, and, although there is some indication that it is the work of McClellan almost entirely (Boydston, 1969), it does indicate something of Dewey's growing interest in educational matters at least as they relate to psychology. Thirdly, the period of Dewey's appointment at the University of Michigan coincided with the development of the Michigan Plan, a college plan for admission based on students who had completed a high school program approved by the University of Michigan faculty. This brought Dewey out into schools and into contact with teachers and curricula below the collegiate level. Finally, and most important to the development of Dewey's theory of education, he became associated with the American Herbartians. Many of the prominent educators who were members had studied at the great German centers in Jena and Leipzig, and, ostensibly at least, they were committed to promoting the educational theories of their master, Johann Friedrich Herbart, although their interpretations of his work are open to some question (Dunkel, 1970). More importantly, however, they served for a relatively brief but intense period as a focal point for a challenge to the old order in education as represented largely by mental discipline and by traditional humanists generally, such as Harris. When, after only eight years of existence, the National Herbart Society changed its name in 1900 to the National Society for the Scientific Study of Education, their specific identification with Herbartian concepts diminished sharply and the challenge to the humanist curriculum was carried forward by reformers representing platforms that bore little or no resemblance to readily identifiable Herbartian concepts, such as correlation, concentration, apperception and culture-epochs. Although some Herbartian ideas were not especially congenial to the burgeoning child-study movement, such as the original Herbartian emphasis on model citizenship, Herbartianism was for the most part absorbed into the developmentalist interest group. In general, the Herbartian emphasis on child growth and development and children's interests blended nicely with the main thrust of the child-study movement.

ii

When Dewey arrived at the University of Chicago in 1894 to head the combined department of philosophy, psychology and pedagogy, the educational world was dominated by the antagonism of two major interest groups representing widely divergent positions as to the future course of American education. Each was led by a dynamic and influential spokesman, and Dewey had had some previous contact with both of them. William Torrey Harris, as editor of the *Journal of Speculative Philosophy*, had provided the encouragement that the young Dewey needed at a critical point in his life.

Granville Stanley Hall had been one of Dewey's professors in his latter year at Johns Hopkins, and Dewey had conducted some psychological experiments in Hall's laboratory there. Harris had, more or less, succeeded Eliot as the central figure among those forces that sought to preserve the humanist ideal by incorporating into the curriculum the finest elements of Western civilization even in the face of the rapidly increasing population of students then enrolling in American schools. Hall, whose personal goal was to become known as the "Darwin of the mind" (Hall, 1923, p. 360), was the epitome of the new breed of social scientists who saw the schools as in need of drastic reform in order to bring their program of studies in line with scientific findings about the nature of child life.

The preeminent figure in the world of education during the last quarter of the nineteenth century was undoubtedly Harris. The fact that he never produced a magnum opus like Hall's *Adolescence* may lead to an underestimation of the pivotal role that he played in the educational affairs of his time. During his long career, he addressed National Education Association national meetings no less than 145 times (Wesley, 1957, p. 48), and one attempt to compile his bibliography listed 479 publications (Evans, 1908). The force of his intellect and his incredible energy were undoubtedly vital ingredients in Harris's national stature, but beyond the question of his personal influence, he gave voice to that large constituency of school teachers and administrators who were made uneasy by the threat of massive reform then looming on the horizon. In particular, Harris helped build a plausible platform for the segment of the educational world that resisted the idea of a major change in the schools of the nation, presumably reflective of the great social transformation that had taken place in American society or, for that matter, the intellectual transformation represented by the rise of science. He was able to strike a tone of moderation in the midst of cries for a revolution in education. Harris, in a sense, was almost the last great spokesperson for a humanistic curriculum that education was to produce from within its midst. Educational leaders in the twentieth century were essentially advocates of change of various sorts, while the banner of humanism in educational policy, usually identified with the school's role in the development of the intellect, was carried by academicians and intellectuals drawn from outside the professional educational establishment. Although Harris's position steadily lost ground among the leaders who regularly assembled at educational conferences and wrote for pedagogical journals, it is likely that Harris's basic position in curriculum matters continued to hold sway with the majority of teachers and administrators across the country for years to come.

Born in 1835, when America was still an agrarian country, Harris was keenly aware of the changes that had been wrought in American society in his own lifetime, but he did not regard these changes as dictating a major reordering of the school's curriculum. Although certain modest adaptations to modern society could be incorporated, the basic function of the school, the development of reason, remained the same. In fact, the restructuring of American society made it even more imperative that the schools perform their distinctive function effectively. Harris's interpretation of Hegelian philosophy permitted him to see industrialization with its profound effect on America's social institutions, not in any apocalyptic sense, but as part of the unfolding of the Divine Will. Harris could, at one and the same time, be an advocate of rugged individualism and believe that the individual achieves realization only by subordinating himself to social institutions, institutions that embody the fruits of civilization. It was through these institutions that the wisdom of the race would be transmitted. A consistent advocate of what he liked to call "self-activity," Harris (1898a) identified that activity with the rational through the exercise of will, and his persistent emphasis on rationality in children put him in direct conflict with the advocates of "education according to nature," like Hall. The school, according to Harris, must train children to gain control over their natural impulses, not to submit to them. "Rousseau's doctrine of a return to nature," Harris said, "must . . . seem to me the greatest heresy in educational doctrine" (p. 37).

As early as 1880, Harris was proclaiming the centrality of the curriculum in educational matters. "The question of the course of study," he said, "is the most important question which the educator has before him' (Harris, 1880, p. 174), and the curriculum, in Harris's mind, should take its cue, not from the vagaries of children's interests nor their spontaneous impulses, but from the great resources of civilization. For Harris, psychological inquiry into child growth and development has its place, but it could never, in itself, direct the course of a proper education. "Self-activity," he said, 'is in every newborn soul as a spontaneity, – a possibility of unlimited action good or bad" (Harris, 1886, p. 92), and essentially, it was the function of the curriculum to direct the development of self-activity in the interest of "a knowledge of truth, a love of the beautiful, a habit of doing the good" (p. 92). Considering the maxim of the self-styled "New Education" – "Learn to do by doing" (a maxim he attributed to the prominent German pedagogue, Friederich Adolph Wilhelm Diesterweg) – Harris was careful to point out that the maxim was incomplete without some "guiding direction" (p. 92). That direction would be provided by a properly constructed course of study. Each branch of study in the curriculum (or, as he liked to call them, "coordinate groups of study") he felt could open the way for an ever-more-adequate appreciation of the Western social and intellectual tradition. His familiar "five windows of the soul," represented by arithmetic and mathematics, geography, history, grammar, literature and art, were chosen because to him they represented the best ways of initiating the child into the kind of self-activity that would lead to a command of the resources of that civilization.

Harris (1888) claimed that the school should first provide the command of language in reading and writing that goes beyond the "colloquial vocabulary" the child acquires in the home (p. 574). That increased command of language emancipated the child from "the thraldom of dependence on the spoken word" (p. 575), and once that were achieved, the child could reach beyond the world of personal experience of oral language, and the first of the "windows," arithmetic, could be opened. Arithmetic permitted entry into the abstract relationships that govern the physical world. Arithmetic, especially exact measurement, represented for Harris a first step in the conquest of nature, and he favored proceeding expeditiously from basic arithmetic to those mathematical operations that were useful in the natural sciences, opposing extensive drill in arithmetic operations (Harris, 1898b, pp. 325–6). Geography, the second of the windows, served to relate the inorganic world to the human world. Harris opposed what he called "sailor geography," the memorization of the names of rivers, islands and cities, in favor of the "dynamics of geography," the inter-relationship between natural forces and human beings that led to different forms of commerce and industry in different parts of the world. History focused directly on the unfolding of the will "realized in institutions rather than in mere deeds of the individual" (Harris, 1888, p. 575). In historical studies, the State and how collectivities made civilization possible should be emphasized. A particular enthusiast for the study of grammar, Harris, waxing poetic, claimed that the window of grammar "lets in a flood of light for the explanation of all problems which human experience can enunciate" (p. 576). For Harris, the logical structure of language was a kind of model for the nature of thinking itself. And, finally, literature opened up that window that permitted us to see life as a totality and to appreciate what is essential in human character. That understanding of human experience, according to Harris, could best be instilled through careful study of standard literary works. These works not only led to an understanding of the roots of human action, but provided the principal form of aesthetic appreciation available in the curriculum.

These basic components of the curriculum, Harris (1888) claimed, were "the five great lines of study that radiate from the center and relate to the five great departments of human learning" (p. 579). Other subjects were not exactly excluded; they were simply subordinate. "Industrial drawing, for example, should have its place in the common school side by side with penmanship" (p. 579). While his position permitted him to support certain proposed changes in the curriculum of the late nineteenth and early twentieth centuries, such as sys-tematic instruction in art, he was probably the leading cham-pion of the continued study of classical literature and never wavered in his support of Greek and Latin, then becoming a lost cause. Harris's defense of the study of classical languages, however, differed in its rationale from that of the typical mental disciplinarian. While Harris seems to have given qualified support to the proposition that mental power could be developed through use, he was skeptical of the mental disciplinarians' belief that mental power developed in one field could be transferred to another. Harris was more in-terested in what the subjects had to offer directly than in their alleged value as vehicles for strengthening innate powers of the mind. Thus, memorizing dates may have some positive effect on "the health of the nervous system," but that activity derived its most immediate justification "on account of the intrinsic usefulness of the data themselves" (Harris, 1898b, p. 178). Although, almost inevitably, Harris found himself using the vocabulary of formal discipline on occasion, his fun-damental justification for retaining Greek and Latin in the curriculum lay in the fact that Greece and Rome were seminal to Western civilization, and no understanding of modern society, Harris believed, would be complete without an appreciation of that heritage. For Harris, it was the content of the subjects rather than their form that was crucial in deter-mining their value. Thus, unlike the reform-minded mental disciplinarian, Eliot, Harris opposed the substitution of French and German for the classical languages. While Eliot could argue that French, properly taught, could discipline the mind as well as Latin, Harris would hold that a knowledge of French simply was not as valuable as a resource of our culture as was Latin. Unlike Eliot, too, Harris was deeply suspicious of electives, advocating substitutions only within each of his five coordinate groups of studies, where content was suffi-ciently similar. By emphasizing the virtues of the content of what was learned instead of disciplinary value, Harris was reconstructing the justification for a curriculum that would preserve the humanist ideal.

The distance that Harris was able to create between his version of a humanist curriculum and the doctrine of mental discipline was particularly important in an era when the psychological underpinning of that doctrine, faculty psychology, was under serious attack by respected psychologists. The rise of experimental psychology was seriously undermining the rationale that faculty psychology had successfully provided during most of the nineteeth century for the continuance of not only Greek and Latin, but other traditional subjects in the curriculum. Undoubtedly, part of the appeal of Harris's rationale was that it did not require any change in the basic organizational structure of the school, since essentially the same things were to be taught, but for different reasons. Moreover, the central role of the school, the development of the intellect, remained substantially unchanged. What remains of humanistic studies in the modern American curriculum follows, at least in broad outline, the program that Harris enunciated.

Although the development of the intellect was always paramount in Harris's educational theory, that development could not proceed without the parallel development of the will. Only in the lowest form of self-activity, sense perception, was the will absent. Here the mind was only the passive receptor of the senses. The true development of intellect began when the will produced attention and with it the ability to select some sense impressions and to neglect others. "Attention," Harris (1896a) argued, "may be regarded as the name of the first union of the will with the intellect" (p. 442). As we proceeded to higher orders of knowing – analysis, synthesis, reflection (analysis and synthesis), and finally to insight or philosophical knowing – the will continued to play a vital role. The training of the will, therefore, especially through correct habit formation, became an essential element in the principal function that education performs, the broadening and deepening of the intellect. Harris's persistent emphasis on the schools' function in the transmission of the

Western cultural heritage through a proper choice of subjects reinforced his reputation as "the great conservator" in the educational world of his time and his identification with the training of the will made him a special target for those reformers in education who saw the existing curriculum as antithetical to the natural impulses and interests of the child, and, therefore, hopelessly out-of-date and unscientific. In his advocacy of a humanistic curriculum in an era when mental discipline was being seriously undermined, Harris actually was not the stereotypic advocate of mindless drill and stern authoritarianism in American schools; but moderate reform at the turn of the century was easily equated with defense of the status quo, and this put Harris in the position of swimming against the strong tide of radical change that the new leadership was advocating.

iii

With Herbartianism losing its early potency as a reform movement, it was the child-study movement that soon posed the most direct threat to Harris's position. Although the leaders of the movement liked to trace their ancestry with some justification to Comenius, Froebel, Pestalozzi and Rousseau, the idea that the key to the curriculum lay in child-study did not really achieve national prominence until the latter part of the nineteenth century. In the 1870s, the cause of child-study gained impetus through the criticism of American education advanced by Charles Francis Adams (1879), especially by his efforts to draw attention to children's mental habits as a way of bringing the light of science to a benighted pedagogy. Adams's high praise for the work of Colonel Francis Parker in the Quincy, Massachusetts, school system not only brought Parker national prominence, but seemed to indicate that drudgery and repression were not, after all, necessary concomitants of schooling. Parker had not simply introduced a much greater measure of freedom for the child than was typical of the regimented schools of that time.

He had, essentially, discarded the old course of study in favor of one that was congenial to the child's penchant for play and activity. He introduced what he called the "word method" of teaching reading, replacing drill in phonics, because it was the "natural" way by which a child learned language. Problems in arithmetic were favored over the mere manipulation of numbers, and rules and generalizations were reserved for later periods of schooling. Formal grammar in the early grades was also discontinued, and natural language activities, such as letter writing, were introduced. The Quincy schools were held up by Adams as a model of schooling, not only because the natural predilections of the child could be used to enrich the spirit of the school, but because effective learning was taking place.

But it was not until Hall returned from Germany in 1880 that the developmentalists found the champion that would make them a potent force in American education. Such was the power of Hall's personality that William James, after a conversation with him, wrote to the president of Johns Hopkins University recommending him for a temporary lectureship for which James himself had been invited, adding, "He is a more learned man than I can ever hope to become" (Ross, 1972, p. 104). Although Hall did not get that appointment, it was then that President Eliot came to the rescue (according to Hall, actually appearing to him mounted on a horse) and offered him a chance to lecture at Harvard on pedagogy and history of philosophy. Hall's lectures on pedagogy were held on Saturdays so that Boston teachers could attend, and they were an immediate and resounding success. The appeal of the pedagogical system based on sound scientific principles must have been enormous at that time. Moreover, Parker's work at nearby Quincy had made Hall's arrival on the scene particularly propitious, and after a period of drift and uncertainty in his life, Hall, at the age of thirty-seven, was suddenly thrust into prominence. He brought to the cause of education according to nature a quality that Parker lacked. Parker's pedagogical reforms were largely instinctive and, although he could be an inspiring speaker, he was not terribly effective in articulating a coherent rationale for his work. Hall, on the other hand, could bring to bear the authority of science to the growing belief that the child's own natural impulses could be used as a way of addressing the question of what to teach. When Hall published "The Contents of Children's Minds" in 1883, it quickly became a kind of model for scientific pedagogy, and the following year Hall accepted the prestigious appointment of full professor of pedagogy and psychology at Johns Hopkins. Hall's success at Johns Hopkins in his appointment as lecturer, beginning in 1882 as well as his soaring reputation as a scientist, had apparently put him in a position to win the appointment over Morris, Dewey's friend and mentor, who had desperately wanted the position. By 1887, Hall helped found the *American Journal of Psychology* and, a year later, he left Johns Hopkins to become the first president of Clark University. When, in 1891, he founded *Pedagogical Seminary* with himself as editor, he was in a position to assume unquestioned leadership of the developmentalist strain in American educational reform. With Hall at the helm, the cause of child-study became identified with scientific and hence valid ways of addressing the great educational issues of the day, while the efforts of the humanists to preserve in the curriculum the great accomplishments of Western culture were increasingly being regarded as speculative and old-fashioned.

Child-study flourished in the 1890s. In 1894, Hall was able to announce at the annual meeting of the NEA that "unto you is born this day a new Department of Child Study" (Hall, 1895, p. 173), and in the same year, the Illinois Society for the Study of Children was also founded. Over the next two years, the Illinois Society's Child-Study Congresses attracted audiences of as many as three thousand persons and, by the end of the decade, at least twenty other state child-study organizations had been founded. To be sure, there were some differences within the burgeoning movement. Some leaders, for example, favored the study of the child under laboratory conditions; others urged an "anthropological" form of data collection in the child's natural setting, a form of observation perhaps best illustrated by Hall's own, "The Story of a Sand-Pile" (1888). Whatever the form, however, there was common agreement that ever more data on the child needed to be gathered. The leaders of the movement were also convinced that, from that mountain of data, direct inferences could be drawn (through what they sometimes called the Baconian method) as to how a child should be educated. Beyond the general proposition that education would proceed according to the child's own nature, however, most leaders of the movement were rather vague. It remained for Hall himself to take the lead in actually spelling out the implications of child-study for school programs.

There was general agreement, of course, among the developmentalists that schools thwarted the child's basic need for activity by treating children as passive receptacles and presenting them with a program of studies that ran contrary to their natural tendencies and predilections. To some reformers, this meant simply the introduction of more active pursuits such as manual training or industrial education and more considered attention to recreation and play activities. But Hall had a much grander scheme in mind, and, although Hall had covered himself in the armor of science, it is significant that his curriculum ideas were drawn, not so much from the scientific data so diligently collected by him and his fellow psychologists, as from his metaphysical, even mystical, assumptions about the alleged relationship between the stages in individual development and the history of the human race.

From his early period of study with the German disciples of Herbart, Hall returned to the United States convinced of the validity of the doctrine of culture-epochs applied to pedagogy. Culture-epochs theory posited the notion that the child recapitulates in his individual development the stages that the whole human race traversed throughout the course of history. In Hall's mind, that recapitulation had strong mythic overtones:

The principle that the child and the early history of the human race are each keys to unlock the nature of the other applies to almost everything in feeling, will, and intellect. To understand either the child or the race we must constantly refer to the other. This same principle applies also to all spontaneous activities. Thus in seeking the true principle of motor education we must not only study the plays, games and interests of the child today, but also try to compare these with the characteristic activities of early man. . . . The child relives the history of the race in his acts, just as the scores of rudimentary organs in his body tell the story of its evolution from the lower forms of animal life. . . . The all-dominant, but of course mainly unconscious, will of the child is to relive this past, as if his early ancestors were struggling in his soul and body to make their influences felt and their voice heard. (Hall, 1904c, pp. 443-4)

The general proposition that "ontogeny recapitulates phylogeny" had been widely accepted as a valid scientific principle from at least the seventeenth century on, but its application to pedagogy – its enunciation as a curriculum theory – was closely identified with both the German and American disciples of Herbart during the late nineteenth century. Its widespread acceptance as a general principle was associated with Darwinian theory. Just as the "gill-slits" in the human embryo were a tie to the beginnings of life in the sea, so the behavior and impulses of the child were considered clues to our ancestral heritage ("Discussion on work," 1901, p. 521). Much of culture-epochs theory's wide appeal in education lay in its association with a scientific order of studies and with the promise it held out for an integration of the curriculum instead of what Hall once referred to as a "mob of subjects." A curriculum comprising interrelated parts rather than isolated entities remained an ideal of curriculum reformers throughout the twentieth century. In the case of culture-epochs, the sequence of epochs in human history, and the actual materials for study, were concentrated around the cultural content of those epochs. Thus, while children were in their "savage" stage of development, they would study materials in all their subjects derived from that historical epoch, such as ancient mythology and fables. What was especially attractive to Hall and others in the child-study movement was that a curriculum organized in this way had a guaranteed appeal to children's interests. Children, they felt, had a natural affinity for materials drawn from a historical epoch which corresponded to their stage in individual development. Not only Hall, but virtually all the child-centered and Herbartian reformers – Parker, Charles and Frank McMurry, Charles DeGarmo – gave culture-epochs theory their firm endorsement. It was widely discussed at national education conferences and figured prominently in textbooks designed for normal schools, such as Charles McMurry's *Elements of General Method*, a work that went through ten editions in the eight years following its publication in 1893.

Although the theory of culture-epochs provided the general configuration for Hall's curriculum, it needed to be supplemented by other principles of child development. Hall remained deeply suspicious of intellectual training for the young largely because reasoning power was not yet part of the child's repertoire. In one of his most influential addresses, Hall pointed out that the etymology of the word "school" derives from leisure, and hence the function of the school was not to impose civilization upon the child, a course of action not only futile, but harmful; rather, the school should, as far as possible, stay out of the child's way, seeking, if anything, to prolong the stages of childhood and adolescence (Hall, 1901b). "The guardians of the young," he proclaimed, "should strive first of all to keep them out of nature's way, and to prevent harm, and merit the proud title of defenders of the happiness and rights of children" (p. 475). Every invasion of the child's leisure "has a certain presumption against it" (p. 475) and, therefore every curricular intrusion must be conclusively justified. One of Hall's most persistent, if not overriding, concerns in this regard was the injury to the child's health that would follow the unwise curtailment of the child's playful tendencies. "Sooner or later," Hall once argued, "everything pertaining to education, from the site of the buildings to the contents of every text book, and the methods of each branch of study must be . . . judged from the standpoint of health" (Hall, 1892, pp. 7–8). Hall's persistent advocacy of health as the school's principal purpose put him, of course, squarely in opposition to Harris, the champion of the development of the intellect as the school's distinctive and central function.

As Hall's criticism of the Committee of Ten's report indicated, another of Hall's preoccupations was with what he called "individualization", leading him to prescribe wide variation in what was taught, not only in terms of the great range of intellectual abilities within the school population, but in terms of other genetically determined characteristics such as gender. Nature not only fixed the stages through which all human beings passed, but determined the limits of human educability and, hence, the nature of the social hierarchy. A strong believer in hereditary determinism, Hall advocated differentiated instruction based on native endowment and even separate schools for "dullards" in the elementary grades (Hall, 1911, p. 605). Segregation by sex, according to Hall, should begin at the outset of adolescence, since marked divergence among the sexes begins suddenly "in the pubescent period – in the early teens" (Hall, 1903, p. 446). Hall noted with some alarm that, although girls until about the age of ten adopt ideals associated with their own sex, statistical studies had shown that, thereafter, girls began to adopt the ideals of males. Citing the concern of one writer that "we shall soon have a female sex without a female character" (p. 448), Hall, while not opposing coeducation *per se*, advocated some segregation within the high school in order to insure "the full and complete development" of both sexes (p. 449). Boys' development, he felt, was endangered by "the progressive feminization of our schools" in a period of their lives that should be dominated by "strong men" and where the curriculum should be geared to the adolescent boy's natural propensities, such as his penchant for studies that maximize content and minimize form (p. 448). Girls predominate in English and history, according to Hall, out of "inner inclination" whereas their preponderance in Latin and algebra was a function merely of "custom and tradition" or, perhaps, "advice" (p. 448). Hall advocated special versions of botany, biology and chemistry designed for girls and toyed with the idea of creating two kinds of high schools for girls, one with a curriculum that emphasized "motherhood and home life" for "the vast majority of women" and another for those who wished to pursue a career (p. 450).

In general, the elementary school curriculum would be dominated, at least until the age of eight, by play, with special care taken not to overtax the child with needless and potentially harmful intellectual tasks. Reading and writing, for example, "should be neglected in our system before eight, and previous school work should focus on stories, the study of nature, and education by play and other activities" (Hall, 1901b, p. 478). Emphasis after the age of eight should be on drill and memorization since "the age of reason is only dawning" (p. 478). The teaching of arithmetic, for example, should be "mechanized" with little emphasis on rules and explanations (p. 479). Since it is still too early to expect good grammar, written work should be sharply reduced and, instead, the "child should live in a world of sonorous speech" (p. 479), which would lay the foundation for correct English once the age of reason was attained. Hall regarded the emphasis on geography in elementary school to be a "relic of mediaevalism" and urged that it be sharply curtailed (p. 481). What remained of this study should respect the stages of growth reflecting culture-epochs. A child's interest in primitive peoples, for example, reached its highest point from nine to ten, while interest in "trade and governmental parts of geography" emerged in the period between sixteen and twenty (p. 480). Latin and Greek, "if they are to be taught" (p. 480), should be introduced not later than ten or eleven when verbal memory is at its highest point. The child should not be presented with unfamiliar passages, but lessons should be based instead on repetition of what the teacher has already done.

When Hall turned his attention back to the secondary school curriculum, he was, curiously, even less tolerant of Latin as a subject. He was particularly distressed by the fact that between 1890 and 1900, a period in which high school enrollment had more than doubled, the percentage of students in secondary schools taking Latin had actually increased from 34 percent to 50 percent, all this in a decade when, according to his figures, the number of students preparing for college had declined from 14 percent to 11 percent (Hall, 1902, p. 261). Why was that "great army of incapables" that Hall referred to in connection with his criticism of the Committee of Ten's recommendations perversely gravitating to such a useless and probably harmful subject? Apart from the fact that it is, compared to science, for example, a cheap subject to teach and that "Latin teaching is more open to women then (sic) science" (Hall, 1901a, p. 655), Hall attributed the disturbing (albeit short-lived) trend toward greater Latin enrollments to "superstitious reverence" (p. 655). On at least two occasions, he compared it to a reference in Booker T. Washington's autobiography alleging that "colored people" had an almost supernatural belief in the power of a knowledge of Latin, however small, to confer superior status (p. 655), a superstition that Washington strove to eradicate. If the high school were successful in eliminating the superstitious reverence for Latin, Hall would replace it with an emphasis on English, but upon its content rather than its form. Since high school boys have passed the Homeric stage in their development, Hall would concentrate literary studies around such legends as King Arthur, Parsifal, Siegfried and Lohengrin, the noblest feature of the feudal period being its emphasis on chivalry and honor. The purpose of literature in the high school, Hall argued, was not so much its aesthetic value, but its positive influence on morals (Hall, 1902, p. 265).

Second only to English in the high school curriculum would be science, with special emphasis on astronomy, since "natural curiosity about the heavens is now almost at its strongest and best" (p. 265), as well as geology and biology. Such content subjects, in general, should be given more emphasis than form subjects, such as language study and mathematics. The third area of emphasis Hall advocated was motor training, which would prepare boys for the "strenuous life of achievement so that every man-Jack of them will want to bring his whole self to bear where he can compete and meet the verdict of his peers" (p. 266). In this connection, Hall boasted that he could do virtually every kind of farm work and that, based on his training in German schools, he could "bind, gild, and cover a book; make a shoe and a broom complete, do a little glass-blowing, plumbing and gold-beating" (p. 267). Such activities served the purpose of training the muscles and training the will at the same time. It was around the triumvirate of English, science and motor activities that Hall would build the secondary school curriculum, with other subjects added, as he put it, *ad libitum*.

Hall never tired of extolling the virtues of science. To him, science represented the culmination of the process of evolution, and it was on his own status as a scientist that his enormous reputation was built. But of the great intellectual traditions that had survived the world of Hall's time, it was ultimately romanticism rather than Darwinism that dominated Hall's thinking. His proposals for reform of the curriculum amounted almost to a denigration of intellect in favor of a sentimentalization of childhood and especially adolescence. Throughout Hall's writings, intellect was subordinated to the virtues of robust health and racial vitality. The development of reason as the chief goal of education, to Hall, was a product of a prescientific era, and to attempt to realize that goal in elementary and secondary schools would serve only to sap energy and impair health. In the concept of adolescence, Hall expressed not simply an idealization of a stage in individual development, but an idealization of a stage in the human race. It was the period when "the floodgates of heredity seem opened and we hear from our remoter forebears, and receive our life dower of energy. . . . Passions and desires spring into vigorous life" (Hall, 1904a). But just as Hall's pedagogical theory reached back eons in time, so it looked ahead ultimately to a race of supermen, a vision which, for him, represented "the highest and final test of art, science, religion, home, state, literature, and every human institution" (Hall, 1901b, p. 488). Hall's "ideal school" held out no promise of social reform except in the mythic sense of "removing the handicaps from those most able . . . in ushering in the kingdom of the superman" (Saunders and Hall, 1900, p. 591). Developmentalism, as represented by Hall's vision, not only found a natural enemy in traditional humanism, but represented a radically different reform thrust from that of the social meliorists.

iv

Dewey's reaction to the rapidly growing child-study movement was at least mixed. As one who was clearly dissatisfied with the state of education in the late nineteenth century, he was drawn naturally to the prospect of reform that the leaders of that movement held out. Moreover, as one who was born in the same year as the publication of *The Origin of Species*, and who, like most intellectuals of his generation, had become imbued with the promise of science in general, Dewey welcomed the scientific study of the child, but he was very cautious about applying such study to the practical exigencies of the classroom. Scientific findings, he felt, could not be converted readily into prescriptions for action, as much of Hall's work implied. He was critical of the insistent demand that science be put to work immediately and directly in transforming school life. "There is no more sense in attacking the scientific investigator . . . because he doesn't provide on demand usable recipes, ticketed and labeled for all pedagogical emergencies," he said, "than there would have been in attacking the early pioneers in electricity because they worked quietly in the laboratory upon seemingly remote and abstruse subjects instead of providing us off-hand with the telegraph, telephone, electric light, and transportation" (Dewey, 1897a, pp. 867–8). The clear implication was that the leaders of the child-study movement were promising that their scientific inquiries would bring about the pedagogical equivalents of those ingredients of modern life virtually in the absence of a basic understanding of what childhood and adolescence were all about. Dewey was also uneasy about the fact that child-study had become isolated from the parent discipline of psychology, resulting in an indiscriminate, almost atheoretical, pursuit of data. He cited William James as arguing that there seemed to exist in the child-study movement "a fear of theory, of speculation, of hypothesis, which is as absurd as pure speculation divorced from fact. The mere collection of facts, uncontrolled by working hypothesis, unenlightened by generalization, never made a science and never will' (p. 868). It was almost as if Dewey were saying that there was more evangelism than science in the movement.

But Dewey reserved his strongest criticism for those within the movement who, behind the mask of science, merely used child-study as an expression of their own sentimentality and therefore as a vehicle for supporting questionable practices. He formulated this criticism by first tracing the development of interest in the child through three major historical stages, each coinciding with a period of social disorganization. To Plato and Aristotle, he attributed the political interest in the child, that is, the proper training of the child in the interest of a desirable social order. "The first source of conscious interest in the child," Dewey said, "was the position of the child as a factor in social organization" (Dewey, 1897b, p. 18). The proper training of children became an important factor in the reconstruction of society, but primarily from the point of view of fitting the child into "the social life-structure they are best adapted to fit into" (p. 20). In its best sense, the political interest in the child represented a recognition that the social order was capable of intelligent direction, and that the proper education of children was an important step in that direction. The pedagogical expression of that ideal "takes shape in the statement that the supreme consideration controlling the whole curriculum of the school lies in the demands of the civilization into which the child is born" (p. 21). The chief weakness of that ideal was that the child was not considered as an individual but exclusively from the perspective of the social order into which he or she was to be fitted. By fixing such an end in advance, according to Dewey, we see only those things which are related to that end, and this impairs both our view of the child and our social vision. "If we have in view a fixed end to which the child is to be adapted," he said, "the things in the child which relate to that end are the only things which we are capable of seeing" (p. 21).

The second great period of interest in the child that Dewey identified was the Renaissance, where the principal perspective from which the child was viewed was aesthetic rather than political. The child, in this period, began to appear prominently in works of art representing a kind of ideal of lost innocence. In children, people saw the spontaneity and the freedom to which they once aspired. In the main, such a view of the child served to soothe emotional stirrings within the adult, rather than as an actual spur to action. "The child," Dewey (1897b) argued, "is taken as affording consolation, as a relief from the ideal, for the adult, and there is no easier or cheaper way of deceiving ourselves than by setting up something as an ideal in order to free ourselves from the responsibility of realizing it" (p. 23). At its best, he claimed, such a view of the child helps humanity formulate its ideal, but, at its worst, the child becomes a mere plaything of the adult in an effort to make life more bearable or pleasurable.

The third and current source of interest in the child Dewey called the scientific, and, like the others, it was associated with a time when older habits and traditions were breaking down, but it was also related to the two earlier periods. Given the fact that this interest in the child was an outgrowth of German romanticism, part of its heritage involved the belief that childhood was somehow tied to the "childhood of humanity," that it was associated with "a lost Garden of Eden," and a return to childhood somehow was connected with idyllic, primitive conditions. (A more apt description of Hall's notions about childhood could hardly be imagined.) It was this sentimental primitivism, Dewey contended, that prevented a fruitful blending of the aesthetic and the scientific interest in the child. While the aesthetic interest in the child provided "the crowning motive for scientific study . . . the return to nature . . . must be literal and not sentimental" (Dewey, 1897b, p. 26). It was when Dewey turned his attention to the relationship between the political and the scientific that he became critical of one of Hall's favorite themes, the notion of a different kind of education for a special role in society based on alleged natural tendencies already present in the child:

> We cannot, whether we approve the fact or regret it, educate the child for special membership on the basis of habit, routine, or tradition. The society for which the child, to-day, is to be educated, is too complex, makes too many demands upon personality to be capable of being based upon custom and routine without the utmost disaster. We must educate him by giving him the widest powers and most complete tools of civilization. Only a study, only the knowledge, of what those powers are and how to master them, and what would instrumentally aid or hinder in their development, and how, is in any way adequate to this task. (pp. 26–7)

Dewey thus set himself against the growing tendency in educational policy, not only to educate the child based on predictions of what the society would be like, but to differentiate the curriculum based on the particular role an individual would be expected to occupy in that society.

v

Within a year of assuming his appointment at the University of Chicago, Dewey made his first major contribution to the literature in philosophy of education, "Interest in Relation to Training of the Will" (1896a), a work that, not surprisingly, dealt with the raging controversy between humanism and developmentalism. Published as a supplement to the first National Herbart Society Yearbook (1895), it provides a significant indication of the direction Dewey was taking in his thinking on the conflict, and, in many respects, is typical of his approach to educational and even general philosophical issues. As the title of his essay indicates, Dewey was trying to shed light on the burning controversy between the advocates of interest, the Herbartians and the child-study advocates on the one hand, and the advocates of the training of the will, the mental disciplinarians and the humanist position represented by Harris on the other.

Characteristically, Dewey took neither side. His approach was first to restate both positions in the "educational lawsuit of interest *versus* effort" (Dewey, 1896a, p. 6), and then, in effect, to find them both guilty of the same fallacy. The advocates of interest according to Dewey's account, seemed primarily concerned with adding a layer of sugarcoating to what was taught to the child, a practice from which the child learned not even the object which has been superficially sweetened: "He soon learns to turn from everything which is not artificially surrounded with diverting circumstances. The spoiled child who does only what he likes is the inevitable outcome of the theory of interest in education" (p. 8).

Dewey's criticism of the doctrine of will was equally sweeping. "The theory of effort," he claimed, "simply says that unwilling attention (doing something which is disagreeable and because it is disagreeable) should take precedence over spontaneous attention" (Dewey, 1896a, p. 6). What the child really learns under these circumstances is to appear "to be occupied with an uninteresting subject, while the real heart and core of his energies are otherwise engaged" (pp. 6–7). In the case of both doctrines, Dewey was obviously trying to draw attention not merely to the ostensible purpose of the activity, but its unintentional and probably more significant consequences. Ultimately, however, he argued that the choice did not lie between engaging the child in mere amusement on the one hand, and forcing the child to pursue disagreeable tasks as part of the training of the will and thereby building moral character on the other. Both sides in the lawsuit, plaintiff and defendant, proceeded, according to Dewey, from the identical assumption: "the externality of the object or idea to be mastered, the end to be reached, the act to be performed, to the self" (p. 9). For the advocates of interest, things that were in fact uninteresting had to be made interesting because they fell outside the scope of the child's real interests; for the advocates of will, strenuous effort had to be expended in order to overcome the distance between the self and the object. Dewey portrayed the self here not as subject to a natural and inevitable unfolding as the developmentalists seemed to feel nor as consisting of innate powers such as the will that could be strengthened by the external application of mental effort, usually of an unpleasant kind. Dewey seemed to be making the case for a child as a striving, active being capable of intelligent self-direction under the proper circumstances. Dewey concluded his essay by pointing out that, like happiness, interest can best be achieved "when it is least consciously aimed at" (p. 33). Instead of mere sugarcoating, or relying on a spurious self-unfolding process, one should first discover the child's own "urgent impulses and habits" and then, by supplying the proper environment, direct them "in a fruitful and orderly way" (p. 33). Interest, under those circumstances, will take care of itself.

Dewey's 1896 monograph thrust him into the forefront of the most important educational controversy of the time. Interest and effort as fundamental concepts in education, after all, were reflective of the historic battle between the Herbartians and Harris that had taken place earlier that year over Harris's report of the Committee of Fifteen, and it must have been evident that Dewey was reconstructing the terms of that debate. Harris, for example, felt impelled to comment on Dewey's criticism. Considering Harris's senior status, his reputation for defiance in the face of attack, and the fact that he was in the middle of his reign as America's most powerful Commissioner of Education, he treated the thirty-six-year-old Dewey with unusual deference. Harris began his reply with effusive praise for Dewey's work, and then, in effect, tried to turn Dewey's analysis into at least a partial defense of his own position. By defining interest essentially as "a form of self-expressive activity" (Harris, 1896b, p. 487), Dewey,

Harris claimed, had actually subordinated the Herbartian concept of interest to a higher principle. Interest in the Herbartian sense covered all sorts of interest "good, bad, and indifferent" (p. 489), but Dewey's term, self-expression, actually introduced a higher defining principle to which mere interest was subordinate: "Interest that lies along the line of self-expression is the desirable interest. The interest should be such that it appertains to this fundamental act of revealing the Divine will in the world – self-expression of all that is highest. Here interest is subordinated to a higher category, the Divine will or the self-expression of reason" (p. 489). Harris was thus enlisting Dewey as a fellow Hegelian and ally against the Herbartians. "Interest," Harris concluded, "must be acknowledged as subordinate to the higher question of the choice of a course of study that will correlate the child with civilization into which he is born" (p. 493). Child-study for Harris was merely one instrument by which the great aim of making the pupil acquainted with the rational order of the universe was accomplished. Harris's claim of Dewey as an ally was clearly an exaggeration. Had Hall bothered to make a similar claim in behalf of child-study, however, it would have been equally far-fetched. Nor would it be quite fair to say that he stood somewhere in between these two antagonists. Dewey was struggling with the possibility that the apparent opposition between the curriculum and the child could be not so much reconciled as vitiated. The problem was not one of choosing between two existing alternatives as it was reconstructing the questions so as to present new ones.

Dewey's guarded optimism about child-study aligned him in a general way with the forces of reform in the educational world, but his reservations about the direction that child-study was actually taking placed him far indeed from the mainstream of that movement as represented by Hall. In fact, his criticisms of an idealized primitivism and a differentiated course of study that amounted to determinism put him squarely in opposition to some of Hall's most cherished ideals. Dewey saw in the child and the adolescent, not the possibility of a mystical union with a primitive paradise or the eventual realization of a super race, but the potential for intellectual mastery of the modern world. In this respect, Dewey was not as far removed from the humanists' emphasis on the development of the intellect as is sometimes imagined. Although he surely differed from someone like Harris as to what the "most complete tools of civilization" were, he shared with both Eliot and Harris a basic optimism about the power of human intellectual capacities that ran contrary to Hall's hereditary determinism and mistrust of intellectual activity in children and adolescents.

Dewey was not exactly a bystander during the heated battle between the humanists and the developmentalists around the turn of the century, but neither was he a staunch ally of either side. Clearly, however, the dispute at the turn of the century between Harris and the humanists on one side and Hall and the developmentalists on the other was providing Dewey with the context for formulating his curriculum ideas. It was in the throes of that effort that the Dewey School was born.

CHAPTER 3

THE CURRICULUM OF THE DEWEY SCHOOL

i

Within two years after John Dewey assumed his appointment as head of the Department of Philosophy, Psychology and Pedagogy at the University of Chicago in 1894, the Laboratory School opened its doors. It is unlikely that Dewey's two years as a graduate student in the city of Baltimore had prepared him for the turmoil and excitement that was Chicago in the 1890s. It was a metropolis of striking contrasts ranging from the Gold Coast to the squalid slums of the newly arrived immigrants from southern and eastern Europe. It was the Chicago rampant with political corruption and a breeding ground of agencies of municipal and social reform, such as the Civic Federation, the Municipal Votes' League, the Chicago Women's Club and, or course, Jane Addam's Hull House. It was the Chicago where "Hog Butcher to the World," Philip Armour, built a huge industrial empire and where Marshall Field and George Pullman amassed vast fortunes; and it was the Chicago where factory inspector Helen Todd (1913) could describe the children of the working class as "a human rubbish pile" (p. 70). It was also the Chicago school system that Joseph Mayer Rice (1893b), in his celebrated series of exposés, had called "the least progressive" (p. 200), but it was the same Chicago school system where Ella Flagg Young had served as District Superintendent for twelve years, the woman Dewey regarded as the "wisest person in school matters" with whom he had ever come into contact (Dewey, 1939, p. 29).

The atmosphere at the University of Chicago must have been heady as well. Although the University was barely four years old at the time of Dewey's arrival, President William Rainey Harper had already assembled a formidable array of scholars in a variety of fields, but particularly in the social arena. Albion Small, a brilliant disciple of Lester Frank Ward's, had been recruited as Head-Professor of the Social Studies, and the subsequent appointment of scholars of such eminence as Thorsten Veblen, W. I. Thomas, George Herbert Mead and Charles Horton Cooley were to make the University of Chicago the nation's citadel in the area of social inquiry. Harper, who had been a renowned teacher of Hebrew at Yale University, had a particular interest in pedagogy and undoubtedly some of the appointments he made reflected his desire to make the University of Chicago a center, not only of scholarship in that area, but a resource for practicing teachers. Harper assiduously sought to build relationships with elementary and secondary schools, a practice quite common in state universities at that time, but unusual in private universities (McCaul, 1959, p. 261).

An early address of Small's, "Demands of Sociology upon Pedagogy" (1896), delivered to a meeting of the National Education Association, illustrates both the interest in pedagogy that pervaded much of the atmosphere in the early years at the University of Chicago and the general intellectual climate that surrounded Dewey in his new position. Three years after the Report of the Committee of Ten was issued, Small began his address by apologizing for reopening "a closed incident of ancient history" in using that Committee's recommendations as a vehicle for proposing a different conception of a proper course of study (p. 174). Small was particularly disturbed by the report of the Conference on History, Civil Government, and Political Economy, a report of a subcommittee that had included among its members James Harvey Robinson and Woodrow Wilson. Small interpreted that subcommittee as assuming that the purpose of education was, first of all, "completion of the individual," and secondly, "adaptation of the individual to such co-operation with the society in which the lot is cast that he works at his best with the society in perfecting its own type" (p. 174). Small felt that, lacking any social philosophy, what we have left and what the report presented was a "classified catalogue of subjects good for study" and no real sense of what it means as a whole. If there was any conception of education as a whole, it was dominated by "a naively mediaeval psychology . . . which would be humorous if it were not tragical" (p. 175). Such a dependence on faculty psychology led the committee to believe, according to Small, that history can train the faculty called judgment, mathematics the faculty called reasoning, and so on as if powers of the mind existed as isolated entities and as if intelligence itself were somehow separated from the rest of existence. "Education" he claimed, "connotes the evolution of the whole personality, not merely of intelligence" (p. 175).

Throughout his address, Small emphasized that subjects as the report treated them were presented as "an unorganized procession of pedantic abstractions" unrelated to the real world and that such a conception served only to make us think of subjects as independent bodies instead of parts of one reality. "The proper educator," he said, "is reality, not conventionalized abstractions from reality" (Small, 1896, p. 176). Turning to the question of whether one subject can serve as a center for the concentration of studies, a position closely associated with the Herbartians, Small simply denied that any such subject exists. Rather, "the rational center is the student himself . . . [and] pedagogy should be the science of assisting youth to organize their contacts with reality," not in thought alone, but "for both thought and action" (p. 178). Students must be led to see the whole if they are to make any sense or derive any meaning from the abstractions from the whole that these subjects presumably represent. Knowledge so far as it is gained at all, Small emphasized, must be seen in its relations "not as self-sufficient knowledges" (p. 180). Not simply the study of sociology, but all branches of knowledge, should begin at the heart of "concentric circles of social activity" starting with the household and gradually extending outward until the "social *desideratum*" is finally reached, whereby "the developing member of society shall become analytically and synthetically intelligent about the society to which he belongs" (p. 182). Small concluded his address with a strong endorsement of the social meliorism of his master, Ward. Educators, he insisted, "shall not rate themselves as leaders of children, but as makers of society. Sociology knows no means for the amelioration or reform of society more radical than those of which teachers hold the leverage" (p. 184). When teachers begin to recognize and accept their social function, rather than thinking of themselves merely as providing "tonics for various kinds of mental impotence" (p. 180), Small concluded, they will begin to fulfill their vital role "in making a better future" (p. 184).

In general, Small's ideas on education reflected increasing impatience with the traditional course of study, but more particularly his ideas foreshadowed the growing tendency to see education not simply in terms of individual development of intellectual powers but in broad social terms. More often than not that tendency emerged from a concern for social stability in the face of a rapidly changing society. In Small's case, and later in Dewey's, the social significance of the curriculum lay in its promise of social progress. Intellectual development, the great purpose of schooling according to the mental disciplinarians, was of course vital, but it had to be reconciled with the school as a social institution and its place in the larger social order.

ii

Ideas do not arise *ab initio*, and it was from the educational and social conceptions of people like Small as well as from his reconstructions of the concepts of Harris, Hall and the Herbartians that Dewey began to forge the basis of what ultimately became the theory of the Laboratory School. Dewey seems to have begun his deliberations for an experimental school associated with the University of Chicago very shortly after his arrival there, and, within a year, he had circulated a privately printed "plan of organization" for what he was then calling the University Primary School. Dewey (1895) began this statement by declaring that, "the ultimate problem of all education is to co-ordinate the psychological and the social factors" (p. 224), a problem that Dewey wrestled with all his life. On the one hand, we had the individual, and education aimed at the fullest possible development of that individual's powers. On the other hand, there was the social environment in which the individual lived, and social environment implied that the expression of the individual's powers would some-how be coordinated with a "social end." One way of achieving such a coordination, Dewey believed, was to make the school a miniature community, where the child lived, participated, and contributed – where, in effect, the child's emerging individuality was at one and the same time used to enrich the social community and tested against the dictates of social reality. Particularly important in such a conception of a school was that the work of the school be directed toward what is of value to the child in the present and not "simply as a preparation for something else, or for future life" (p. 224). Such a conception of education rejected both the notion that the function of education was to prepare the next generation to operate efficiently in the existing social order and the idea that the present interests of the child must be subordinated to future rewards whether they were represented by vocational competence or by a command of the cultural heritage. The process of leading the child from present interests to an intellectual command of the modern world, however, re-mained for Dewey a controlling purpose, and the critical problem was to construct a curriculum that best facilitated that process. It was with this in mind that Dewey conceived of the proposed school as a laboratory by which theoretical designs for how this could be accomplished would be tested in a world of real teachers and real children.

At various times, both before and during the operation of

the Laboratory School, Dewey considered the extant theories of curriculum in the light of what he had set forth as the controlling purposes for his school. Dewey was vitally interested in "the theories which have attempted to give some principle or philosophy for the various subjects of the curriculum," and Harris's position was certainly one of them (Dewey [1966, p. 187], 1899a). Harris was generally sympathetic to the idea of representing in the course of study the whole of human experience, and through his five groups of studies, was attempting to do just that. It was important in the curriculum, Dewey thought, "to represent and present, with a certain degree of symmetry, all the intrinsic factors in human experience" (p. 189). The problem was that Harris's five subject areas just did not do that in any sort of cohesive way. Each of the groups of studies was taken, more or less, "ready made," Dewey felt, and each taught as isolated from the next with "no real principle of unity given us" (p. 189), thus reflecting the criticism the Herbartians had made of Harris's subcommittee report on that "immortal day in Cleveland" a few years before. As a result of this isolation of subject areas, the study of any given subject suffered: "geography loses much of its meaning when separated from history, and history loses a good deal of its content, if you isolate it entirely from geography" (p. 191). The distinctions among the various groups of studies, therefore, were formal and artificial, particularly in the way a child would see them. While such a system of organization and classification of subjects may make sense to the mature mind "to introduce them to the child as distinct from the start, is to disorganize and disintegrate, instead of coordinate and connect" (p. 193). Even at the highest levels of scholarship, neat demarcation among the various branches of knowledge may not be a good thing. Dewey recognized, for example, even at the turn of the century, that some of the most exciting experimental work being done in biology was the result of the introduction of concepts and methods from physics and chemistry (p. 194).

A related problem arose when subjects were presented in a more or less finished form. Dewey was convinced that it just made it all the more difficult under those circumstances to see organized knowledge as related to human needs and human aspirations. Organized bodies of knowledge, Dewey was fond of pointing out, were, after all, the outcomes of a long period of historical development. Rather than springing up full-blown as rarefied abstractions, they were the outgrowths of human conditions and the attempts of people to do the things that had to be done. "Even mathematics," Dewey (1899a) claimed, the most abstract of the subjects commonly taught in schools, "originally sprang up, not out of the ground, not out of nature, but out of human life and human needs" (p. 191). To present school studies as finished abstractions not only distorted their origins, but widened the gulf between knowledge and human affairs. Dewey's basic objection to Harris's position, then, was not with its attempt to bring to the child the intellectual fruits of Western civilization, but with the fact that this was being attempted without respecting the way children see their world and with a view of knowledge that exaggerated and distorted distinctions among the branches of study and that obfuscated rather than enhanced their relationship to human purposes. Moreover, the promise of unity among the major subjects in the curriculum was not fulfilled as long as each of Harris's five areas of study were treated independently from one another. In bringing these criticisims to bear on Harris's basic position on curriculum, Dewey was aware that he was also criticizing the standard curriculum of his day, since what Harris advocated bore a striking resemblance to what the curriculum already looked like.

One curriculum that held out some promise for change in the right direction was, of course, culture-epochs; but Dewey had mixed feelings about its efficacy. Part of its appeal lay in its attempt to take children's interests directly into account in constructing a course of study. If children at a given stage in their development had a natural interest in the heroes of Norse mythology, why not take that as the starting point for leading on to something else? Furthermore, a culture-epochs curriculum proposed to move progressively from the early stages of human evolution to more or less contemporary civilization, and it was with the ability to deal effectively with the modern world that Dewey felt the school curriculum should ultimately lead.

As an active member of the National Herbart Society, it was almost inevitable that Dewey should have to come to grips with the theory that, by common agreement, was the foundation of their approach to the course of study. The immediate occasion for Dewey's considered reaction to culture-epochs was a lengthy article on the subject by C. C. Van Liew (1895), a leading Herbartian and prominent figure in the child-study movement. Dewey (1896b) saw the theory in general as addressing the critical problem of finding a principle "that will give correspondence between child and subject-matter" (p. 233), and culture-epochs theory posited a sympathetic correspondence between what is contained in an historical epoch and what appealed to the child. While Dewey was careful to say that he did not question the fact of correspondence in a general way, he argued that its application to education was not really a fact but an analogy to biological recapitulation, and to draw implications from that analogy was a rather tricky business. "No one proposes," he said, "that the mother shall modify her diet when the human embryo has reached the 'fish' phase, or take any practical note of it" (p. 234). There were, then, two problems to be considered: one was that the parallelism between the child and the race was not as literal as was sometimes supposed and, therefore, one could not merely make inferences from race development to individual development without some sort of independent verification as to whether a corresponding stage actually existed in the child. If one were to recapitulate the historical epochs too literally insofar as the curriculum were concerned, one would certainly run the risk of "arresting development" (p. 234) by prolonging unduly some aspect of study simply because the human race had experienced a prolonged historical period in its development. At best, the existence of an historical epoch could suggest the possibility of a corresponding developmental stage in the child, and, even then, it was not clear that we should single out that interest as supreme, making the corresponding epoch the chief basis for what the child studied. In Dewey's view, it would have to be further recognized, even if these corresponding interests were identified in the child, that they exist among other interests. "There was never a mind," Dewey (1899a) said, "simply mythical or simply heroic" (p. 207). In an apparent reference to the sort of reasoning so often employed by Hall and others in the child-study movement, Dewey argued that "any one can set out and collect lots of instances of the spontaneous myth-forming by children," but this does not warrant "the inference that the child at this stage of his being is essentially a myth-forming person and therefore is in the same kind of emotional atmosphere that the primitive people were when they formed myths" (p. 207).

The second major aspect of the culture-epochs curriculum to which Dewey objected was the practice, in both Germany and the United States, of using the cultural products of the historical period as the basis of what was taught. In practice, actually, the culture-epochs curriculum sometimes used such products of historical periods as the legends produced by the people of that era, but often it was not so much a true artifact of that period as it was a kind of literary representation of an historical epoch, such as the common practice in the United States of using Longfellow's *Hiawatha* to represent to children undergoing the "savage" stage in their development the corresponding stage in human history. This made Dewey's criticism all the more cogent. If there were such a thing as an agricultural stage in a child's development, Dewey (1896b) argued, it "requires, according to the true analogy, to be fed in just the same way in the child in which it was fed in the race – by contact with earth and seed and air and sun and all the mighty flux and ebb of life in nature" (p. 235). Dewey was here not so much objecting to the idea of a basic analogy of recapitulation guiding the curriculum as he was rejecting the common assumption of culture-epochs theory that history and literature had to be made the basis of study when such a parallelism was assumed. Myths, for example, so far as children were concerned, "are a very excellent thing" when regarded simply as stories, but, in another reference to the way Hall would interpret their pedagogical value, Dewey took the position that "it is self-deception to suppose that they have a value other than that of a story – that by some inner affinity to the child's nature, he is being morally introduced into the civilization from which the myth sprung, and is receiving a sort of spiritual baptism through "literature" (p. 236). Dewey concluded his analysis by alluding to the ability of children to engage in serious intellectual endeavor, a position almost directly opposite to that of Hall's: "Let us treat the intellectual resources, capacities, and needs of our children with the full dignity and respect they deserve, and not sentimentalize nor symbolize the realities of life, nor present them in the shape of mental toys" (p. 236). While Dewey was intrigued by the Herbartian concept of culture-epochs, he was obviously a long way from giving it his complete endorsement.

In developing the curriculum theory that was to guide the Dewey School, Dewey thus rejected the two alternatives that presented themselves most forcefully around the turn of the century. While each had its own appeal to Dewey, neither was able to deliver, in his view, on the claims made for it. The humanist curriculum, as exemplified by Harris, sought merely to impose a collection of subjects on the child, and, although the ultimate aim of intellectual development through the study of these subjects was a noble one, that curriculum had neither the coherence nor the appeal to the child's interests that Dewey sought. It was that appeal that attracted Dewey to culture-epochs as a curriculum theory, but, upon examination, the promise of a sympathetic relationship between the child and an historical epoch in human history appeared more symbolic than real. The promise of a curriculum sympathetically attuned to children's interests was simply unrealized. It remained for Dewey to construct out of those rejected theories something that could stand as the curriculum theory for the Dewey School.

iii

Early one Monday morning in January 1896, Dewey's school, with a complement of two teachers and sixteen pupils, held its first session. So far as has been recorded, that morning's activities consisted of a song, a tour of the premises at 389 Fifty-Seventh Street, including the garden in back, the construction by the children of a paper container for their school materials, a story told by one of the children, and, finally some physical exercise ("The model school," 1896, p. 707). The curriculum that was to guide that school's activity in the years to come had not as yet been fully worked out in Dewey's mind, and, in the first couple of years of its existence, a casual observer could have construed it as a culture-epochs course of study. "Superficially," Dewey admitted, "there was a similarity to the 'recapitulation' theory in this method of enlarging the intrinsic experience of the children by means of subject-matter drawn from the development of the culture of mankind" (Dewey, 1936, p. 472). The skeleton of Dewey's curriculum did, in fact, bear a marked resemblance to that of culture-epochs, especially in its progression from early stages in human history to later ones, but the flesh, muscles, and tissue were of a quite different order. In those early years, the youngest groups concentrated on the "building of the homes of the primitive peoples" (Mayhew and Edwards, 1936, p. 43), and "reinvented Ab's trap for the sabre-toothed tiger" (p. 44), while older groups dealt with the ancient Greeks and progressively later historical periods; but beyond those superficial resemblances, there lay a fundamental transformation that Dewey had wrought in what was to be the unifying center of the course of study. Like Small, Dewey felt the Herbartians to be misguided in assuming that any of the existing subjects, such as history or literature, could serve to provide the unity in the curriculum that he sought.

Instead, Dewey found that unifying concept in what he called *occupations*. The term, perhaps, was an unfortunate one because it could easily be identified with vocational education or with an overriding emphasis on overt activity, but Dewey, at various times, took pains to explain the special meaning he attributed to that concept. Perhaps the fullest explication of the importance that he attached to the notion of occupations is found in one of his most brilliant essays, "Interpretation of the Savage Mind," a work written during the period of the Dewey School, but not on any pedagogical topic. In that essay, Dewey, usually a gentle critic, was uncharacteristically harsh in attacking the anthropological interpretations of Herbert Spencer. He was disturbed by the fact that Spencer, in his interpretations of so-called primitive peoples, seemed to take his own civilization as the standard for which to measure others, as if the savage mind could be gauged on some kind of "fixed scale" (Dewey, 1902, p. 218). Primitive people were always seen as lacking this or that quality that the civilized mind possessed. But, as Dewey asserted, "the psychical attitudes and traits of the savage are more than stages through which the mind has passed, leaving them behind. They are outgrowths which have entered decisively into further evolution, and as such form an integral part of the framework of present mental organization" (p. 217). Curiously, he pointed out, such a positive view was commonly accepted in the case of the evolution of animals, but was lacking in the work of Spencer and some anthropologists in their interpretations of human evolution. Rather than seeing the human mind on some kind of hierarchical scale, Dewey urged that we see human intellectual activity and indeed the culture as a whole in relation to the characteristic activities in which the individual or society engages and the ability of those individuals to achieve command of their environment. "The biological point of view," he argued, "commits us to the conviction that mind, whatever else it may be, is at least an organ of service for the control of environment in relation to the ends of the life process' (p. 219). Hunting peoples, agricultural peoples and so on cannot be judged by the extent to which they have mastered or adopted the trappings of what we call civilization, but in relation to the dominant activities required by the kind of world in which they live. "The occupations," Dewey said, "determine the chief modes of satisfaction, the standards of success and failure. Hence they furnish the working classifications and definitions of value. . . . So fundamental and pervasive is the group of occupational activities that it affords the scheme or pattern of the structural organization of mental traits" (pp. 219–20). Not only did an understanding of fundamental occupations give us insight into present mental operations, but it provided a way of understanding other features of a culture – art, religion, marriage, laws.

In a manner similar to the way Hall applied "ontogeny recapitulates phylogeny" to the construction of a course of study, Dewey took his own interpretation of the evolution of the human species and tried to reconstruct it in the curriculum of the Dewey School. In an important sense, like that of Hall and the Herbartians, Dewey's curriculum was also an historical recapitulation, but what it recapitulated was not the historical stages through which the human race had presumably passed; instead, it traced the evolution of the basic social activities that Dewey called occupations. "This simplified social life," he hoped, "should reproduce, in miniature, the activities fundamental to life as a whole, and thus enable the child, on one side, to become gradually acquainted with the structure, materials, and modes of operation of the larger community; while, up on the other, it enables him individually to express himself through these lines of conduct, and thus attain control of his own powers" (Dewey, 1896c, p. 418). For Dewey, then, a curriculum built around fundamental social occupations would provide the bridge that would harmonize individual and social ends – what for him was the central problem to be resolved in any educational theory. It would also serve to tie together the various component parts of the curriculum and give it the kind of unity that Dewey saw as lacking in Harris's course of study. The question of whether children would be interested in such matters or whether the program of studies had the desired effect were things that simply had to be discovered in the setting of the Laboratory School, and modifications would have to be introduced based on the results of that experiment in curriculum.

About a year after it opened, Dewey outlined the general organization of the school and the framework of studies as it had evolved to that point. Insofar as organization was concerned, the nine years of the elementary school had been broken down into three subdivisions: the first included children from four to seven; the second from seven to ten; and the third from ten to thirteen. In the elementary period as a whole, Dewey (1897d) saw the distinguishing aim, not as providing technical knowledge or the "possession of a certain amount of information," but to build into the child's consciousness "an orderly sense of the world in which he lives" beginning with that part of the world that touches the child most directly, the family, and moving gradually outward to the school, the neighborhood, and further to the larger society (p. 74), a general aim strikingly similar to that of Small's. The course of study had three main subdivisions: manual training, history and literature, and science. Dewey saw the purpose of manual training not in terms of the development of useful motor skills, but in terms of the opportunities it presented "for cultivating the social spirit" and "supplying the child with motives for working in ways positively useful to the community of which he is a member" (p. 72). As basic social activities, furthermore, they could provide the starting point for tracing their evolution to the abstractions represented by the organized bodies of knowledge: "Cooking, for example, is a natural avenue of approach to simple but fundamental chemical facts and principles, and to a study of the plants which furnish articles of food" (p. 72). The introduction of carpentry work was not for the purpose of developing the skills of sawing and hammering, but because it presented an excellent opportunity for introducing calculation within a natural context and for the opportunity it provided in "cultivating a genuine number sense" (p. 72). Dewey was obviously interested in the child gaining a command of chemistry and arithmetic, and he thought this could be best accomplished by introducing them to the child in a manner similar to the way they first became matters of urgent necessity to the human race.

From such social occupations, such as growing food, constructing shelter and making clothing, conventional subject matter was expected to evolve, but in a more vital and constructive way than in the typical curriculum. Arithmetic, for example, was expected to emerge from cooking activity. In one extant report by the cooking teacher, Miss Scates reported that the fractions 1/3, 2/3 and 3/3 and the ratio of 1:2 were included in the cooking of flaked rice and flaked wheat, although she noted that the "experiment was not a great success on account of poor scales" ("Scrapbook IX," 1900). Children also were called upon to evaluate their own handiwork on occasion as an apparent culmination of the effort to involve children, not only in the planning stages of their activities, but at their conclusion as well. Dewey's nine-year-old son, Fred, for example reported:

> We made a wigwam. My wigwam is not made well. I could not make a good Indian. Harper's wigwam was very nice. William had a good one too. Yesterday we looked for thread in a sheep's knee. We found it. It was the tendon. ("University Primary School," 1896).

Dewey was concerned as well with the child's mastery of organized subject matter such as science, but he felt that the surest path to that achievement would be by initiating the child into the fundamental social occupations from which science arose. In 1900, for example, Group V tested seeds that would later be used in the garden to determine what percentage would germinate in the spring ("Group V," 1900). In a history class conducted by Miss Camp, children, through some smelting work, discovered the advantages of charcoal over wood in the smelting process ("Group IV," 1900). In another group, children who had been creating a story about a tribe that had left their caves and started down a river expressed a desire to use the clay that the Indians in the story used and began experimenting with the uses of clay.

In developing the activities that were to constitute the curriculum of the Dewey School, Dewey was not reaching for a compromise between the positions of, say, Harris, and Hall.

Rather, he was trying to reconstruct the issue of the child versus the curriculum in such a way as to make their opposition unnecessary. Dewey tried to illustrate his point by reference to certain subject matter. "Geography," he said, "is not only a set of facts and principles, which may be classified and discussed by themselves; it is also a way in which some actual individual feels and thinks the world" (Dewey, 1897c, p. 361). To Dewey, the point of education was unquestionably the latter, but the problem lay in the apparent gap between the way the child sees the world and the way a mature adult does. "To the child," he said, "simply because he is a child, geography is not, and cannot be, what it is to the one who writes the scientific treatise on geography. *The latter has had exactly the experience which it is the problem of instruction to induce.* . . . We must discover what there is lying within the child's present sphere of experience (or within the scope of experiences which he can easily get) which deserves to be called geographical" (p. 361). There was, for Dewey, no body of knowledge which has been "eternally set off" and defined as geography or any other subject. If we had a square mile of land, for example, there was no objective reality which would determine that the way of seeing it was geographical, or trigonometric, or botanical, or geological, or, for that matter, historical. The reference point of the individual viewing that territory was the starting point for any kind of logical organization of its features. So far as Dewey was concerned, the first curriculum question was, "how, out of the crude native experience which the child already has, the complete and systematic knowledge of the adult consciousness is gradually and systematically worked out" (p. 364).

As time progressed and the Dewey School grew both in terms of size and recognition, Dewey continued to report on the school's activities as well as to refine his theory of the course of study. A matter of increasing concern to him was the apparent opposition that existed in the pedagogical world between the psychological position, insisting on the primacy of the mental operations of the child, on the one hand, and the logical position, insisting on the primacy of the organized bodies of knowledge, on the other. He interpreted the tone of "comparative worthlessness" directed toward the psychological position in Harris's Report of the Committee of Fifteen to the existence of a dualism that unnaturally separated "the subject-matter of experience" from "the mental operations involved in dealing with it" (Dewey, 1897c, p. 357). While Dewey recognized that the ordinary teacher does not usually raise such questions but simply follows the curriculum as laid out, he emphasized that those who deal theoretically with the curriculum as well as those responsible for laying it out cannot ignore the question of such an untenable dualism. Regarding Harris's position, one which he characterized as "the most philosophic answer which has yet been given to these questions in America," Dewey did not oppose the general proposition that "the standard for selecting and placing a study is the worth which it has in adapting the pupil to the needs of the civilization into which he is born" (p. 359), but he did take issue with the implication in the Committee of Fifteen Report and in other writings of Harris that such a social determination of the curriculum somehow excludes a psychological one. Dewey was thus not taking sides in the continuing battle between the humanists and the developmentalists. He was essentially saying that they were fighting over a false issue.

The way history was studied in the Dewey School also illustrates how Dewey was using the school to help him reconstruct the curriculum concepts that were being put forward by the various interest groups of his time. "To study history," he said, "is not to amass information, but to use information in constructing a vivid picture of how and why men did thus and so; achieved their successes and came to their failures" (Dewey, 1900, p. 199). The general aim of teaching history was to lead the child to an appreciation of the values of social life and to let the child see the forces that led to effective co-operation among human beings. The record of human history in Dewey's view was a record of how human beings used intelligence to gain command of their environment – "how man learned to think, to think to some effect, to transform the conditions of life so that life itself became a different thing" (p. 200). This applied to the study of how human beings in early times developed tools which helped them overcome adversity. It applied to the study of the American frontier period where people were required "to cope with a raw and often hostile nature, and to regain success by sheer intelligence, energy, and persistence of character" (p. 201). Thinking of history as social history rather than a rendering of events also "prevents any tendency to swamp history in myth, fairy story, and merely literary renderings" (p. 201), a reference to what the Herbartians preached and practiced. "I cannot avoid the feeling," Dewey said, "that much as the Herbartian school has done to enrich the elementary curriculum in the direction of history, it has often inverted the true relationship existing between history and literature" (p. 201). While he had no objection in principle to using *Robinson Crusoe* as a kind of idealization of how a human being can gain intelligent control over an adverse situation, it would be far better, he thought, to carry that theme through American colonial history. The same would be true of *Hiawatha* as a vehicle for the study of so-called savage life. Why not study the accomplishments of the American Indian firsthand and how their social life emerged from the conditions that they had to face and overcome rather than through an idealized literary representation? Although Dewey clearly saw much value in the study of history, he questioned the need to follow a strict chronological rendering as implied in Herbartian culture-epochs. In determining the appropriateness of various periods, remoteness in time was not a guiding consideration. What was important was nearness "in spirit" to the child's own psychological outlook. Thus prehistoric life was much closer to the child than, say, the Babylonian period or the Egyptian period, because, in Dewey's words, either of the latter ones "does not simplify enough and it does not generalize enough; or, at least, it does not do so in the right way" (p. 202).

In the Laboratory School, therefore, there was nothing of what we would call today a survey of history. Instead, there was an attempt to introduce at appropriate periods in a child's development those aspects of history that provided insight into the social life of people with a particular emphasis on their typical occupations, occupations that served to shape that social life. For the first group, therefore, the six-year-olds, there was an initial period of studying the occupations of people who live in urban and rural areas; seven-year-olds looked at inventions and how they grew out of the need to overcome certain obstacles; and the eight-year-olds studied explorers and discoverers as a transition from the child's immediate surroundings to things that are further removed in time. Chicago and the United States generally provided the main focus for the second group, with the third year of that group's work devoted to a transition by examining connections between European and American life. Finally, in the third group, chronological order was introduced, beginning with the ancient world and leading to a more conventional study of European and American history. The order of study, Dewey (1900) was careful to point out, was "the outcome not of thought but of considerable experimenting and shifting of subjects from year to year" (p. 203).

Perhaps the most dramatic, and, in the long run, most controversial departure from the conventional curriculum of the day was the manner in which the so-called three Rs were treated, and, in particular, reading, which for many people, then as now, was the touchstone of a successful elementary school curriculum. In general, Dewey believed that reading, writing and arithmetic could be most effectively taught within the context of use and especially in connection with the basic occupations around which the curriculum revolved. Part of this belief was rooted in his overall curriculum theory and partly from his conception of changing American life. In an era when reading and writing meant the difference between being educated and uneducated, "all the meaning that belongs to these ends naturally transferred itself to the means through which alone they could be realized" (Dewey, 1898, p. 316). With the breakdown of the isolation that once existed, the immediate importance of reading and writing as a gateway to a "richer and wider mental life" (p. 316) had been diminished and the advent of the telephone and the telegraph, the great growth in newspapers and magazines, and various forms of amusement, at least in cities, had lessened the motive power that was associated with "those banks termed books" (p. 317). Instead of facing up to the fact of this change in how reading was regarded and then adapting our curriculum accordingly, Dewey felt that we had continued reading "as the centre and core of our course of study, and dressed it out with a variety of pretty pictures, objects, and games, and a smattering of science" (p. 318).

Dewey was obviously concerned that reading be taught successfully, but as long as reading was being taken out of its natural context, it appeared inevitable to him that the child would regard reading merely as a task to be accomplished without any sense of what a book is for. In characterizing the isolation of reading as a subject, Dewey (1898) deplored the fact that a book had become a "reading-lesson" (p.322), and reading itself was nothing but uttering sounds and recognizing words. "When the bare process of reading is thus made an end in itself," he said, "it is a psychological impossibility for reading to be other than lifeless" (p. 322). The reading books themselves exemplify the "fatal divorce between the substance and the form of expression" in the utter triviality of their content. "Take up the first half-dozen or dozen such books you meet with," Dewey implored, "and ask yourself how much there is in the ideas presented worthy of respect from any intelligent child of six years" (p. 322).

The teaching of reading was so much an outgrowth of the basic activities of the Dewey School that one distinguished former student, a man of remarkable memory, could not ever recall being taught to read. (H. K. Tenney, personal communication, October 18, 1976). Reading, writing and arithmetic were things that occurred naturally in the course of building a clubhouse, or cooking, or raising a pair of sheep. In this way, Dewey was trying to avoid two common effects of the prevailing methods of teaching reading. The first was "exhibited in the paradox of the combination of slavish dependence upon books with real inability to use them effectively" (Dewey, 1898, p. 324) and the other was that "the regimen of the three R's" (p. 325) simply crowded out very important educative activities that children between four and eight or nine could be engaging in. Art, for example, in its various forms – music, drawing, modelling and so forth – was much more fitted to what the child needed at that age than a concentration on written symbols. Even literature and history suffered because reading material was not chosen for its intrinsic value, but because it presumably matched the child's ability to recognize verbal symbols. What Dewey did not anticipate at this point was that the rise of standardized achievement tests in the twentieth century would sharply accelerate the tendencies in the teaching of the three Rs that he so much deplored and would help make his own emphasis on the relationship between reading and human purposes the object of scorn and caricature.

iv

At the same time that Dewey was establishing the order of studies in his school and the manner in which the subjects should be treated, he was also seeking to articulate the theoretical conceptions that guided that work. In April of 1899, Dewey delivered three lectures to an audience of parents and others in which he tried to express the basic rationale for the school, and these lectures formed the heart of *School and Society*, which, when it was published that year, added immeasurably to the fame of the school and spread Dewey's ideas to a worldwide audience. In "The School and Social Progress," the first of the lectures, Dewey attempted to link the basic core of his curriculum, the occupations, to the mighty changes that had been wrought in American society, particularly the arrival of what Dewey called the factory system. Dewey was not so much expressing nostalgia for the days when "the whole process of getting illumination stood revealed in its toilsome length, from the killing of the animal and the trying of fat to the making of wicks and dipping of candles" (p. 19), as he was trying to point out that such a process, toilsome as it was, was an educative activity in a way that flicking a switch and filling a house with electric illumination could never be. Those activities of an earlier day, furthermore, provided opportunities for cooperative action toward a common goal and for a sense of accomplishment that was not as readily available in a modern technological society. For the "city-bred child of today" (p. 21), such opportunities were no longer present, and the educational problem then became one of recreating in the school something of the occupations that in former times not only provided a sense of real purpose, but linked intelligence and cooperative action to what the work of the world required.

The way to accomplish this, according to Dewey (1899b), was to create in the school "a miniature community, an embryonic society" (p. 28), and as various forms of social occupations were introduced, "the entire spirit of the school is renewed" (p. 27) and the school becomes a place to live rather than "only a place to learn lessons" (p. 28). Dewey was again careful to emphasize the social side of these occupations rather than their utilitarian value in what ultimately turned out to be a mostly futile effort to deflect the idea that he was mainly interested in teaching practical skills. "There is nothing which strikes the average intelligent visitor as stranger," he said, "than to see boys as well as girls of ten, twelve, and thirteen years of age engaged in sewing and weaving. If we look at this from the standpoint of preparation of the boys for sewing on buttons and making patches, we get a narrow and utilitarian conception – a basis that hardly justifies giving prominence to this sort of work in the school" (pp. 29–30). The children in the school sheared sheep, made the cards used to card the wool, and then spun the wool on a spinning wheel, hardly practical activities in a modern industrial society. Here, they were following through something that they designed and created from its most elementary form to a finished product. Dewey once recalled that Plato defined a slave as one who had none of his own ideas, but was always expressing those of someone else. How much more urgent it must be in a modern industrial society than it was in Plato's time, Dewey mused, that somewhere people learn to develop and bring to execution their own ideas. "When occupations in the school are conceived in this broad and generous way," he felt, "I can only stand lost in wonder at the objections so often heard, that such occupations are out of place in the school because they are materialistic, utilitarian, or even menial in their tendency" (p. 34). The miniature community that Dewey envisioned was designed to initiate the child into effective social membership and, by "providing him with the instruments of effective self-direction," in the words of one of Dewey's most oft-quoted statements, "we shall have the deepest and best guarantee of a larger society which is worthy, lovely, and harmonious" (p. 40).

In his two subsequent lectures, Dewey tried to indicate how the activities that characterized the school, not only had the social value he expressed in the first lecture, but followed the instincts that children brought with them to school. In "The School and the Life of the Child," he amplified the four instincts or impulses that he believed characterized children's behavior: the social or communicative instinct, the constructive instinct – the desire to make things, the expressive impulse, which grows out of the first two and, finally, the artistic impulse. These impulses, Dewey (1899b) felt, were in fact connected somehow with primitive life, as culture-epochs theory implied, and that because "there is a sort of natural recurrence of the child mind to the typical activities of primitive peoples" (p. 58) one could use that correspondence in constructing a course of study. Despite Dewey's reservations about Herbartian theory, certain aspects of their ideas seemed to have made a lasting impression on him. When Dewey turned to the theme of "Waste in Education" in his third lecture, he was careful to delineate his version of waste from the typical emphasis on efficiency, then only in its incipient stages but destined to become a dominant theme in American education in the twentieth century. Dewey declared that he was not so much interested in "waste of money or the waste of things" (p. 75), but the waste in human life that is created by the isolation of the school from social life and, because "all waste is due to isolation," also to the waste created by the isolation of one subject from another as well as "to the lack of coherence in . . . studies and methods" (p. 74).

Increasingly, Dewey was associating the work of the Laboratory School with his epistemological ideas, and, in fact, with his overall philosophy. "The underlying theory of knowledge," he said of the Laboratory School, "emphasized the part of problems, which originated in active situations, in the development of thought and also the necessity of testing thought by action if thought was to pass over into knowledge. The only place in which a comprehensive theory of knowledge can receive an active test is in the process of education" (Dewey, 1936, p. 464). It was for this reason that Dewey tried to see the school as embodying a form of social life, one where cooperative social living in miniature could provide the setting for the development of thought. Dewey specifically denied that there was any desire to " 'adjust' individuals to social institutions, if by adjustment is meant preparation to fit into present social arrangements and conditions" (p. 366). It was rather that mental development was essentially a social process and required a congenial social setting in which to develop effectively. In the long run, it was intellectual development that Dewey sought to effect through the curriculum, not only because it gave the individual command of his or her environment, but because intelligent social action held out the most promise for a better society. Dewey's rejection of the traditional course of study was not because it emphasized intellectual content; it was precisely because it lacked it. "Custom and convention," Dewey asserted, "conceal from most of us the extreme intellectual poverty of the traditional course of study, as well as its lack of intellectual organization" (p. 468).

In designing a course of study for his school, Dewey, as usual, rejected both the alternatives that were presented. One was "to follow the traditional arrangement of studies and lessons"; the other was "to permit a free flow of experience and acts which are immediately and sensationally appealing, but which lead to nothing in particular" (Dewey, 1936, p. 469). The solution that he sought in the curriculum of the Laboratory School was to find those things within the child's life and interests that offer the best opportunity to lead gradually to a command of the abstract subject matter we associate with logically organized bodies of knowledge. Because Dewey's school, throughout its existence, was essentially an elementary school, and because Dewey left the University of Chicago before any attempt was made to develop a program of secondary education, we tend to get a truncated version of what Dewey envisioned as an appropriate course of study, emphasizing primarily children's interests and active occupations and slighting the importance that he attached to a command of the intellectual resources of one's culture.

Written two years before he left the University of Chicago, Dewey's *The Child of the Curriculum* is unquestionably the best-known and, in most respects, the clearest exposition of his theory of curriculum. As usual, Dewey was trying to dispel what he regarded as an untenable dualism. On the one hand, we had "certain social aims, meanings, values incarnate in the matured experience of the adult" and on the other, "an immature, undeveloped being" (Dewey, 1902a, p. 4). The differences between those two "fundamental factors" were obvious. The world of the adult was logically arranged with reference to general principles; it is classified and abstracted from the real world. The child, on the other hand, lives in a world of immediate and direct experiences, and Dewey elaborated on what these basic factors implied when the course of study was considered. Conventionally, subjects are divided into topics and topics into studies and each study into lessons, and finally each lesson into specific facts or skills to be learned. "The road which looks so long when viewed in its entirety," he said, "is easily traveled, considered as a series of particular steps" (p. 8). On the other side, the child and the facts of child development are taken as the starting point. The standard for what is taught lies in the child not with bodies of subject matter.

Dewey saw the solution in reconstructing the problem in such a way as to make that apparent opposition disappear. He believed that he found the key to that dilemma in the concept of *experience*. One had "to get rid of the prejudicial notion that there is some gap in kind (as distinct from degree) between the child's experience and the various forms of subject-matter that make up the course of study." Once that was accomplished, the child and the curriculum (the course of study) became "simply two limits which define a single process" (Dewey, 1902a, p. 11). What Dewey was constructing, essentially, was a continuum of experience, and it was the function of the course of study to move along that line from one defining point, the immediate, chaotic, but integral experience of the child, to the other defining point, the logically organized, abstract, and classified experience of the mature adult. What was being reconstructed in the curriculum, therefore, was not the stages in the development of human history as the Herbartians advocated, but stages in the way human beings gained control of their world through the use of intelligence – stages in the development of knowledge.

But that reconstruction could not be strictly a logical one; it had to be psychologized. Dewey (1902a) pointed out that, while there was no direct opposition between the viewpoint of the scientist and the science teacher, neither were they "immediately identical" (p. 22). The scientist was primarily interested in advancing knowledge, in developing new hypotheses and trying to verify them. While the teacher was also interested in the subject matter of science, his or her primary interest was in how that knowledge become part of the child's experience. It is not so much with knowledge itself that the teacher was concerned but in the effect that knowledge has on the child. As the child progressed in the educational process, the child's experience would begin to take on the form of the logically organized bodies of experiences that we call knowledge and which evolved over many centuries. Dewey was thus hoping at one and the same time to put children in command of the intellectual resources of their culture and to break down the barriers that life in a technological society had erected between knowledge and human affairs. By reconstructing the evolution of knowledge in the curriculum, Dewey was hoping not only to educate children but to restore to modern life the role that he believed knowledge had once played in a pre-industrial society.

v

Dewey left the University of Chicago in 1904 after an unfortunate, almost tragic, dispute with President Harper. The Laboratory School continued to exist, but gradually lost the particular character that Dewey gave it. His appointment at Columbia University was in its philosophy department, and, although he maintained some connection with Teachers College, his work in his long career at Columbia reflected, in the main, general philosophical interests. Although his magnum opus in education, *Democracy and Education*, was not published until 1916, it is largely a comprehensive synthesis of the ideas that Dewey developed during his Chicago period. Dewey had established himself as an educational statesman continuing to interest himself in educational questions throughout his lifetime, and his pronouncements often attracted national attention. But, although all sorts of changes in educational policy and programs were attributed to Dewey's influence during his long career at Columbia, and although his work attracted devoted disciples, nowhere do we find a coherent and lasting attempt to implement his course of study. While it would be obvious exaggeration to say that Dewey's influence on the curriculum of America's schools was nil, other reformers with quite different conceptions of what should be taught were far more successful, or to put it more accurately, their ideas were more congenial to the forces that in fact influenced the course of study in the twentieth century than were Dewey's.

What was there about Dewey's ideas that caused them at best to be translated into slogans and at worst to be distorted altogether? Dewey himself may have had the most significant insights into that question. In a paper given during the period of the Dewey School, he considered the general question of education reform and why it fails (Dewey, 1901). He tried to draw a picture of how innovations are introduced into the curriculum. First, he said, someone feels that a school system is behind the times, that there are new and exciting things going on elsewhere. Public sentiment is aroused and, after letters are written, editorials appear, and lobby groups do their work, the change is instituted: "The victory is won, and everybody – unless it be some already overburdened and distracted teacher – congratulates everybody else that such advanced steps are taken" (p. 334). Within a short time, however, complaints are heard that children do not read as well as they used to or that their handwriting is bad; there develops a public outcry to rescind the reform, and there is a return to the status quo ante.

One reason, Dewey (1901) felt, that these cycles occur is that there is "no conscious educational standard by which to test and place each aspiring claimant" (p. 335). Every movement for change, whether it be a new way of teaching arithmetic or a new subject such as manual training, is seen as isolated and independent from the rest of the curriculum; what we have is a multiplicity of standards for judging the worth of each reform, and these standards can easily work at cross-purposes. Secondly, Dewey called attention to what he termed "the mechanics of school organization and administration" (p. 337). Although such things are usually seen as peripheral to the main business of the course of study, in fact the organizational features of the school are often controlling factors in what gets taught. As long as the grouping of students, the selection of teachers, and the system of rewards remain the same, the reform is doomed. "We forget," Dewey said, "that it is precisely such things as these that really control the whole system, even on its distinctively educational side" (p. 338). The changes that Dewey sought in the curriculum were so sweeping and so revolutionary that they had to be accompanied by an equally great transformation in the way schools were run, and the key organizational features of any school are far more permanent affairs than any branch of study in the curriculum.

Moreover, the things that Dewey sought to promote through his curriculum were difficult to measure and therefore difficult to fit into a system that depended on "that kind of external inspection which goes by the name of examination." "Technical proficiency," he said, "acquisition of skill and information, present much less difficulty" (Dewey, 1901, p. 340). Dewey also called attention to the minimal role that the teacher normally had in designing a course of study. It is, after all, the teacher "who alone can make that course of study a living reality," and "as long as the teacher, who is after all the only real educator in the school system, has no definite and authoritative position in shaping the course of study, that is likely to remain an external thing to be externally applied to the child" (p. 341). What Dewey called the question of democracy was also involved, but the practical question was derived from the fact that the teacher was the most important figure insofar as the curriculum was concerned, and there was simply no point in attempting a reform of the course of study without the active participation of the teacher and without taking into account the teacher's abilities, interests and desires. Curriculum change, therefore, required not simply a new conception of the course of study, but a complex process of interaction involving both the organizational structure of the school and those people who were to be instrumental in bringing it to the classroom. From all accounts, such interaction did exist in the Laboratory School where Dewey had assembled a superb corps of teachers, but accomplishing that same dedication and commitment in the typical public school was another matter. With remarkable prescience, Dewey predicted that, without considered attention to the processes of change itself, "we shall be forever oscillating between extremes: now lending ourselves with enthusiasm to the introduction of art and music and manual training because they give vitality to the school work and relief to the child; now querulously complaining of the evil results reached, and insisting with all positiveness upon the return of good old days when reading, writing, spelling, and arithmetic were adequately taught" (p. 346).

Bandwagonism and pendulum swings from reform to conservatism in educational affairs did, in fact, become a persistent and almost mysterious phenomenon in the twentieth century. But beyond the shifts themselves, there remained a fundamental resistance to the sorts of changes that Dewey sought to introduce. In a larger sense, it is likely that what Dewey saw as the basic function of education, the development of the kind of intelligence that would lead to a command of the conditions of one's life and ultimately to social progress, was not what most people saw as the major requirement of a modern industrial society. The appeal of a stable social order with each person efficiently fulfilling his or her appointed tasks was far more compelling. John Dewey, the quintessential American philosopher, may, paradoxically, have been out of step, in at least some significant respects, with dominant American values, and while, personally, he was much revered in his own lifetime, his educational reforms remained confined largely to the world of ideas rather than the world of practice. The question of why certain proposed reforms do not become translated into practice, however, may be, in the long run, of equal importance to the question of why others do.

CHAPTER 4

SCIENTIFIC CURRICULUM-MAKING AND THE RISE OF SOCIAL EFFICIENCY

i

Of the varied and sometimes frenetic responses to industrialism and to the consequent transformation of American social institutions, there was one that emerged clearly dominant both as a social ideal and as an educational doctrine. It was social efficiency that, for most people, held out the promise of social stability in the face of cries for massive social change, and that doctrine claimed the now potent backing of science in order to insure it. This was a vastly different science, however, from either Hall's natural order of development in the child or Dewey's idealization of scientific inquiry as a general model of reflective thinking. It was a science of exact measurement and precise standards in the interest of maintaining a predictable and orderly world. In a period when the influence of certain social institutions such as family and church were believed to be in a state of dangerous decline, the functions of schooling had to be restructured radically in order to take up the slack. The scope of the curriculum needed to be broadened beyond the development of intelligence to nothing less than the full scope of life activities, and the content of the curriculum had to be changed so that a taut connection be maintained between what was taught in school and the adult activities that one would later be called upon to perform. Efficiency became more than a byword in the educational world; it became an urgent mission. That mission took the form of enjoining curriculum-makers to devise programs of study that prepared individuals specifically and directly for the role they would play as adult members of the social order. To go beyond what someone had to know in order to perform that role successfully was simply wasteful. Social utility became the supreme criterion against which the value of school studies was measured.

In a general sense, the advocates of social efficiency were educational reformers. The fact that their brand of reform differed dramatically from that of Hall's and was the virtual antithesis of Dewey's should not obscure the fact that the basic intention of its proponents was to overthrow the established order in education as represented by the traditional humanist curriculum. Nor should one assume that the humanitarian impulse usually associated with reform was completely absent. That humanitarian impulse, reflected earlier in the work of Joseph Mayer Rice, expressed itself largely in a concern that the existing curriculum was of no interest and of no value to the new population then entering school, particularly secondary school. Beyond their interest in social stability, many leaders of the social efficiency movement indicated a genuine concern for the dissatisfaction that many children expressed about school and for the high rate of dropouts. The answer lay in a curriculum tied to direct utility and to tangible, albeit remote, rewards.

The social theory that guided the development of social efficiency educators is probably best represented by the work of the renowned American sociologist, Edward A. Ross. Ross was not a sociologist of education, but his social ideas, especially as expressed in the most famous of his many books, *Social Control* (1901), strongly influenced the work of such educational sociologists as David Snedden, Ross Finney, Charles Ellwood and Charles C. Peters and they, in turn, devoted themselves to developing curricula consistent with Ross's ideas. By modern standards, Ross was more of a social philosopher than a sociologist, but, in his own day, Ross's work had the full support of science. Ross himself had, early in his life, experienced disillusionment with speculative philosophy, particularly Hegel, and he thought of his own work as an effective counterpoint to the vagueness and imprecision of philosophical thinking. *Social Control* had its inception in a series of twenty-seven articles that Ross wrote for the *American Journal of Sociology* in the 1890s. By the turn of the century he had completed his editing of that work and, in 1901, it was published in book form. The book reveals Ross to be beset by a kind of intellectual schizophrenia. On the one hand, he could scarcely conceal his admiration for "the restless, striving, doing Aryan, with his personal ambition, his lust for power, his longing to wreak himself, his willingness to turn the world upside down to get the fame, or the fortune, or the woman he wants," especially when compared to "the docile Slav or the quiescent Hindoo" (p. 3). In many respects, Ross identified personally and intensely with "the dolichocephalic blonds of the West" (p. 3) and admired the rugged individualism he believed they personified.

On the other hand, he saw civilized society teetering on the edge of a precipice. Modern industrial society, which he generally equated with capitalism, had corrupted those instincts that had once been appropriate in the Teutonic forests, and so American individualism, "the product of the last, most Westerly decanting of the Germanic race" had to be curbed (p. 17). Ross generally rejected the idea of a natural law insuring progress so prevalent in the work of Spencer and urged massive intervention in the interest of preserving society. "*Society*," Ross fervently believed, "*is always in the presence of the enemy*" (p. 190), and *Social Control* is, in a significant sense, a compilation of the weapons of self-protection in the arsenal of society. So powerful were these weapons in his view that he was impelled to issue a warning at the end of his book:

> I confess that no light responsibility is laid upon the investigator who explores the mysterious processes that take place in the soul of a people, and dissects in public the ideals and affirmations elaborated in the social mind. The fact of control is, in good sooth, no gospel to be preached abroad with allegory and parable, with bold type and scare headlines. The secret of

order is not to be bawled from every housetop. The wiser sociologist will show religion a consideration it has rarely met with from the naturalist. He will venerate a moral system too much to uncover its nakedness. He will speak to men, not to youth. He will not tell the "recruity," the street Arab, or the Elmira inmate how he is managed. He will address himself to those who administer the moral capital of society – to teachers, clergymen, editors, law-makers, and judges, who wield the instruments of control; to poets, artists, thinkers, and educators, who guide the human caravan across the waste. In this way he will make himself an accomplice of all good men for the undoing of all bad men. (p. 441)

The weapons of social control that Ross had amassed in his book were so powerful as to be dangerous in the hands of anyone but the most upright.

Education was one of the most effective of those weapons in society's arsenal, particularly in the light of the decline of other modes of social control. "Underneath the medley of systems," Ross (1901) observed," we find *an almost world-wide drift from religion toward education* as the method of indirect social restraint" (p. 176). Unfortunately, according to Ross, American schools had been infused with "an intellectual bias" and, while the development of the intellect was not "without a moral value," that bias had led American schools to "become less an instrument of social control than an aid to individual success" (p. 176). The crisis represented by modern capitalism, he felt, required that the schools adopt a much more direct and more pronounced social purpose.

The decline in the influence of the family was another factor to be taken into account in the design of a proper educational system, but Ross's interpretation of that phenomenon was not entirely consistent with that of other reformers of his time. For Dewey, for example, the decline of the influence of the family meant that the school should build a closer tie between home and school and that the teacher should assume something of the role of an ideal parent by introducing into the course of study those household occupations now lost in an industrial society, social occupations that had once had such great educational value. The decline of a beneficent and educative family influence was, for Dewey, a loss that the school had to retrieve somehow. Ross (1901), on the other hand, happily welcomed the same phenomenon. The school in his view was actually in a better position than the family to instill "the habit of obedience to an external law" (p. 164). Anyone can be a parent, while the certification of teachers is a matter of state control. As a result, Ross explained,

> Another gain lies in the partial substitution of the teacher for the parent as the model upon which the child forms itself. Copy the child will, and the advantage of giving him his teacher instead of his father to imitate, is that the former is a picked person, while the latter is not. Childhood is, in fact, the heyday of personal influence. The position of the teacher gives him prestige, and the lad will take from him suggestions that the adult will accept only from rare and splendid personalities. The committing of education to superior persons lessens our dependence on magnetic men (pp. 164–5).

Rather than decrying the loss of family influence, Ross obviously welcomed the opportunity to put the child in the hand of "picked" persons as one more way of curbing anti-social tendencies. Ross, of course, was not the first to think of schools as an instrument of social control. The general idea of shaping individuals through a system of schooling is at least as ancient as Plato. For Ross, however, the social control function was overwhelming and urgent. Although both Dewey and Ross drew implications for schooling from the same perceived social change, one saw the need to restore in a different setting certain valuable experiences, while the other saw an opportunity to exercise a direct and desirable form of social control. The contrast between these two interpretations is one indication that the relationship between social change and educational doctrine is not so much a direct consequence of the change itself as it is social change as filtered through the perceptions of powerful individuals and groups.

ii

Besides the direct and explicit social control that Ross envisioned, the other key ingredient in social efficiency as a curriculum movement was efficiency itself. Here the principal figure was Frederick Winslow Taylor, the so-called father of scientific management. Like Ross, Taylor did not concern himself directly with education, although, through his disciples in the educational world, his indirect influence was enormous. In fact, the field of curriculum as a distinct area of specialization within the educational world was born in what may be described as a veritable orgy of efficiency, and the after-effects of that orgy have been felt throughout the twentieth century. The bureaucratization of the American educational enterprise would likely have occurred anyway; it had already been under way for some time (Tyack, 1974), but it was aided immensely by the metaphors, procedures and standards of excellence that were drawn from the scientific management movement.

The immediate aim of Taylor's system of scientific management of factories was increased production at lower costs, but beyond that economic purpose lay a penchant for order and regulation that was at least the equal of Ross's. Nor was a moral dimension lacking. In Taylor's first paper before the American Society of Mechanical Engineers (1895), Taylor, in making the case for a "piece-rate system," expressed concern for loafing on the job (what was then called "soldiering") and for the techniques that would insure an honest day's work (p. 856). "If a man won't do what is right," he once said, "*make him*" (Copley, 1923, p. 183). Like Ross, Taylor (1903) believed that certain natural tendencies in human beings, such as laziness, had to be curbed, but there was promise in the fact that the output of a "first-class man" was considerably greater, "two to four times," that of the average worker (p. 1365). The work of the first-class man, then, could be used as a standard for how quickly and how well a particular job was to be done (p. 1365). Once the standardization of the techniques of production were achieved, the task of bringing the average worker up to the required level of work could be accomplished. In wage incentives, Taylor thought he had found the means that would at one and the same time be in the best interests of the worker and raise the production level of the average man to that of a first-class man. There were limits, of course, to the amount to be paid. "If over-paid," he warned, "many will work irregularly and tend to become more or less shiftless, extravagant, and dissipated" (p. 1346), but a carefully developed economic incentive could eliminate "systematic soldiering" (p. 1351) and bring higher production at lower cost.

By the time Taylor published his classic *Principles of Scientific Management* (1911), he was already recognized as the prophet of a new order in industrial society. The heart of scientific management lay in the careful specification of the task to be performed and the ordering of the elements of that task in the most efficient sequence. Taylor summarized the series of steps in this way:

> *First.* Find, say 10 or 15 different men (preferably in as many separate establishments and different parts of the country) who are especially skillful in doing the particular work to be analyzed.
> *Second.* Study the exact series of elementary operations or motions which each of these men uses in doing the work which is being investigated, as well as the implements each man uses.
> *Third.* Study with a stop-watch the time required to make each of these elementary movements and then select the quickest way of doing each element of the work.
> *Fourth.* Eliminate all false movements, slow movements, and useless movements.

Fifth. After doing away with all unnecessary movements, collect into one series the quickest and best movements as well as the best implements. (pp. 117–18)

The technique is probably best illustrated in Taylor's (1911) account of how his colleague, Frank B. Gilbreth, analyzed the "art of bricklaying" (p. 77). Every movement of expert bricklayers was analyzed, and, through the elimination of waste, a standard and carefully laid out sequence of movements toward the accomplishment of that standard was established. The key, really, to performing any complex task was to break it down into its most elementary components, each part so simple that it would not tax the ability of the worker and, thereby, error would be reduced and production increased.

But apart from the mere increase in production, Taylor foresaw that once his system were adopted, a new era in labor relations would emerge. It was in this way that his humanitarian impulse was expressed. In testimony before a Special House of Representatives Committee charged with investigating the Taylor system, Taylor argued that scientific management would bring about "the substitution of peace for war; the substitution of hearty brotherly cooperation for contention and strife; of both pulling hard in the same direction instead of pulling apart; of replacing suspicious watchfulness with mutual confidence; of becoming friends instead of enemies" ("Taylor's testimony", 1912, p. 30). Here was the reformist's zeal that prompted Taylor in carrying through his mission to reconstruct American industry. His watchword was efficiency, but through efficiency he was trying to achieve the higher purpose of a more orderly and less contentious society. It was a reform that political conservatives could easily embrace.

With the rage for efficiency in full swing by the second decade of the twentieth century, it was inevitable that criticism of the inefficiency of American schools, criticism initiated by Rice's muckraking journalism, should soon be heard. The application of Taylor's system of managing factories to the management of schools was the most immediate and most natural step. In time, however, the use of scientific management techniques went far beyond the application of Taylor's ideas to the administration of schools; it ultimately provided the language and hence the conceptual apparatus by which a new and powerful approach to curriculum development would be wrought. The route by which scientific management became the basis for an education doctrine is actually no mystery. Those educational leaders who forged the new doctrine made no secret of the source of their ideas, self-consciously and conspicuously following the principles of Taylorism in an effort to make the curriculum a direct and potent force in the lives of future citizens and, ultimately, an instrument for creating a stable and smoothly functioning society.

iii

No one epitomized the new breed of efficiency-minded educators more than John Franklin Bobbitt. In fact, his work represents in microcosm the development of a field of specialization within education, the field of curriculum. It is probably this identification of social efficiency with the emergence of the field itself that is a significant factor in the persistence of many of its most central ideas today in only a slightly modified form. Bobbitt was brought to the University of Chicago in 1909 by Charles H. Judd, a psychologist who had just been recruited from Yale to head the Department of Education. Judd himself was a major exponent of the scientific study of education, and he probably saw in the young Bobbitt a kindred spirit. In the following year, Bobbitt, now promoted from lecturer to Instructor of School Administration, introduced a course entitled, simply, Curriculum. In his third year, that course, apparently a great success, was expanded to include both the autumn and the winter quarters. By 1912, Bobbitt published his first significant article on curriculum, "The Elimination of Waste in Education," and his career as a curriculum leader was launched.

A major portion of Bobbitt's (1912) article was devoted to extolling the virtues of the school system that had been developed by Superintendent Willard Wirt in Gary, Indiana, a "city having been practically created by the United States Steel corporation" (p. 259). Wirt had devised a system, popularly called the "platoon system," which was designed to increase efficiency in the use of space within a school building by shifting students from classrooms to other indoor space, such as the auditorium, and to the playground in systematic fashion. Bobbitt was impressed by the fact that "the usual plant, if it is fully equipped is operated during school hours at about 50 per cent of efficiency," but that "the educational engineer at Gary was to formulate a plan of operating his plant during school hours at 100 per cent efficiency" (pp. 260–1). While the platoon system was clearly more managerial than curricular as an educational innovation, Bobbitt's use of such terms as "educational engineer" to refer to the superintendent of schools and "plant'" to refer to the school was no merely decorative use of language; it had implications far broader than the pedestrian question of space utilization. It provided the emerging curriculum field with the root metaphor on which a new and powerful theory of curriculum could be built.

In enumerating the four principles on which an efficient school would be based, Bobbitt's first three, such as optimal use of the school plant, were basically administrative. But in enunciating his fourth principle of scientific management applied to education, he extended the factory metaphor to the question of how curriculum should be constructed:

> Work up the raw material into that finished product for which it is best adapted. Applied to education this means: Educate the individual according to his capabilities. This requires that the materials of the curriculum be sufficiently various to meet the needs of every class of individuals in the community; and that the course of training and study be sufficiently flexible that the individual can be given just the things that he needs. (Bobbitt, 1912, p. 269)

Individual variation in ability had, of course, been recognized well before Bobbitt's time, but Bobbitt was now asserting that the curriculum be carefully adapted to each "class of individuals" as part of the drive for the elimination of inefficiency in education. People, after all, should not be taught what they will never use. That was a waste. In order to reduce waste, educators had to institute a process of scientific measurement leading to a prediction as to one's future role in life. That prediction would then become the basis of a differentiated curriculum. Within the framework of the new theory, "education according to need" was simply another way of saying, education according to predicted social and vocational role. Boys, for example, whose "needs" were different from girls in terms of such matters as vocation, recreation and citizenship were to be given a different course of study from girls in these respects (p. 270). Future men and women were destined to perform different roles in society, and it was simply inefficient to train them in the same way. Bobbitt's concern for the "raw material" in the context of his theory was not so much a concern for individual well-being as it was part of an effort to eliminate waste in the curriculum and, by extention, in the social order generally. The doctrine of social efficiency held out the then very appealing prospect of scientifically attuning the curriculum to the requirements of the new industrial society.

iv

One of the most tangible and far-reaching manifestations of the drive to create a more directly utilitarian curriculum had its inception in a resolution passed in 1905 by the Massachusetts Senate and House of Representatives creating what came to be known as the Douglas Commission. That resolution authorized Governor William L. Douglas to appoint a Commission on Industrial and Technical Education in order to investigate the needs of the state in various industries and to determine "how far the needs are met by existing institutions," as well as to "consider what new forms of educational effort may be advisable" (Massachusetts Commission, 1906, pp. 1–2). A social scientist, Dr Susan M. Kingsbury, was appointed as "expert investigator," and within a year the Commission issued its report based on twenty public hearings held in major cities around the state and on the testimony of 143 witnesses including manufacturers, farmers, representatives of labor unions and school officials. The report indicated general agreement between the "broader-minded students of education" on the one hand and, on the other, those "men and women who have been brought into intimate contact with the harder side of life": the "old-fashioned" curriculum of Massachusetts's schools was too far removed from the demands of life created by an industrial society and that in practical trade training lay the answer (p. 4). The justifications for this solution were drawn, as would be expected, from the doctrines being so insistently espoused by the emergent reform interest groups of the time. From the developmentalists, there came the expressed concern for the "fullest development of the child" and from the social meliorists the idea that such education could be useful "in the reformation of wayward and vicious children at reform and truant schools" in much the same way "that it is being used to elevate the colored race in the south" (p. 4).

Most pervasive was the insistence that the schools undertake the task of preparation for earning a livelihood. The report indicated that at almost every hearing they were told that "the processes of manufacture and construction are made more difficult and more expensive by a lack of skilled workmen" (p. 4). In that regard, the Commission chided the advocates of manual training for taking too narrow a view, emphasizing its value as a "cultural subject a sort of mustard relish, an appetizer, – to be conducted without reference to any industrial end" (p. 14). By contrast, the Commission cited with approval the establishment of textile schools in Lowell in 1897, in New Bedford in 1899, and in Fall River in 1904 as affording the kind of education that would serve best both the citizens and the Commonwealth of Massachusetts. While the

Commission recognized that direct trade training was regarded with "suspicion and hostility of many of the labor unions of the State," on the grounds that the labor market was being expanded in order to lower wages, they felt those suspicions to be largely unwarranted (p. 6). Although the Commission did not engage in the open and often vitriolic attacks on the academic curriculum that became common in the educational world in later years, their sympathies clearly lay with a new system of education tied to the "callings in life . . . professional, commercial, productive and domestic" (p. 14). In fact, as they viewed it, the decline of the apprenticeship system made such a change a social necessity. Whereas at one time, the report argued, the system of schooling and the institution of apprenticeship were kept in a kind of balance in terms of their influence on youth, that balance had now been destroyed to the point where a dangerous bias had been created with children and youth devoting their time exclusively to academic studies in school. That balance could be rectified by restructuring the curriculum in schools to include the functions once performed by the apprenticeship system. This was exactly the kind of argument that appealed to those leaders in American life who sought a restructuring of social institutions in line with what they saw as a major social transformation.

An important addendum to the main report was Kingsbury's "Report of the Sub-committee on the Relation of Children to Industries;" a report that focused on the 25,000 children between fourteen and sixteen who were not in school. After a detailed and considered attempt to survey a sample of that 25,000, Kingsbury found that five-sixths of them had not completed an eighth-grade education and that virtually none had ever attended high school. As Helen Todd, the factory inspector, was to find seven years later, it was not economic deprivation that was the principal cause of leaving school to work in factories. The chief blame for the unfortunate state of affairs that Kingsbury found lay in the "dissatisfaction" that children felt with their schoolwork and the fact that "the parent does not know where to find an occupation for his child" other than the unskilled labor available at the textile mills and other factories (Massachusetts Commission, 1906, p. 44). Moreover, with proper training, she argued, "our cloths can compete with the foreign market" and the state would prosper (p. 46). The chief obstacle to that prosperity as well as to the well-being of the child was a curriculum removed from any prospect of reward in occupational terms. Under those circumstances, neither the child nor the parent could see any point to continuing school much after the sixth grade.

Kingsbury's was a powerful and timely case. The issue of school-leavers brought into focus elements from several reform streams and promised to become one of the most debated questions in twentieth-century education. But Kingsbury's temperate and balanced treament of the issue left open the terms that would define that debate. The most powerful of these reform streams, however, social efficiency, soon moved to reconstruct the issue in its own terms. Three years after the Douglas Commission Report, Leonard Ayres published his enormously influential *Laggards in Our Schools* (1909), one of the first avowedly "scientific" treatises in education. Ayres, who had once been superintendent of schools in Puerto Rico, had gotten a grant from the Russell Sage Foundation in 1907 to study the effects of retardation in schools. (The term "retardation" did not have the psychological connotations it has today but was used simply to refer to the problem of children not making normal progress in schools.) Ayres opened his report by alluding to the 1904 report of Superintendent William H. Maxwell of New York City indicating that 39 percent of the students in the elementary grades were too old for the grade they were in (pp. 1–3). The problem as he saw it was to discover why this situation existed and to suggest remedies that might correct it.

Ayres's study was conducted through the careful examination of school records, not through the observation of schools themselves as Rice's had been. The key to the problem as he saw it was that retardation represented a great loss in efficiency. Students who were supposed to be making their way smoothly through the grades were, in an alarming number of cases, taking twice as long to complete a grade as they should. The problem lay, of course, with the curriculum. *"These conditions,"* Ayres (1909) asserted with finality, *"mean that our courses of study as at present constituted are fitted not to the slow child or to the average child but to the unusually bright one"* (p. 5). In defining the problem in this way, he was sounding a theme that social efficiency reformers were to echo through most of the twentieth century: the "college-preparatory" curriculum that had held sway for so long needed to be replaced by a curriculum attuned to the needs of a new population and a new industrial order. As a result of an inefficient curriculum, Ayres pointed out, "in the country as a whole about one-sixth of all the children are repeating and we are annually spending about $827,000,000 in this wasteful process of repetition in our cities alone" (p. 5). No well-run manufacturing establishment would tolerate such waste.

To correct this scandalous situation, Ayres developed his famous Index of Efficiency which he applied to fifty-eight urban school systems. Given that Index, the production metaphor applied to the curriculum could be used with ruthless precision. Ayres wanted to know, for example, the number of students who begin each school year so that "the relation of the finished product to the raw material" could be computed. He sought to calculate the "conditions of maximum theoretical efficiency" in each grade so that the "relations of the actual plant in size to the theoretic requirements" could be determined. "Suppose," he argued, "we had a factory which instead of utilizing all its raw material (100 per cent) embodied only 50 per cent in its finished product" (Ayres, 1909, p. 176). That factory would be even less than 50 per cent efficient if it were also found that the "theoretical product" of the plant were higher. Using the Index of Efficiency, it was evident that the schools of the nation were even more inefficient than the raw data indicated (pp. 176–7). More importantly, the genuine issue of the appropriateness of the curriculum to the school population that the Douglas Commission raised had been reduced to a problem of simply efficiency and cost-effectiveness. The power and appeal of the factory metaphor applied to curriculum issues was all too painfully evident in the way Ayres reconstructed the problem, a power and an appeal that was to put the social efficiency interest group in a commanding political position in the decades ahead.

In the next few years, the notion that the problem of "retardation" was primarily a problem of curriculum inefficiency became a constantly recurring theme. It was so persistent, in fact, that one of the leaders of the social efficiency movement, Charles A. Ellwood, a professor of sociology at the University of Missouri, complained just six years after Ayres's report that nearly everyone now seems "to think that the only way to remedy this evil is to make the curriculum of our public schools more 'attractive', so as to hold the child's interests longer." While "not opposed to the making of curricula attractive," Ellwood was more concerned with the loss of social control that the problem of "elimination" presented (Ellwood, 1914, p. 572). He was worried about the fact that children, under existing compulsory education laws, could simply "soldier" until they are fourteen and then leave school before their "efficiency as citizens" had been established. Since it was clear to Ellwood that "a *definite* sentence is the greatest of all impediments" in reforming deliquent children, why not impose on all the children of the nation an indefinite sentence of schooling? "If the indefinite period of detention in an industrial or reform school is good for the delinquent child," he insisted, "why is not an indefinite period of instruction and training in our public schools good for the normal child?" (pp. 574–5). In this way, schools would perform the "social service" for which they were intended, fitting the child to the demands of modern society. Even further, the schools, given enough time, could identify the feebleminded that the psychologist, H. H. Goddard's investigations had dramatically brought to the fore, and appropriate action could be taken before they "are allowed to go out into life, and by the laws of heredity . . . inevitably pass on to future generations their defects and even diffuse them in the population as a whole" (p. 576). In this way, consistent with Ross's ideal of the school as a weapon of social control, the school could serve the social function it so long failed to perform. While Ellwood's recommendations never were implemented in the form he proposed, they illustrate that along with simple efficiency the other key element in the powerful social efficiency equation was social control. It was principally in terms of efficiency and control that the complex and critical issues of "retardation" and "elimination" and their relationship to curriculum were defined for at least a half century.

v

Two closely interrelated movements in psychology lent vital support to the way proponents of social efficiency defined the key curriculum issues that were to emerge in the twentieth century. One was the development of a psychological theory to replace the moribund faculty psychology, one which fitted in neatly with the basic presuppositions of social efficiency; and the other was the mental measurement movement which provided the technology necessary for the kind of assessment and prediction that a curriculum based on social efficiency doctrine required. These two movements, both flowering in the first quarter of the twentieth century, placed the social efficiency interest group in a dominant, although not supreme, position *vis-à-vis* the others.

One of the most critical points in the development of a new psychology consistent with the emerging ideas of the scientific curriculum-makers centered on the psychological concept that is conventionally called "transfer of training." It is universally assumed that what one learns in school somehow carries over to situations different from that particular time and that particular setting, but the process by which that transfer takes place was and still remains a subject of great debate. It is, in a sense, part and parcel of what we call learning, and without a plausible account of how we learn, no curriculum theory could really gain widespread acceptance. James had in 1890 fired one of the first salvos at the mental disciplinarian notion of transfer when he reported that his experiments on memory had failed to show any improvement in what mental disciplinarians had imagined to be a discreet faculty of memory. If memory could not be improved by memorizing, then it could hardly be justified as a pervasive school activity, since much of the things being memorized were hardly worth committing to memory in the first place, and they were most likely to be forgotten in any event.

By the early twentieth century, experimentation to discredit the mental disciplinarian concept of transfer became a cottage industry (Rugg, 1916) and leading the way was James's brilliant and illustrious student, Edward Lee Thorndike. Thorndike had been brought to Teachers College, Columbia University by Dean James Earl Russell as part of what turned out to be a successful effort to build the preeminent institution for the study of education. Thorndike's first major foray into the intricacies of the problem of transfer was a series of experiments he conducted with his student, R.S. Woodworth, that were published under the general heading, "The Influence of Improvement in One Mental Function Upon the Efficiency of Other Functions" (Thorndike and Woodworth, 1901). In a variety of mental operations, such as estimating the areas of rectangles, subjects were given intensive training until they achieved a high degree of proficiency. Then they were given a similar task, such as estimating the areas of figures of the same size but of different shapes, and the amount of transfer from one learning task to the other was computed. This was repeated with such other tasks as estimating the lengths of lines or estimating the weights of objects. The effectiveness of the special training in the learned task was not at issue – only the extent to which learning that task carried over to a similar one. Thorndike's conclusion based on these experiments was devastating to commonly held beliefs about transfer: "Improvement in any single mental function need not improve the ability in functions commonly called by the same name. It may injure it"

(p. 250). In a major book published a dozen years later, Thorndike extended that conclusion to cast doubt on even the existence of such mental operations as memory, perception, reasoning, and observation. They were, in effect, fictions and should be discarded along with a lot of other conceptual baggage left around by faculty psychologists (Thorndike, 1913, pp. 363–5) But without those concepts the whole value of general education was cast into doubt.

In place of a concept of mind comprising a limited number of discrete faculties, Thorndike and other psychologists in the early twentieth century sought to construct something more consistent with their experimental evidence. The mind that Thorndike envisioned was a machine in which there were thousands – millions – of individual connections, each one bearing a message having little in common with the next. The mind in his view consisted not of large capacities such as memory and reasoning waiting there to be developed, but of "multitudinous separate individual functions" (Thorndike and Woodworth, 1901, p. 249), a kind of switchboard with innumerable wires (bonds) connecting discrete points.

As if this were not enough, Thorndike conducted an experiment two decades later that was even more unsettling to traditional curriculum beliefs. This time it was the value of particular school subjects that was called into question. Between 1922 and 1923, Thorndike administered two forms of the same intelligence test to 8,564 high school students. He then divided that population according to groupings of subjects they had studied over the course of that year to the extent that that was possible. Once he had corrected for such factors as initial ability and special training, the value of these courses of study in raising intelligence levels could then be computed. We would then know how much better Latin or mathematics was in raising general intelligence than, say domestic science. Thorndike's conclusion in this study amounted to another bombshell: "We find notable differences in gain in ability to think as measured by these tests, but they do not seem to be due to what one studies. . . . Those who have the most to begin with gain the most during the year.

Whatever studies they take will seem to produce large gains in intellect" (Thorndike, 1924, pp. 94–5). There may be some question as to whether Thorndike was warranted in drawing such sweeping conclusions on the basis of this as well as his 1901 experiments, but the ready inference that curriculum-makers drew was that improving intelligence, in effect, teaching students to think through a course of study designed for that purpose, was a pipe dream. What really mattered was native intelligence.

By 1924, Thorndike's attacks on mental disciplinarian concepts already had a sympathetic audience. Not only was mental discipline dead as a formal theory, but the new scientific curriculum-makers such as Bobbitt and Charters were developing a theory of curriculum entirely consistent with the concept of mind inherent in the new psychology. If transfer from one task to another was much less than had been commonly believed, then the curriculum had to be so designed as to teach people specifically and directly those exact skills required for the tasks that lay before them in life. Gilbreth's atomization of the "art of bricklaying," Thorndike's image of mind as consisting of innumerable tiny functions, and Bobbitt's scientific curriculum drawn from a laborious analysis of the multitudinous tasks that comprise human life were all of one conceptual piece.

So was the companion movement in psychology that was to affect the curriculum of American schools profoundly, the calibration of intelligence into minute units – I.Q. points. The sources of mental testing lie in the efforts of Francis Galton in England to trace the components of genius as well as the experimental laboratories established in Germany by Wilhelm Wundt, but most directly in the work of Alfred Binet, who was charged by the French Ministry of Education to find a way of identifying those French schoolchildren who needed special education. The simple scale of tasks he developed in that regard underwent a kind of sea change once it was transported to American shores. In the hands of psychologists such as H. H. Goodard, Lewis H. Terman, R. M. Yerkes, and Edward L. Thorndike, that scale became not just a diagnostic device, but a powerful tool by which society could be regulated (Gould, 1981).

As Ross had foreseen, a vital force in the creation of such a stable and orderly society was a system of schools dedicated to that purpose, including, most specifically, a curriculum tied to the destined roles that future citizens were to perform. Since future citizens were to perform different and complementary tasks, a differentiated curriculum was needed in line with the determination of native capacities that a scientific system of mental measurement would provide. In particular, secondary education would be that period when the differentiation should be the sharpest. In fact, the creation of a new educational institution, the junior high school, was given special impetus by the perceived need to "explore" children's needs and capacities before entering upon the high school period.

Thorndike himself was unequivocal on the need for differentiation in the high school curriculum. "The problem before the high school," he declared, "is to give the boys and girls from fourteen on who most deserve education beyond a common school course such a training as will make them contribute most to the true happiness of the world" (Thorndike, 1906, p. 180). That task required exactly the kind of "prognostication" that Hall had earlier proposed and that Eliot, in his defense of the Committee of Ten report, had so vehemently opposed. Thorndike was in absolute agreement with his fellow psychologist Hall that "no high school is successful which does not have in mind definitely the work in life its students will have to perform, and try to fit them for it" (p. 180). The majority of students entering high school, he felt, were not "efficient at dealing with *ideas*, but whose talent is for the manipulation of *things*" (p. 181) making them more suited for cooking than for writing compositions or performing experiments. Moreover, in a modern industrial society, schools had to supply the knowledge that once was the province of other institutions. "The time has passed," Thorndike affirmed, "when the rule of thumb was enough for the building trades; when science was a luxury to the farmer, when old wives' lore passed on from mother to daughter was the best available education for housewifery and motherhood" (p. 181). He went on to estimate that not more than a third of the secondary student population should study algebra and geometry since, in the first place, they were not suited for those subjects and, in the second, they could occupy their time much more efficiently by studying those subjects that would fit them more directly for what their lives had in store. The curriculum for the new education needed to be expanded far beyond the traditional subjects that the Committee of Ten had recommended just a few years before, and curriculum differentiation became a necessary concomitant to that expansion. In the drive to implement such a reform, the mental measurement movement performed a vital legitimating function.

At the same time that psychologists were shaping a new psychology consistent with the emerging field of curriculum, those sociologists of education who had embraced the social efficiency ideal were not only endorsing the scientific work of their colleagues in psychology, but elaborating the social theory that was to guide the curriculum changes they sought. Ross Finney, for example, an influential professor of sociology at the University of Minnesota, saw clear implications for how the curriculum should be organized from the experience gained from the Army Alpha mass testing. What angered Finney was the persistence of the "rise-out-of-your-class" philosophy of society that continued to dominate educational policy in the face of conclusive evidence that "the great majority are *predestined* never to rise at all" (Finney, 1928, p. 180). From Plato to Charles Horton Cooley, Finney felt, social theorists were continuing to make the mistake of assuming that people actually can be taught to recognize or somehow to "discern the one man in the right" when establishing a good society (p. 385). Fortunately that question had been unequivocably settled. "And now come forward the psychologists," Finney announced, "with scientific data for headlining what we all knew before, namely, that half the people have brains of just average quality or less, of whom a very considerable percentage have very poor brains indeed" (p. 386). In spite of that evidence, the mistaken notion persisted that the school's function was to teach people to think, a position he attributed (correctly) to James Harvey Robinson and "Doctor" John Dewey. "But this solution," Finney pointed out, "will hardly bear inspection. In the first place, the barber's I.Q. is only .78, according to the army tests. I.Q.'s below .99+ are not likely to secrete cogitations of any great social fruitfulness" (p. 388). His solution was to teach that half of the population without the power to "secrete cogitations", to follow dutifully what those who have that power tell them to do. In fact, in curriculum terms, he envisioned one curriculum for leadership and another for "followership" designed for that purpose. Finney's is one case in point among many of how the concept of I.Q. and mental measurement generally fit perfectly into the idea of a curriculum tied to the particular qualities of the "raw material," rather than assuming anything like the ability to think across the entire student population.

Probably the most eminent of the new breed of educational sociologists was David Snedden. Snedden first came under Ross's influence while an undergraduate at Stanford University, beginning in 1895. After completing a doctorate at Teachers College, Columbia University, he became an adjunct professor of education there. Later, as Commissioner of Education in Massachusetts, he was in a position to help guide the course of American education, especially in his efforts to enlarge the scope of vocational education and to create a socially efficient curriculum generally. It was in his period as Commissioner that he appointed two men who were to put their own marks on the future course of the curriculum in the United States. Snedden chose his former student, Charles Prosser, as Deputy Commissioner for vocational education who, over his long career, became the pivotal figure in the development of vocational education in the United States and who emerged after World War Two as instrumental in the ill-fated life adjustment movement. His second appointment, in 1912, was Clarence Kingsley, a high school teacher from Brooklyn, New York, as his assistant in secondary education. Six years later, Kingsley was to engineer, almost single-handedly, the Cardinal Principles Report, a major landmark in secondary education in the United States. In 1916, Snedden returned to Teachers College to accept a professorship in educational sociology and thus was able to point that fledgling discipline in the direction of his master, Ross. For the next two decades, Snedden was a central figure in a group of educational sociologists that included Ross Finney, C. C. Peters, and Charles Ellwood.

In terms of his ideas on the curriculum, Snedden was in agreement in almost every detail with the preeminent scientific curriculum-makers such as Bobbitt and W. W. Charters, but he had a much grander and more explicit social vision. Writing in 1921, Snedden predicted that "by 1925, it can confidently be hoped, the minds which direct education will have detached from the entanglements of our contemporary civilization a thousand definite educational objectives, the realization of which will have demonstrable worth to our society" (Snedden, 1921, p. 79). Snedden recognized, however, that it was not necessary nor was it even desirable for all persons to achieve all the objectives that had been so determined. Objectives had to be set in relation to what he called "case groups" defined as "any considerable group of persons who in large degree resemble each other in common possession of qualities significant to their school education" (Snedden, 1923, p. 290). Like his contemporaries, Snedden felt that the junior high school period was where "differences of abilities, of extra-school conditions and of prospects will acutely manifest themselves, forcing us to differentiate curricula in more ways, probably, than are as yet suspected" (Snedden, 1924, p. 740), and thus the creation of case groups was particularly germane to that institution.

The curriculum itself would be built of "peths," tiny units of which a single spelling word would be an example (Snedden, 1925, p. 262). Persisting in his penchant for neologisms, Snedden then proposed that peths be organized into "strands," built around "adult life performance practices" such as "health conservation through habitual safeguarding practices," for which something like 50 to 100 peths would serve. A strand for anything as simple as becoming a streetcar motorman would require only 10 to 20 peths, but to produce a good farmer or a good homemaker, anywhere from 200 to 500 peths would have to be assembled (pp. 288–9). Snedden (1924) also created the " 'lotment' . . . the amount of work that can be accomplished, or the ground considered, by learners of modal characteristics (as related to the activity covered) in 60 clock hours" (p. 741). Snedden's vision of a school and its curriculum was almost a caricature of Taylor's vision of a factory and the manufacturing process virtually replete with the stopwatch which had become practically a symbol of industrial efficiency.

But Snedden's penchant for quaint terminology should not obscure the fact that he was representing what amounted to the dominant curriculum ideology of his day. When in 1923–24, for example, George S. Counts conducted his study of high school curricula, the wide acceptance of different curricula for different segments of the high school population was clearly evident. He reported 18 different curricula in Los Angeles secondary schools and 15 in Newton, Massachusetts (Counts, 1926, p. 13). In the very same school year, Robert and Helen Lynd (1929) discovered in the schools of Middletown a "manifest concern . . . to dictate the social attitudes of its young citizens" that was reflected in a variety of required courses in civic education, a curricular emphasis second only to vocational training.

Snedden's protégé, Clarence Kingsley, the mathematics teacher from Brooklyn, was the man who in 1918 produced the document that proved to be the capstone of the quarter-century of furious efforts at curriculum reform that began with the Committee of Ten Report. The Report of the Commission on the Reorganization of Secondary Education or, as it has been popularly called, The Cardinal Principles Report (National Education Association, 1918) met with almost universal approbation when it was issued, and, unlike Eliot's Committee of Ten report (which had by this time fallen into almost universal disfavor), continues to be cited as embodying the highest wisdom in curriculum matters. It was perhaps inevitable, given the intense and largely successful efforts at curriculum reform since 1893, that some form of repudiation of Eliot's report should be forthcoming and that it should reflect the growing belligerence toward academic subjects through the ascendence of social efficiency in the educational world. Given the pervasiveness of that doctrine and the calls for a radical transformation of the curriculum, Kingsley's report was rather moderate. By far the most prominent portion of the 32-page report was the statement of the seven aims that would guide the curriculum: "1. Health. 2. Command of fundamental processes. 3. Worthy home-membership. 4. Vocation. 5. Citizenship. 6. Worthy use of leisure. 7. Ethical character" (pp. 10–11). With the possible exception of the second one, these aims each represented an area of life activity, and the curriculum would be directed toward efficient performance within that area. Thus would a much closer connection be maintained between education and the actual activities that people are called upon to perform in their daily lives. Unlike the Committee of Ten report, where the four programs of study represented the heart of the recommendations, the Cardinal Principles Report centered on something beyond the curriculum itself. The curriculum became the instrument through which the aims were to be achieved.

Although a significant shift in emphasis, this represented a rather temperate stance, given the pedagogical climate of the times. Social efficiency proponents such as Bobbitt, Charters and Snedden were calling for the elimination of the conventional subjects in favor of subjects that were themselves areas of living such as citizenship and leisure. Kingsley, however, did not call for the elimination of history and English – only that they reorient themselves toward the achievement of at least one, and preferably several, of the seven aims. Snedden, Kingsley's erstwhile mentor, decrying the fact that vocation appeared lost amid the full list of seven aims, declared the report to be "almost hopelessly academic" (Snedden, 1919,

p. 522) and accused the Commission of being "chiefly preoccupied with the liberal education of youth" (p. 526).

Neither did the report go as far as Snedden would have liked in the direction of differentiated curricula. Although the report refers to "curriculums," there was more than a passing reference to the need in a democracy for the school to perform a unifying function through common experiences in school, including the high school period (National Education Association, 1918, pp. 22–3). In that regard, the Commission was unequivocal in its support of the comprehensive high school, a position that in 1918 was being widely debated, with social efficiency educators leading the way in calling for different forms of secondary education for different kinds of youth. As a whole, however, the report reflected with reasonable accuracy the winds of change that had swept the educational world in the previous quarter-century. So widely accepted were Kingsley's recommendations that 1918 may be regarded as the year when the humanist position reflected in Eliot's Committee of Ten report was forced to go on the defensive, no longer playing the dominant role it once did in the battle for the American curriculum.

vi

By 1918, social efficiency as a curriculum theory was almost at its zenith, and attention to curriculum reform had reached the point where curriculum was being recognized as a vital subspeciality within the broader spectrum of education. One sign of the new status accorded the curriculum was the publication of the first modern book devoted exclusively to that topic, a book entitled simply, *The Curriculum* (Bobbitt, 1918). In it, Bobbitt summarized the state of the art up to that point. He also provided what is probably the most concise and at the same time most explicit definition of the theory that he and his fellow social efficiency educators were advocating:

The central theory is simple. Human life, however varied,

consists in the performance of specific activities. Education that prepares for life is one that prepares definitely and adequately for these specific activities. However numerous and diverse they may be for any social class, they can be discovered. This requires only that one go out into the world of affairs and discover the particulars of which these affairs consist. These will show the abilities, attitudes, habits, appreciations, and forms of knowledge that men need. These will be the objectives of the curriculum. They will be numerous, definite, and particularized. The curriculum will then be that series of experiences which children and youth must have by way of attaining those objectives. (p. 42)

Almost every sentence in Bobbitt's summary of the theory marks off a vital facet of what was the ascendant mode of thinking about the curriculum in the twentieth century. There was first its simplicity. Compared to Dewey's conceptually complex version of recapitulation or the mystical romanticism of Hall's culture-epochs, simplicity itself must have had a tremendous appeal. That simplicity was expressed largely in a conception of curriculum planning that could be reduced to a series of steps, an idea perfectly consistent with Taylorism and one that has maintained its appeal even to the present. There was also the appeal to specificity, an ideal drawn from scientific management as well as Thorndike's connectionism, and, in the minds of many, from science itself. Imbedded in Bobbitt's description of the essentials of the theory was the mechanism by which the curriculum would actually be constructed, a mechanism that Bobbitt (1918) was convinced was "a scientific technique" (p. 42). Activity analysis or, as it was sometimes called, job analysis, consisted of a procedure whereby one first created an inventory of the "particulars" that comprised human life. These were the things that people in fact did, and those things would be converted into curricular objectives. The next step was simply to create that "series of experiences" that would most efficiently achieve each objective. What Bobbitt was proposing was essentially that Gilbreth's technique for analyzing bricklaying be applied, not simply to "vocational labors" as in the case of scientific management, but to all the activities in which human beings engage, to "their civic activities; their health activities; their recreations; their language; their parental, religious, and general social activities" (p. 43). The scope of the curriculum would be nothing less than "the mosaic of full-formed human life" (p. 43).

Bobbitt (1918) recognized that the total range of human activity was so vast that no curriculum could encompass it all, but he found a solution to that problem in the idea of "directed and undirected experiences" (p. 43). Some objectives, Bobbitt asserted, may be "attained without conscious effort" and although the "curriculum-discoverer" must be aware of these as well, "he will be content to let as much as possible be taken care of through undirected experiences." Fortunately, the schools did not have to teach everything. Some things are simply learned through a natural process of socialization. "*The curriculum of schools*," Bobbitt emphasized, "*will aim at those objectives that are not sufficiently attained as a result of the general undirected experience*" (p. 44). Those abilities not so attained Bobbitt called *shortcomings*, that is, the deficits that people exhibited once the full range of activities had been discovered. (Shortcomings is the counterpart of the contemporary concept of "needs" in curriculum construction.) He cited approvingly, for example, the research that his like-minded contemporary, W. W. Charters, had conducted in discovering the errors made by Kansas City children in both oral and written language. Each of the noted errors in grammar, once classified by type, constituted a shortcoming that had to be addressed. "Only as we list the errors and shortcomings of human performance in each of the fields," Bobbitt concluded, "can we know what to include and to emphasize in the directed curriculum of the schools" (p. 52).

Neither Bobbitt nor Charters gave extensive attention to the implications of their conception of curriculum to larger social questions or to the role of the school in relation to social progress. In the main, they saw themselves simply as bringing the light of science to a field that had been governed by drift, tradition and fruitless speculation. In *The Curriculum*, for example, Bobbitt seems to have seen the relationship between social progress and what is taught in schools almost exclusively in terms of instrumental efficiency. "As agencies of social progress," he maintained, "schools should give efficient service. And efficient service, we are nowadays coming to know, is service directed, not by guess or whim or special self-interest, but by science" (p. 69). Schools, in other words, were charged with providing society with what it needed as determined by scientific analysis.

Their own perceptions notwithstanding, there was a highly significant social dimension to the work of the scientific curriculum-makers. This is perhaps best illustrated in some of the works of Charters. Charters, even more than Bobbitt, devoted himself to the actual task of activity analysis in a variety of fields. Most of his influential research was related to various occupational roles such as librarian and veterinarian, applying Gilbreth's bricklayer analysis to many other fields as a basis for vocational training in those fields. His *Analysis of Secretarial Duties and Traits* (with I. B. Whitley, 1924), for example, became a classic in the area of business education. But it was when he turned to the more general activities that human beings engage in that some of the techniques that seemed so plausible in a vocational context began to exhibit strong social overtones and where some weaknesses were exposed.

Around 1920, Charters was asked by Stephens College of Columbia, Missouri, a private women's college, to devise a new curriculum. It seemed clear to Charters that the job of being a woman was of the same order as any other job, requiring the same techniques of curriculum development that he had employed in relation to other occupational roles. Charters took the occasion of his first report on that curriculum to reaffirm the urgency with which he viewed the matter of curriculum reform. "The curriculum situation has become acute," he began. "The masses who send their children to school are growing restive under what they consider to be the useless material taught in the grades" (Charters, 1921, p.

224). One of the main missions that social efficiency reformers set for themselves was that of replacing what was useless and merely symbolic in the curriculum with what was directly useful. According to Charters, this involved a combination of an analysis of the activities that human beings engage in along with a determination of the ideals that will control those activities. In accordance with one of the most central principles of social efficiency, he believed that "we should define curriculum on the basis of what people are going to do" (Charters, 1926a, p. 327). Just as we would not provide the same education to a prospective doctor as to a prospective engineer, we should not prescribe the same education for women as for men. As Bobbitt had discovered, men and women were destined to do different things.

In order to secure a scientific inventory of women's activities, Charters solicited from the women themselves a statement of what they did during the course of one week. In all, an incredible 95,000 replies were received, and the activities were initially broken down into about 7,300 categories. These were then further divided into categories such as food, clothing and health, and these categories, in effect, became the subjects in the curriculum. Attention was given to those activities that were characteristic of "homemakers" as opposed to "unmarried women" with only those categories shared by both groups destined to become the required subjects. The study of clothing would be required of all women, but an "appreciation of art . . . would be purely elective" even though the study seemed to point to the conclusion that "the aesthetic is sufficiently prominent among women to presume that they may get greater appreciation from these than from other subjects" (p. 329). Unlike someone like Hall, who would consider interest to be a crucial criterion in determining a curriculum, the social efficiency educators were primarily concerned with efficient performance in a future social role, and, using that criterion, aesthetics hardly mattered.

In considering a curriculum for homemakers in particular, Charters decided to present a list of 48 traits to a group of

3,440 judges who were asked to rate them as (1) most important, (2) neither unusually important nor unimportant, and (3) least important (Charters, 1926b, p. 680). When these rankings were subjected to statistical treatment, it was discovered that Care of Health, e.g. "She plans her family's diet to meet their physical needs" (p. 676) ranked first, and Honesty, e.g. "She shows no deceit in handling of the family finances" (p. 678) and Love, e.g. "She has an ideal of love and expresses this love for her husband, children, and home" (p. 678) were tied for second. Ranking last was Philanthropy, e.g. "She is engaged in some organized club work that has a philanthropic purpose" (p. 679). Such a trait study would be used, according to Charters, to build a curriculum first by infusing some attention to these traits in "every subject taught" and secondly by directly training women to secure these traits when an "individual profile chart" showed them to be weak in some of them (p. 684).

As Charters's efforts to create a curriculum for women indicate, scientific curriculum-making almost inevitably was tied, first of all, to the social status quo, with the activities that people already were engaging in serving as the norm for what people ought to do, even when, as Charters never tired of saying, those activities would have to be "idealized" before they could serve as legitimate objectives in a course of study. The curriculum lacked any utopian component, social progress being seen in terms of simply performing more efficiently what one would do anyway. Little or no attention was given to the potential for social change having the effect of transforming the nature and scope of those activities. Secondly, despite the persistent invocation of science in the interest of a curriculum tied to direct utility, the technique of activity analysis almost inevitably resorted in the end to consensus. Whatever may have been the scientific procedure used to create the list of activities or traits originally, they were incapable of standing on their own as elements in the curriculum without the intervention of human judgment.

This was the case, for example, in Bobbitt's celebrated Los Angeles school survey, a study which culminated in his most influential book, *How to Make a Curriculum* (1924). Although Bobbitt insisted that the method of activity analysis required that "at all stages of the analyses, attention should be fixed up on the *actual activities of mankind*" (p. 9), the list of curricular objectives he presented in the book represented not direct observation of actual activities but "the practically unanimous judgment of some twenty-seven hundred well-trained and experienced adults" and even, in a few cases, "only majority approval" (p. 10). (In point of fact, Bobbitt arrived in Los Angeles with a long list of objectives that his graduate students at the University of Chicago had prepared and then presented them for approval by the Los Angeles teachers (Bobbitt, 1922, pp. 4–5).)

Whatever may have been the practical difficulties of activity analysis, one persistent legacy of the scientific curriculum-makers is the continued insistence upon stating precise and definite curricular objectives in advance of any educational activity. This is, of course, an argument by analogy from the world of manufacture where, at least according to Taylor, precise specifications and standards had to be established in advance in order to achieve the desired product with maximum efficiency. "The first step in curriculum-making," Bobbitt (1924) asserted, "is to decide what specific educational results are to be produced" (p. 32), and the fact that his injunction has become a vital ingredient in the predominant approach to curriculum planning in the twentieth century is testimony to the success of the overall position he represented. The idea of stating numerous, precise and definite objectives, by contrast, never seems to have arisen in the work of Harris, Hall or Dewey.

Moreover, the scientific curriculum-makers' conception of education as preparation for what lies ahead has become thoroughly infused into contemporary educational thought. As Bobbitt (1924) made this point, "Education is primarily for adult life, not for child life. Its fundamental responsibility is to prepare for the fifty years of adulthood, not for the twenty years of childhood and youth" (p. 8). Dewey regarded his own position as one that "contrasts sharply" with any doctrine based on education as preparation. He objected to placing children on a "waiting list," a kind of "probation for another life" (Dewey, 1916, p. 63). That kind of education, he insisted, had no motive power and puts "a premium . . . on shillyshallying and procrastination" instead of capitalizing on the natural powers of attention and energy that children bring with them to school (pp. 63–4). In the end, he claimed, "the principle of preparation makes necessary recourse on a large scale to the use of adventitious motives of pleasure and pain" just because a remote future has no power to direct children's energies. It has cut itself off, he claimed, from the "possibilities of the present" (p. 64). Resorting to a system of education based on preparation also, in Dewey's view, subverted the ethical force of education. "Who can reckon up the loss of moral power," Dewey (1909) once said, "that arises from the constant impression that nothing is worth doing in itself, but only as a preparation for something else, which in turn is only a getting ready for some genuinely serious end beyond?" (pp. 25–6).

Profound differences of the sort that existed between the social efficiency educators and Dewey on such a fundamental matter as whether education should be seen as a form of preparation or not signifies, not a single reform thrust aimed at dislodging the old order in education, but several. And insofar as effect on actual school practice is concerned, the prominence and persistence of the basic ideas of the scientific curriculum-makers indicates that someone like the relatively obscure Bobbitt may have been far more in touch with the true temper of his times than the world-renowned Dewey.

CHAPTER 5

SUBJECT REALIGNMENT AND VOCATIONALISM

i

It was perhaps because he sensed the danger of a massive transformation of the traditional school subjects that Eliot, in a startling, almost inexplicable, repudiation of his long-standing position, declared in 1908 that "teachers of the elementary schools ought to sort the pupils and sort them by their evident or probable destinies" (pp. 12–13). There was, he even emphasized, "no function more important" (p. 12). Alluding to the issue of manual training, Eliot agreed that it had been "rightly introduced" and that it was "a very useful element in the curriculum," but he urged that trade schools should be added that are distinctly preparatory for "a life of skilled manual labor" (p. 10–11). Without equivocation, the architect of the Committee of Ten report was rejecting one of the Committee's most critical recommendations and accepting Hall's stand that the curriculum should be tied to the probable destination of students (and even extending it to the elementary school level), a position he had passionately rejected only three years before (Eliot, 1905). If the humanist values he cherished could not be instilled in the entire school population, as Eliot would have undoubtedly preferred, it could at least be preserved in that segment whose "destiny" it was to go on to college. Without that compromise, it must have seemed conceivable, at least in the context of educational reform during the first decade of the twentieth century, that humanist values might be eradicated altogether from the American school curriculum. Curriculum-makers and leaders in the professional education community more and more saw the temper of American life in the early twentieth century and, to some extent, mass public education itself as inconsistent with humanist values and traditions, and this perception served to isolate the humanist tradition from the mainstream of American educational policy-making. With the tide of educational change running against them, humanists seemed to be reaching an undeclared détente with the social efficiency educators whereby the traditional academic curriculum would be preserved, but only in connection with a select portion of the school population, increasingly defined as "college-entrance" students.

As America moved toward the second quarter of the twentieth century, educational leaders became increasingly strident in their denunciations of the schools for their failure to change their curricula in line with the new ideas that reformers like David Snedden and Charles Prosser were espousing. Despite the vigorous efforts of extremist social efficiency educators, many traditional subjects somehow managed to survive. Whatever had been the high hopes of those educational reformers who wanted to wipe the curricular slate clean, they were almost bound to fall short simply because the nature of the reforms proposed were often so far reaching. Snedden's dream of replacing subjects with peths and strands as the basic building blocks of the curriculum remained unrealized. But sometimes lost in the disappointment over the seemingly slow pace of curricular change was the fact that reformers had in the century's first two decades also achieved a few notable, even astounding, successes in the direction of the social efficiency ideal.

There had, after all, been a whole new institution created, the junior high school, and, with the influx of mental testing into the schools on a mass scale after the First World War, that institution could devote itself to determining the true nature of the "raw material," leaving the high school free to provide the differentiated curriculum that the social efficiency reformers so insistently demanded. One of the candidates for the honor of being the first junior high school in America, for example, was the school built in 1910 during the superintendency of Frank F. Bunker in Berkeley, California. Bunker unabashedly drew from Ayres's research on "laggards" and "retardation" as well as from similar studies by other educational leaders such as Thorndike. The curriculum he reported for that school reflected precisely the vocational orientation that the social efficiency leaders argued would eliminate the waste accruing from the failure of many students to proceed expeditiously through the grades (Bunker, 1916). Much of the rationale for the new institution had also been built around putative evidence brought forward by the developmentalists to the effect that pre-adolescents were best kept separate from older, post-pubescent students. The large-scale incorporation of the junior high school into the American educational ladder is one instance where the success of an important innovation benefited by the fact that the ideas of two or more powerful interest groups intersected at that point.

A second indication of some success was that many of the traditional school subjects, although not being cast out of the curriculum as the more extreme social efficiency reformers demanded, were quietly transforming themselves in line with the new utilitarian curricula. History, for example, was gradually being replaced, or at least supplemented, by other social studies, some of which were aimed directly at the development of efficient citizenship (Sivertson, 1972). Even when the name of a subject like history remained intact, the subject itself frequently took on a new character in line with the demands of the citizenship aim as the Cardinal Principles Report had recommended (Lybarger, 1981). With concern about an undesirable class of immigrants on the rise, it was to the schools generally and to the social studies in particular that American leaders turned as the most efficacious way of introducing American institutions and inculcating American norms and values.

A pivotal figure in the reconstruction of the social studies

along directly functional lines was the Director of the Depart-
met of Research for the Hampton Institute, Thomas Jesse
Jones. Jones evolved a new social studies at Hampton that
was designed to equip America's underclass with the skills
that would bring them to the level of the white middle class.
The prevailing rationale at Hampton and many other educational institutions designed specifically for Blacks and American Indians was that while those races were not inherently
inferior, they were in an earlier stage of development than the
white race. By designing the program of studies so as to
introduce the more advanced white social institutions and
social practices to the less advanced races, their progress
toward a state of civilization could be speeded up. As Jones
(1908) put it, "Because the Negro and Indian races have not
had time to develop, they are not equal to certain other races;
with time to develop, they may become the equals of other
races" (p. 5). The course in economics at Hampton, for
example, was a direct attempt to get Blacks and American
Indians to abandon certain undesirable practices in specific
areas of practical concern such as the purchase of clothing and
the consumption of food. Emphasis was given to the "Negro's
preference for ham instead of beef, for fats and sweets instead
of the more nutritive foods, for fancy and brilliantly colored
garments instead of the more substantially made clothes"
(Jones, 1908, p. 12). In these respects, the "uneducated
Indian was said to be even more reckless than the Negro" (p.
13). Efforts were made to inculcate the habit of saving
because "saving results in capital which can be used both to
increase the income of the individual and to assist in the
general welfare of the community" and to introduce students
to various forms of saving institutions (p. 14). "The study of
economics," Jones reported, "reminds the pupil of social
gradations based on wealth, and enlightens him as to some of
the individual characteristics and social forces that have
brought about these gradations and that will enable him to
pass from one grade to another" (p. 40). When it came to the
study of sociology, Jones emphasized that "possibly the most
impressive contributions in the sociological course at Hamp-

ton is the realization of the truth that beyond differences in physique, in economic possessions, and in literacy, there are other vital differences in the dispositions, in the mental characteristics, and in the social organizations of races" (p. 40). Census reports were studied in order to point up differences among the races in such areas as marriage relations, occupations and crime. By studying the actual census figures in these matters, the students at Hampton would learn not to be influenced by data that are "exaggerated and distorted by the inflamed imagination of some 'social reform' novelist" (p. 40). Other topics included comparisons of Negro and white birth and death rates with special emphasis on the responsibility to give "careful consideration" to "economic outlook" before undertaking to have children (p. 42). Social studies at Hampton Institute was obviously designed to have a directly beneficial effect on the lives of its students through the development of what were deemed to be socially desirable habits and ideals, and, as early as the turn of the century, the program at Hampton was attracting national and largely favorable attention (Shaw, 1900).

It should not be surprising, therefore, that Jones, as the guiding force behind such widely acclaimed reforms, should be appointed by the National Education Association to head the subcommittee on social studies of the Commission on the Reorganization of Secondary Education. When the preliminary reports of the various subject subcommittees were issued (National Education Association, 1913), it was clear that the recommendations for the reconstruction of the social studies would follow the lines that Jones had pursued at Hampton. "Good citizenship," the report declared, "should be the aim of social studies in the high school," and this meant that "facts, conditions, theories, and activities that do not contribute rather directly to the appreciation of methods of human betterment have no claim" (pp. 16–17). With a passion rarely seen in government reports, Jones sought to redirect the old academic study of history toward the production of good citizens through such new forms of social studies as community civics, to be "offered to the pupil as early as his powers of appreciation allow" (p. 18). Within a short time, the effort to reshape the social studies in line with the citizenship aim mushroomed in terms of scope and intensity (Sivertson, 1972), with civic virtues being defined largely in terms of "obedience, helpfulness, courtesy, punctuality and the like" (National Education Association, 1915, p. 36). When the report of the Commission's Committee on Social Studies was issued, it included a direct endorsement of the social studies program at Hampton Institute, declaring that it could find "no better illustration" of its recommendation for the schools of the nation than could be found there (National Education Association, 1916, pp. 53–6). Given the almost obsessive concern with social disintegration and an erosion of tradition-al American values, it is not surprising that a curriculum originally developed for a social underclass should eventually emerge as a model for the majority of America's school-children.

Other subjects were also undergoing internal transforma-tions. The teaching of reading, for example, the heart of the elementary school curriculum, became increasingly domin-ated by a torrent of scientific studies of word frequency such as Thorndike's *The Teacher's Word Book* (1921) and by efforts generally to base reading instruction on scientifically determined findings (Gray, 1925). Similar efforts were also carried forward in the area of arithmetic which included systematic testing of persons in various occupations for the purpose of setting curricular standards based on commercial uses (Courtis, 1913). In this way, the scientific curriculum-makers' ideal of an array of school subjects keyed to objec-tively determined demands of modern life was gradually approaching realization.

ii

The most dramatic and, in the long run, the most far-reaching of the successful curricular innovations was vocational educa-tion. In 1893, the Committee of Ten had excluded vocational education entirely from their four model programs of study. Given their basic mental disciplinarian orientation, the members of the committee simply did not deem it a fit subject for a school curriculum, even one, as they saw it, that was designed for "life" as opposed to college entrance. But by 1917, vocational education came to be regarded as such an urgent necessity as to require major federal aid. The significance of the success of vocational education was not simply that a new subject had been added, nor that a major new curriculum option had been created, but that many existing subjects, particularly at the secondary level, were becoming infused with criteria drawn from vocational education. This became evident in the increasing popularity of such courses as business mathematics and business English as legitimate substitutes for traditional forms of those subjects. In very visible ways, the whole curriculum for all but the college-bound was becoming vocationalized. Superintendent Bunker (1916), for example, pointed with pride to the emphasis being given practical subjects in the new junior high school.

Deliberate efforts to introduce an element of practicality into the traditional humanist curriculum in the United States go back at least as far as the late eighteenth century with the founding of Benjamin Franklin's academy and were even reflected in the controversy leading to the Yale report of 1828. One of the most successful of these efforts was the one by farm and manufacturing groups to enact the Land Grant College (Morrill) Act. When it was finally passed and then signed by President Abraham Lincoln in 1862, it led, eventually, to the founding of a number of colleges devoted to including the practical arts such as mechanics and agriculture in their curricula. The dominant form of secondary education in the nineteenth century, the academy, had a distinctly practical orientation (Sizer, 1964) and, in general, schools in the nineteenth century were continually preaching the virtues of hard work and the dangers of sloth as part of moral training, reflecting a tradition of some relationship, however ill-defined, between work and school. In addition, as America's industrialization continued into the later nineteenth century, so did the effort to provide an improved professional education especially for engineers, as represented by the creation of Rensselaer Polytechnic Institute organized around a European model, and the infusion of engineering into the curriculum of the United States Military Academy at West Point, New York.

But of all these portents of a drive for a practical curriculum, especially one tied to occupational competence, the most immediate and significant precursor to the emergence of vocational education as a potent force in the American curriculum was the manual training movement. Manual training, actually, was tied in its very early years to the training of engineers. Under the leadership of John O. Runkle, the president of the Massachusetts Institute of Technology and a professor of mathematics, and Calvin M. Woodward, Dean of O'Fallon Polytechnic Institute at Washington University in St Louis, Missouri, the manual training movement met with almost unprecedented success. Early in their careers, both Runkle and Woodward had devoted themselves to reforming the professional education of engineers especially by seeking to infuse into their training a more practical knowledge of tools and basic mechanics than was typical for that period. A turning point in that effort came when Runkle and some of his colleagues attended the Russian exhibit at the Philadelphia Centennial Exposition in 1876. Runkle was enormously impressed with the fact that Victor Della Vos of the Imperial Technical School at St Petersburg had developed a series of graded exercises designed to teach the very skills that Runkle had thought were so lacking in the education of engineers in the United States. Practical skills, in other words, could be arranged into an orderly sequence, a curriculum that could be taught in schools. Runkle's admiration for that training was such that he soon extended his proposals for the Russian system beyond the professional training of engineers to public education generally. The new programs he envisioned would be as applicable to future mechanics as to engineers.

Woodward's enthusiasm for the new manual training was no less ardent. In 1879, Woodward opened the Manual

Training School of Washington University with a three-year program for boys between fourteen and eighteen years of age. According to Woodward (1885), the curriculum of the school was designed "to foster a higher appreciation of the value and dignity of intelligent labor, and the worth and respectability of intelligent laboring men" (p. 623) not for specific trade training. As his work with the school evolved and as the school gained national visibility, his emphasis tended to waver between the relatively narrow aim of improving pre-professional training for engineers and the much grander vision of reconstructing the curriculum of the public schools in such a way as to redress the imbalance between the essentially literary humanist curriculum and the handiwork that was a mark of modern life. Although he strongly maintained that manual training should be seen in terms of "a wholesome intellectual culture" (Woodward, 1887, p. 245), he also emphasized the "honor and comfort" of work as mechanics, engineers or manufacturers in contrast to those who "eke out a scanty subsistence as clerks, book-keepers, salesmen, poor lawyers, murderous doctors, whining preachers, penny-a-liners, or hardened 'school-keepers' " (p. 172). For Woodward, manual training was essential not only for proper intellectual and moral education but as a way of restoring the dignity of hand labor, an avenue for youth to a respectable and rewarding occupation, and a way to make the country prosper. In short, manual training was being advertised in terms that all the reform groups of the period could easily embrace.

As a publicist for the new education, Woodward was unsurpassed. Whether by instinct or calculation, he recognized that the power of the humanists was still too strong in the late nineteenth century to be vulnerable to a frontal attack. "It is scarcely necessary," he declared in 1885, "to add that the 'New' education includes the 'Old.' We tear down no essential parts of the old temple" (p. 614). What he proposed instead was that education add two "wings" to the edifice. One was the wing of natural science which the humanist curriculum had undervalued; the other, of course, was manual training which completes the old education by introducing "an education through the senses of touch and sight, through the hand and the eye" (p. 614). Unlike Hall's, for example, Woodward's reforms were represented as a relatively minor adjustment that would painlessly bring traditional education in line with the demands of modern society. He was even able to promote his innovation in mental disciplinarian terms, arguing that "manual training is particularly strong in furnishing the knowledge and experience, in establishing the major premises essential to logical reasoning" (Woodward, 1890, p. 204). That was an argument of considerable appeal to someone like Nicholas Murray Butler, the president of the New York College for the Training of Teachers (later Teachers College). "Manual training is mental training through the hand and eye," said Butler (1888), "just as the study of history is mental training through the memory and other powers" (p. 379).

But with claims of such scope, it was almost inevitable that a few objections should be heard. William Torrey Harris (1889), for example, speaking for the Committee on Pedagogics of the National Education Association, found it necessary to "insist that manual training ought not to be begun before the completion of the twelfth year of the pupil, nor before he has had such school instruction in the intellectual branches of school-work, namely, in reading, writing, arithmetic, geography, grammar, and history" (p. 417). Harris was not one to surrender the primacy of his "windows of the soul" without a fight. He claimed that the early imposition of manual training on children could not be accomplished "without dwarfing their human nature, physically, intellectually, and morally, and producing arrested development" (p. 418). Harris was ready to accept the case for the intellectual value of the study of science but not manual training. "While the student is learning a method of doing something his brain is exercised" he said; "when the process has become a habit it is committed to his hand, and his intellect is not required again except for new combinations" (Brown, Hoose, Parr and Harris, 1889, p. 95). Harris was thus denying the intellectual value of manual training that its major proponents persistently claimed, but the voice of "the great conservator" was increasingly a lonely one, especially on that subject.

While the nationally known proponents of manual training such as Woodward and Butler preferred to advance their cause in terms of intellectual development, it was the potential for a practical and especially an occupational payoff that school administrators found most appealing. One early debate over manual training's practical value followed in the wake of the founding in 1867 of a manual training school for Blacks and American Indians in Hampton, Virginia, by Samuel Chapman Armstrong, the Superintendent of the Freedmen's Bureau. Like Woodward, Armstrong, the son of missionaries in Hawaii, maintained that the "training of the hand is at the same time a discipline of the mind and will" (Peabody, 1918, p. xv). He exalted labor for Blacks, particularly menial labor, by both men and women. In the dignity of labor and the Puritan ethic, Armstrong saw the salvation of the Black race from poverty and degradation. Armstrong's disciple, Booker T. Washington, sought to instill a similar ethos in his Tuskegee Normal Institute founded in Alabama in 1881. Through manual training, the "downtrodden child of ignorance, shiftlessness, and moral weakness" would be converted into a "thoroughly rounded man of prudence, foresight, responsibility, and financial independence" (Washington, 1905, p. 7).

The practical value of training in menial labor did not go unchallenged. W. E. B. DuBois, for example, the first Black man to be awarded a PhD from Harvard University, argued that the sort of hand labor being promoted at Tuskegee was essentially an anachronism in modern industrial society and that Blacks were being denied the intellectual training and professional skills that a twentieth-century economy demanded and therefore being denied a chance at true equality. Moreover, as early as 1902, DuBois had pointed out that the range of "callings" was so great that, even if trade schools were to be made much more efficient, they could not serve their intended purposes. "The factory system," he pointed out, "with its minutely developed division of labor . . . renders it absolutely essential that the apprentice should learn his trade in the factory." The second major problem he cited was "the strong opposition of trade unions to Negro labor in all lines save those where the Negro already has a foot-hold" (DuBois, 1902, p. 82). Beyond these questions of the efficacy of manual training, DuBois raised some broadly philosophical questions:

> Industrial schools must beware of placing undue emphasis on the "practical" character of their work. All true learning of the head or hand is practical in the sense of being applicable to life. But the best learning is more than merely practical since it seeks to apply itself, not simply to present modes of living, but to a larger, broader life which lives to-day, perhaps, in theory only, but may come to realization to-morrow by the help of educated and good men. . . . The ideals of education, whether men are taught to teach or to plow, to weave or to write must not be allowed to sink to sordid utilitarianism. Education must keep broad ideals before it, and never forget that it is dealing with Souls and not with Dollars. (p. 81)

Thus, in the context of the education of Blacks, were the practical and moral virtues associated with manual training being questioned even as it was being extended to the public schools generally.

But whatever may have been the high-minded justifications for manual training that advocates like Woodward put forward or the principled objections that detractors like Harris and DuBois raised, its implementation at the school level was largely a combination of trade training and the standard academic curriculum of the day. Some school systems managed to combine these elements for a time, but, for the most part, when local school groups debated proposals for the introduction of manual training in major cities such as Boston and Milwaukee, those debates were framed largely in terms of economic benefits to the boy or girl receiving the training or to the overall economy of the municipality. Although the debates at the local levels were also infused with a concern for the immigrant poor or for the inadequacy of the existing curriculum in terms of holding the children of the masses in school, it was through trade training that this was to be accomplished, not "mental training through the hand," as Butler preferred to define it. Butler's characterization gave it a legitimacy in the councils of the National Education Association and among leaders in education generally, but rarely was manual training so regarded in terms of school practice. One probable side-effect of that characterization, however, was to avoid so sharp a differentiation in curriculum as to exclude academic subjects, such as foreign languages, science and higher level mathematics from the early manual training programs. The programs of manual training and industrial education developed in the early years of the manual training movement, such as those in Fitchburg, Massachusetts and Milwaukee, Wisconsin, exhibited a rigor and even a high status rarely evident after the vocational education movement was in full swing. In many cases, for example, those early programs were designed to meet college entrance requirements and did not, therefore, represent an educational dead end. The earliest effects on the curriculum of the manual training movement were primarily in terms of grafting on instruction in areas like drafting and mechanics to what was already in place rather than transforming the curriculum entirely for a target population (Ringel, 1980; Kean, 1983).

iii

Even in the face of reluctance on the part of educational leaders to accept a definition that equated manual training with direct trade training in the nineteenth century, the movement toward specific vocational education proceeded apace once the new century began. It was in the long run the direct benefits of occupational skills rather than the remote values associated with completing a liberal education through the hand that had the greater appeal. That appeal in fact was so great that the major impetus for vocational education began to shift from the relatively obscure journals of education and other professional forums to the larger social and political arena. One turning point was the founding in 1896 of the National Association of Manufacturers which from the outset made school policy a centerpiece of their deliberations. Of particular concern to the National Association of Manufacturers was competition for world markets from Germany. Germany's system of separate and specialized technical schools was held in such high esteem that, one year after its founding, the Association's annual convention adopted a resolution declaring that since technical education was so critical in the development of industry, its members should support "manual training or other technical schools" ("Resolutions," 1897, p. 92).

In his presidential address of 1898, Theodore C. Search again emphasized the example of Germany's success in industry and manufacture, also attributing that success to its system of technical schools and citing the fact that England was following its example. In the competition for foreign trade, he felt, America's failure to take into account "the obvious demands of industry and commerce" in its educational system put it at an obvious disadvantage. That disadvantage could be redressed by "the establishment of educational institutions which would give us skilled hands and trained minds for the conduct of our industries and our commerce" (Search, 1898, p. 22). By 1905, a year before the Douglas Commission report, the Association's Committee on Industrial Education had picked up the theme of an American school curriculum that was failing the large majority of the schools' inhabitants. The report cited alarming statistics on the dropout rate:

> Eighty per cent of our public school pupils drop out of the schools before attaining to the high school, and 97 per cent of all our public school pupils, from the primary grades to the high schools, drop out before graduation from the high school. Out of 16,225,093 pupils enrolled in the schools of the whole country only 165,000 are students in the colleges or high schools; only one in one hundred has the benefit of a higher training. ("Report," 1905, p. 142)

The report went on to allude to the decline of the apprenticeship system and the failure of manual training to fill the gap in industrial skill development created by that decline. Again, the answer lay in the creation of "trade schools in which the youth of our land may be taught the practical and technical knowledge of a trade," a matter that the report characterized as "the most important issue before the American people to-day" (p. 143). In subsequent years, the National Association of Manufacturers, through its Standing Committee on Industrial Education, never wavered in its continuing effort to redirect American education toward the system so admired in Germany. The Philadelphia Board of Education, for example, came in for special commendation at the 1907 meeting for being the first to establish a trade school as part of its public school system as did the State of Wisconsin, which was singled out as the first state to enact a law creating a system of trade schools ("Industrial," 1907, p. 122). Reflecting a now familiar theme, the committee's 1912 report accused the American school system of a distinct literary bias which resulted in a curriculum directed toward "abstract-minded and imaginative children, who learn readily from the printed page" (p. 156) and ignoring the majority who are not so blessed.

Again borrowing from the German system, the Association endorsed part-time continuation schools for youth between sixteen and eighteen who were not in school. They recommended a minimum of five hours a week of instruction for such students, as was the case in Wisconsin, and urged employers to pay students their regular salaries for that time. Needless to say, the continuation school should be infused with instruction related to industrial occupations, although continued education for citizenship ought not to be neglected ("Industrial," 1912, pp. 159–60). In general, the curriculum for boys would consist of such courses as mechanical drawing, machine shop and carpentry and, for girls dressing, millinery and domestic science.

The response on the part of organized labor to the challenge of vocational skill training in the public schools and to its unqualified support by the National Association of

Manufacturers was equivocal. The American Federation of Labor, which was undergoing a period of tremendous growth just after the turn of the century, appointed a Committee on Education in 1903, but no clear-cut stand emanated from that committee nor from the American Federation of Labor generally, reflecting uncertainty and conflicting views on educational policy. Dissension emerged as to the extent to which unions should run their own schools as well as to whether the institution of apprenticeship should actually be abandoned. For Samuel Gompers, who by now was the acknowledged leader of organized labor, the ideal solution lay in the creation of schools by the labor unions themselves that would serve in place of the old apprenticeship system. A lack of enthusiasm on the part of the rank and file, however, proved troublesome. The introduction of the Linotype into the printing trade in 1890, for example, represented one opportunity to retrain workers by labor itself, especially in view of the cooperation of one Linotype company. The New York local, however, decided in favor of setting up one more committee to study the matter rather than to establish their own programs for the retraining of workers. Even when other printing locals developed their own programs and the International had set up a correspondence course in 1907, there was little support on the part of the workers themselves (Fisher, 1967). Setting up a union-sponsored system was an expensive and risky undertaking. As a result, no concerted opposition emerged from organized labor to the stream of National Association of Manufacturers pronouncements on the importance of vocational education.

The course that organized labor was eventually to follow in this matter was foreshadowed by their ready participation in the organization that became the principal lobby group for vocational education, the National Society for the Promotion of Industrial Education. The idea of a national organization to promote industrial education emerged at a meeting called by two prominent educators, James, P. Haney, Director of Manual Training at Teachers College, Columbia University, and Charles R. Richards, Director of Arts and Manual

Training in the New York City public school system. Meeting at the Engineers' Club in New York in 1906, the invited group decided to see whether a new organization could be formed that would represent the combined interests of business, labor and professional educators. Almost immediately, that organization struck responsive chords from many quarters. On May 24, 1907, for example, President Theodore Roosevelt wrote to the president of the new society, Henry S. Prichett, that the American school system has been "well-nigh wholly lacking on the side of industrial training, of the training which fits a man for the shop and the farm. . . . We of the United States must develop a system under which each individual citizen shall be trained so as to be effective individually as an economic unit, and fit to be organized with his fellows so that he and they can work in efficient fashion together" (Roosevelt, 1907, p. 6).

Although the prospects seemed exciting, the exact direction that the new organization would follow was not clear from the outset. The early debates reflected some uncertainty as to the respective forms that vocational reeducation should take. Some discussion seemed to indicate a desire to revivify the apprenticeship system with the actual work site becoming the setting where the trade training took place (Deems, 1908). The president of one large Connecticut firm declared his general support for industrial education but thought on-site training to be indispensable. "We must take the boys that go into our shops and educate them for our particular work," he declared, "The schools cannot do this" (Bullard, 1909, p. 51). On the other hand, one study of the shoe industry indicated that workers were reluctant to lose time teaching apprentices and that learning a new job was unpopular among workers because it frequently meant a reduction in productive labor and therefore in their earnings (Dean, 1908). Frequently, the German model of continuation schools was represented as an ideal combination of factory and school-based instruction.

Within a few years of the Society's founding a consensus began to emerge in the organization to the effect that the most appropriate course was direct trade training in· the public schools. A word of caution, however, was expressed by Dewey's friend, Jane Addams, head of Hull House, in Chicago. Although she had a year earlier idealized the German model of industrial education as one not so much designed to advance industrial development as to promote "human welfare" (Addams, 1907, p. 39), she now expressed distinct reservations about the emphasis on direct trade training. Industrial education in public schools, she thought, should aim at educating youth "to live intelligently in an industrial community" (Addams, 1908, p. 95) and not at specific trade training. Alluding to the way modern industry had through its high degree of specialization transformed the nature of work, she declared that "it would be a very brave person who would now assert that the worker enjoys such a life" (p. 96). Addams confessed to being "confused" by some proponents of vocational education who were alluding to modern industrial conditions making extensive trade training obsolete while others pointed to a revival of the apprenticeship system within factories themselves. By this time, however, the momentum in the direction of school-based trade training was far too strong to be denied. Organized labor was suspicious of skill training in factories under the aegis of the manufacturers themselves, yet labor was unable to mobilize its own alternative. Trade training in the public schools seemed to be the most acceptable option. Gompers personally endorsed that policy in 1910 (1910, p. 40–2).

Another question to be resolved was the role of vocational education for women. Within a year after its formation, the National Society for the Promotion of Industrial Education appointed a Sub-Committee on Industrial Education for Women with Jane Addams and Susan Kingsbury among its members. Their report, issued in 1907, was careful to point out that women have always worked, and that, therefore the working should not be taken to be "a peculiar feature of modern times, an interloper as it were, usurping a place which does not rightly belong to her" (Marshall, 1907, p. 6). One major thrust of the report appeared to be an effort to head off any possible attempt to define vocational education for women strictly in terms of domestic science. Another theme, continually being raised by Addams, was related to the changing nature of work brought about by the division of labor. "The tendency to divide and subdivide every operation," the report said, "means that girls can go to work at a very early age, at the same time learning only one minute part of their work and having no chance to see its relation to any other part. Thus they find their progress retarded and growth and development impossible" (pp. 12–13). In this vein the report called for more study, not just in terms of the effect on industry but on the women themselves, before a suitable form of training be introduced.

Some of the discussions on vocational education for women were tinged with allusions to women's rights. In one address delivered in 1910, a representative of the National Woman's Trade Union League indicated that some forms of trade training were depriving women of their "breadwinning capacity":

> There is an agricultural school in one of our Eastern cities, where the girls and boys are taught the possibilities of breadwinning as agricultural laborers, agriculturists, gardeners, florists, or whatever you will. When it comes to the boy, he learns the chemistry of the soil, and gets down to the fundamental things in those particulars, but the girl is taught cooking and sewing. I am not saying that cooking and sewing are not necessary, but when we cheat a girl out of the training she ought to have for her breadwinning capacity, and substitute something which has nothing to do with the trade she is trying to learn, then we make a great and grave mistake. (Robins, 1910, p. 78)

She concluded her address by underscoring the "need of teaching the girl the value of her labor power" and improving the conditions of laboring women (p. 81). Another speaker at the same meeting in Milwaukee, the president of the Young Women's Christian Association from Hamilton, Ontario, in making the case for a more effective program in homemaking, argued that too much attention was being given to cooking. "I think that is one very clear evidence of man's hand in our educational organization, because he has provided more liberally for cooking lessons than for any other branch of industrial education for girls" (Hoodless, 1910, p. 181). Her address ended with a call to women to participate fully in developing educational programs for women (p. 184).

iv

By the second decade of the century, the main issue before the National Society for the Promotion of Industrial Education was not the form that industrial education should take but how it should be controlled. There were initial efforts in the period around 1910 and 1911 to work with individual states in improving their systems of trade training, but the possibility of developing a unified policy through massive federal intervention soon proved to be an irresistible prospect. By 1911, a bill had been proposed by Senator Carroll S. Page of Vermont to provide federal funds in the area of industial education, one of a series of such measures going back to the Davis Bill in 1907. Snedden (1912) took the lead in arguing for the efficacy of federal legislation in the area, although he felt that states and local communities should contribute as well (p. 128). He also held out the intriguing prospect that the National Society for the Promotion of Industrial Education could help administer the federal legislation once it were enacted. In fact, Snedden as Commissioner of Education in Massachusetts and Prosser as his Deputy Commissioner and new Secretary of the Society worked closely with Senator Page in framing the legislation (Page, 1912, p. 118). Similar legislation involving agricultural education, the Smith–Lever Bill, was a complicating factor. Both bills after being passed died when a Joint Conference Committee could not reconcile the two bills, but the Smith–Lever Bill was later reintroduced and signed into law in 1914.

It took more modification to shepherd vocational education through Congress successfully. Alongside the drive for industrial education, a parallel drive among agricultural interests had been emerging since the nineteenth century. Although prompted by almost opposing impulses, one to preserve the virtues of agrarian life and the other to bring the country in line with the new industrial age, the destinies of the two movements were to be eventually intertwined in the Smith–Hughes Act of 1917 as they had been earlier in another major piece of federal legislation involving higher education, the Morrill Act of 1862. One of the most effective campaigns to incorporate agricultural work into elementary and secondary schools had its origins in the work of Liberty Hyde Bailey who, as a professor in the College of Agriculture at Cornell University, sought to introduce nature study in rural schools. Like the original manual training movement, Bailey's emphasis was not on earning a livelihood and even the introduction of scientific methods of farming was not, for him, a paramount concern. Rather, he preached a reverence for the soil and for farm life, a way of life that he saw as in danger of disappearing. Although he favored introducing agriculture into the school curriculum, Bailey (1908) was concerned about the possible detracting effect it would have on the spiritual values that would be derived from nature study.

As early as 1894, Bailey was able to obtain funds from the New York State legislature and soon his work was being disseminated to rural schools throughout the state. Within a decade, some three thousand teachers were receiving instructional material from Bailey. When a Rochester, New York, seed dealer offered seed packets for sale at one cent per packet, school-children purchased eleven thousand of those packets within two weeks (Keppel, 1960, p. 67). Whatever may have been the high romanticism implicit in Bailey's campaign, it struck a responsive chord among those who felt threatened by the intrusion of the new industrial society. Very similar crusades emphasizing the virtues of rural living were undertaken at the same time by "Uncle Henry" Wallace, the editor of *Wallace's Farmer* and William Dempster Hoard, editor of *Hoard's Dairyman*. Hoard, in particular, sought to rally farmers to make rural schools more attuned to the agricultural community.

The National Society for the Promotion of Industrial Education appeared almost oblivious to the popularity these movements enjoyed in the farming community, but Congress was not. Somehow, the increasingly insistent demands for industrial skill training in the public schools had to be balanced against the still potent demands of rural leaders for the preservation of their way of life, and once again Congress found it expedient to link the needs of industry and agriculture under the general aegis of the national interest. The national interest in the case of agriculture was usually expressed in terms of improved methods of farming such as in the Hatch Act of 1882 where agricultural stations had been set up for the purpose of disseminating the results of agricultural experimentation. When President Woodrow Wilson appointed a commission in 1914 to study the question of federal aid to vocational education, the joining of industrial trade training with farmer's interests was almost a political necessity. Indeed, when the commission reported, the two main recommendations treated the claims of the two groups together. One recommendation called for federal support for the training of teachers in trade and industrial as well as agricultural and home economics subjects and the other provided funds for paying teachers in those areas. With President Wilson's strong endorsement, the measure finally passed less than two months before America's entry into the First World War.

By 1917, the main direction of vocational education was sealed – job skill training in the public schools supported generously by the federal government. The National Society for the Promotion of Industrial Education, now the National Society for Vocational Education, had succeeded in mounting a drive for federal intervention that gave even further impetus to a movement that had already achieved high visibility. When the Executive Staff was appointed to administer the new law, it was natural for Prosser to be its director, with other members of the organization serving as members. With money, powerful lobby groups, energetic leadership in high places and a sympathetic public, vocational education was well on its way to becoming the most successful curricular innovation of the twentieth century. While some compromises were necessary, the appeal of the social efficiency interest group was clearly reaching its peak.

v

Three years before the actual passage of the Smith–Hughes Act, a bitter debate erupted over the direction that the new vocational education was taking. While that dispute had no dramatic effect on the pending legislation, it illustrates that beneath the mainstream of social efficiency ideology, there existed a small undercurrent of opposition. Writing in the first volume of *New Republic*, Dewey (1914) took the occasion of the appointment by Congress of a Commission on National Aid to Vocational Education to denounce in uncharacteristically harsh language the nature of the proposals that had been emanating from the supporters of the legislation.

In an apparent reference to the continuing admiration for the German system of education that had flowed from the pronouncements of the National Association of Manufacturers, Dewey (1914) cast doubt on its appropriateness as a model for American education. The German educational system, he pointed out "has been frankly nationalistic." Its actual effect on the well-being of workers had been negligible, Dewey argued. Statistics indicated that skilled workers in Germany received virtually the same salary as unskilled workers. In Germany, he maintained, the "well being of the state as a moral entity is supreme" and the "promotion of commerce against international competitors is one of the chief means of fostering the state." The system of education that had been developed in Germany was openly and directly "a means to this means," which as a model of educational policy he described as "extraordinarily irrelevant to American conditions" (p. 11).

Dewey (1914) applauded the efforts in cities like Chicago, Gary and Cincinnati to adapt instruction in order to keep children in school longer, but this effort, he insisted, should take the form of "making their instruction significant to them" and not "to turn schools into preliminary factories supported at public expense" (p. 12). Throughout his article, Dewey used the term industrial education rather than vocational education. Although these terms were often used interchangeably, Dewey undoubtedly used industrial education to indicate that in his view the introduction of such study ought to have a much broader purpose than simply trade training. Consistent with the reservations expressed earlier by Addams, he pointed out that narrow forms of skill training may not even serve the intended purpose since "automatic machinery is constantly invading the province of specially trained skill of hand and eye". Dewey deplored the fact that there were no educators appointed to the new commission, since he regarded the issue to be "primarily an educational one and not a business and technical one as in Germany" (p. 12). He took as his example of the "wrong kind" of legislation a new law in Indiana which, in setting up the continuation schools that the National Association of Manufacturers had advocated, provided state funds only if the instruction "deals with the subject matter of the day employment" and where that purpose was extended even to regular schools (Dewey, 1915b, p. 71). Such a narrow interpretation of industrial education he described as "theory run mad" (p. 72).

Snedden, who along with Prosser had emerged as one of the twin stalwarts of the trade training movement, seemed genuinely surprised and dismayed by Dewey's direct attack. Indicating that he had grown accustomed to attacks by educational "reactionaries," he nevertheless found Dewey's criticism to be "discouraging" (Snedden, 1915, p. 40). He found it "incredible" that the cause of vocational education be regarded as "beneficial chiefly to employers" and argued that "greater productive capacity" would ultimately be shared by the laborer (pp. 41–2). He went on to argue that the question of whether vocational education should be part of the general

system of education in a state or whether it should be administered as a separate system as in the case of Wisconsin was
"merely one of securing the greatest efficiency" (p. 42).
Dewey's reply to Snedden did not minimize the extent of their
differences. Dewey (1915a) characterized Snedden's position
as "the identification of education with acquisition of specialized skill in the management of machines at the expense of an
industrial intelligence based on science and a knowledge of
social problems and conditions" (p. 42). He alluded to Snedden's support of the Cooley Bill which had been introduced in
the Illinois legislature in 1913, a bill drafted by the former
superintendent of schools of Chicago that would provide a
dual system of education, one general and the other vocational. That, Dewey felt, would result in a typically "bookish"
education for one group and narrow trade training for the
other. Dewey concluded his reply by emphasizing that his
difference of opinion with Snedden was "not so much narrow-
ly educational as it is profoundly political and social. The kind
of vocational education in which I am interested," Dewey
insisted, "is not one which will 'adapt' workers to the existing
industrial regime; I am not sufficiently in love with the regime
for that" (p. 42). In a period when vocational education was
going virtually unchallenged even by organized labor, Dewey
had emerged as its most ardent and perhaps even its most
vocal opponent.

Dewey's *Democracy and Education* (1916) appeared while
the drive for direct trade training in the schools was at its
height. Alluding to other untenable dualisms, theory and
practice, body and mind, mental states and the world, Dewey
thought that much of the confusion over vocational education
was derived from an unwarranted opposition between labor
and leisure. This leads us, he believed, to single out the one
aspect of a person's life which distinguishes one person from
others and to ignore those shared with others. In the effort to
prepare someone for earning a livelihood, the most significant features of one's education can easily be neglected.
Typically, Dewey tried to take terms like occupation and
vocation and redefine them in his own terms:

> The only adequate training *for* occupations is training *through*
> occupations. The principle . . . that the educative process is its
> own end, and that the only sufficient preparation for later
> responsibilities comes by making the most of immediately
> present life, applied in full force to the vocational phases of
> education. The dominant vocation of all human beings at all
> times is living – intellectual and moral growth. In childhood and
> youth, with their relative freedom from economic stress, this
> fact is naked and unconcealed. To predetermine some future
> occupation for which education is to be a strict preparation is to
> injure the possibilities of present development. (pp. 362–3)

Dewey was thus trying to superimpose his own broad conception of an occupation, "a continuous activity having a purpose" (p. 361), on the common use of the term, a ploy which
probably led to further misinterpretation of his position. One
thing he was clear on, however, was that current trends in
vocational education could easily lead it to become "an
instrument in accomplishing the feudal dogma of social predestination" (p. 372). Speaking to a meeting of the Public
Education Association on the eve of President Wilson's
signing of the Smith–Hughes Act, Dewey (1917) argued that
the bill "settled no problem; it merely symbolizes the inau-
guration of a conflict between irreconcilably opposed educational and industrial ideals" (p. 335). In an apparent allusion
to the original manual training position, Dewey held that
vocational education conceived as a part of "a liberal education and generous education already supposed to exist" to be
"pure romance" (p. 332). The key issue was "whose interests" would be served by its introduction (Dewey, 1917, p.
332). He asked rhetorically whether the new vocational
education was being directed at an "increase in the industrial
intelligence and power of the worker" or whether laborers
are to have their skills developed in order to "add to the
profits of employers . . . by avoiding waste, getting more out
of their machines and materials" in the hope that they will
ultimately share in the profits "as an incidental by-product"
(p. 333). Whatever may have been Dewey's disillusionment
with what passed for a liberal education in his day, he was far

from supportive of the alternative that social efficiency doctrine dictated.

vi

In 1924, when Robert and Helen Lynd undertook their classic study of Muncie, Indiana, in America's heartland, they found that the beginning high school freshman was expected to choose from twelve courses of study: general, college preparatory, music, art, shorthand, bookkeeping, applied electricity, mechanical drafting, printing, machine shop, manual arts and home economics (Lynd and Lynd, 1929, p. 192). Although English was still required for the first two years, it was replaced by commercial English in five of the courses and was an option in the fourth year. "The most pronounced region of movement," they found, "appears in the rush of courses that depart from the traditional dignified conception of what constitutes education and seek to train for specific tool and skill activities in factory, office, and home" (p. 194). Lacking the long and honorable tradition of the academic subjects, the new vocational subjects "frankly adopted the canons of office and machine shop" (p. 194). What is more, these were the courses to which the members of the Rotary Club and the public generally pointed with pride. The head of the school board made his own preferences clear and, at the same time, offered an apt summary of the educational transformation that social efficiency had wrought in little more than a quarter-century: "For a long time all boys were trained to be President. Then for a while we trained them all to be professional men. Now we are training boys to get jobs" (p. 194). Insofar as the curriculum for girls was concerned, the home economics program began in the seventh grade with the study of food, household management, and selection of food and clothing. In the high school, it included instruction in dressmaking, millinery, hygiene and home nursing. In the scant three decades since the Committee of Ten recommended its four model "programmes," each with different but distinctly academic emphases, direct training for one's future occupational role had emerged as a major, if not the predominant, element in the high school curriculum for that segment of the school population whose "probable destiny" did not include attendance in college.

Vocational education was the most successful curriculum innovation in the twentieth century in the sense that none other approaches it in the range of support it received and the extent to which it became implemented into the curriculum of American schools. Although a wide range of studies has adduced no persuasive evidence that vocational education as a substitute for traditional curricular offerings results in a net gain either in employment or salary for students in those programs (Boyer, 1983), the faith in job skill training through the school system continues unabated. Even more important than the particular programs that have evolved has been the effect on the American curriculum as a whole. Preparation for the particular occupational role, including attending college as a form of occupation, has permeated the justifications for virtually all school subjects. These justifications, in turn, profoundly affect the selection of materials to be studied and the manner in which they are organized for instruction.

On one level, the success of vocational education can be attributed to the fact that it acted as a kind of magic mirror in which the powerful interest groups of the period could see their own reflected ways of reforming what was increasingly regarded as a curriculum out of tune with the times. Virtually the only opponents of any consequence were the humanists like Harris who saw in vocational education a threat to the subjects that developed the intellect and passed on the cultural heritage. DuBois's arguments that trade training in schools was not as effective as was commonly supposed and that it also served to deprive a segment of the school population of the intellectual training they needed were also distinctly humanistic in tone and in general orientation but probably reached a very small and unsympathetic audience. Humanist influence in the period was so clearly on the wane that even Eliot, at least temporarily, was forced to come to terms with the prevailing effort to direct the schools' curriculum along the lines of probable destination. Dewey's opposition, significant though it was, was to the particular direction industrial education was taking and to what it could (and in fact did) become. If anything, Dewey's vague and loosely defined identification as an educational reformer seeking to infuse active occupations into what had become a passive, almost archaic, curriculum, probably served to associate him in the popular mind with the very position he tried to oppose.

vii

That vocational education represented a triumph for the forces of social efficiency can hardly be doubted. The key figures in the shaping of the Smith–Hughes legislation and, equally important, in the way it was implemented in later years were people who shared the perspectives of Charles Prosser and David Snedden and not Jane Addams or John Dewey. Vocational education also fits perfectly into the social efficiency ideal of education as preparation for a specific social and occupational role, and, in this sense, it was the most important step in the direction of a policy of curriculum differentiation in order to achieve that ideal. But the existence and the influence of other interest groups meant that it was not a complete victory. Contrary to the distinct preferences of leaders in the vocational education movement, like Prosser and Snedden, as well as the National Society for the Promotion of Industrial Education generally, vocational education did not emerge under dual control with separate educational institutions created specifically for a predefined school population. Although separate vocational high schools do exist here and there in the United States, the comprehensive high school established itself as the typical if not the quintessential American educational institution, with curricular tracking, both formal and informal, attending to the differentiating function that social efficiency educators considered so critical. While Dewey's appeal to democratic values was not sufficiently persuasive actually to stem the tide of direct trade training, it may have helped to force the compromise that kept a system of schooling where at least in principle all children share a common setting for their education. If nothing else, that compromise preserves the possibility that elements of a common curriculum could reemerge or, at least, that mobility among the various curricular tracks could be facilitated. Moreover, the fact that early manual training programs deliberately avoided some of the most damaging effects of educational predestination often attending curriculum differentiation means that the course that vocational education took in the twentieth century was by no means inevitable. There were other options.

To be sure, the particular course that vocational education in fact followed was influenced by social conditions existing at the time that the drive was at its height. There was after all not only a rising tide of industrialism but a decline of such institutions as apprenticeship, and there is no question that these factors were involved in the campaign for vocational education and its overwhelmingly favorable reception. But these events were filtered through the lenses of particular ideologies that presented not only certain conceptions of the relationship between work and schooling but a vision of a desirable social order. Vocational education did not emerge as a supremely successful curricular innovation because social changes made it so but because certain ways of interpreting social change made the infusion of vocational education into the public school curriculum the most plausible and politically expedient, although not necessarily the most efficacious, response to those perceived changes.

CHAPTER 6

FROM HOME-PROJECT TO EXPERIENCE CURRICULUM

i

On the face of it, industrial training in city schools and vocational agriculture in rural schools were natural counterparts. Both made the school a bridge to the world of work, one by providing youth with the skills that were required by industry and commerce and the other by attending to the skills needed to run a productive and successful farm. That tie was, if nothing else, a politically expedient one to the framers of the Smith–Hughes legislation who essentially treated the two as of one piece (along with home economics). In the eyes of Congress, both were also no doubt deemed to be in the national interest. The value of a skilled and abundant industrial labor pool seemed self-evident, and through vocational agriculture, the school could become the center for the dissemination of scientific methods of farming just as experimental stations had been under the Hatch Act. Although both were regarded as forms of vocational training, and in one sense they obviously were, the difference between vocational agriculture and industrial training turned out to be more significant than their similarities. While both can be seen as responses to industrialism and urban growth, one was framed in terms of simply meeting the needs of the new industrial society by training a skilled labor force in schools while the other had its origins in the effort to preserve certain values associated with rural living in the face of that new society.

Even beyond their differences in origin, the two forms of vocational education as they actually emerged exhibited a profound pedagogical difference. The population served by vocational programs tied to manufacturing were preparing youth for a future that was remote both in time and in setting. Students in those programs were being taught skills in the hope that, some time in the future, those skills would stand them in good stead in the workplace. Unlike the apprenticeship system which school-based industrial training was intended to replace, it was rare that many of those being trained had any direct experience in the real world of manufacturing, much less the particular kind of factory that would one day, presumably, be the source of their employment. The population served by vocational agriculture programs, by contrast, was not only familiar with their workplace, they were, in almost all cases, in daily contact with it. The relationship between school, work and even home was real and intimate. From the perspective of curriculum, this was potentially a factor of tremendous significance. It bore directly on the question, for example, of whether the curriculum should be seen as a preparation for future living as the social efficiency proponents demanded or tied to issues or problems of immediate interest and value to the learner.

The first known program growing out of the important relationship between home and school that was embedded in vocational agriculture was conceived by Rufus W. Stimson, a teacher at Smith's Agricultural School in Northampton, Massachusetts. In 1908–9, he implemented what he called a home-project plan in order to help "the boys in applying the teachings of the school in their home farm work" (Stimson, 1914, p. 16). Even in the context of vocational education, there was, in Stimson's view a danger of "too much reflection, not enough action" (p. 10). Not only could that problem be immediately resolved through the home-project, but improved farm procedures could be directly introduced. For example, since it was, in all likelihood, "part of the boy's business to assist in feeding the cows," that boy could be assigned to weighing one cow's rations and calculating the cost to feed her. Samples of the cow's milk could be brought to school for bacteriological tests. The effect of introducing a larger component of clover into the cow's feed could be observed (p. 14). In some cases, students actually earned money in connection with their home-projects. By 1911, Stimson's plan had become so successful that the Massachusetts legislature provided additional state aid in order to spread the idea, and two years later, United States Commissioner of Education, P. P. Claxton, asked Stimson to prepare a government publication describing the virtues of agricultural home-projects. In short order, the Massachusetts home-project plan, as he called it in the Bureau of Education Bulletin he wrote, was attracting national attention as a way of organizing the curriculum in vocational agriculture.

An educational innovation of such promise did not escape the attention of Charles Prosser, who, in his new position as Director of the Executive Staff for the Federal Board of Vocational Education, asked F. E. Heald, a specialist in agricultural education assigned to the United States Department of Agriculture, to prepare a special comprehensive bulletin on the subject. In 1917, Heald had published an article reporting that the project had already "gained a recognized standing in educational and scientific circles" (p. 166). In describing the project, he emphasized the importance of pupil interest "at the outset" and "in which there is some problem more or less new" (p. 167), thus identifying two of the most important characteristics that were to appeal to certain reformers in the educational world in later years.

The report that Heald wrote a year later at Prosser's request, "The Home Project as a Phase of Vocational Agricultural Education" (1918), was far more extensive. It included an historical account of the development of the idea as well as some of the controversies that had developed over the definition of a project. There were also practical suggestions involving how records should be kept and a strong suggestion that a contract be signed by teacher, pupil and parent setting forth the terms of the project and the level of achievement to be reached. There were also illustrations of projects that could successfully coordinate the work done in school with the farm at home. Although he recognized that financial gain was sometimes a factor in home-projects, Heald thought it was "not always the controlling one" (p. 11), arguing that the "main factor" ought to be "the personal interest of the pupil" and even that "the immediacy of motive has a considerable bearing on the final success" (p. 10).

That emphasis contrasted with the position taken by Prosser in the foreword to the bulletin. Prosser reminded the reader that the purpose of the Smith–Hughes legislation was "to fit for useful agricultural employment" (Heald, 1918, p. 5). As would be expected, he urged that "final economic profit should be a definite aim of all such project work, as it is the aim of the farming business as a whole," adding that "economic development should be emphasized as a final goal" (p. 6). Within a decade of its introduction, the home-project was beginning to be seen in sharply contrasting terms depending, of course, on the ideological stance of the observer. From a social efficiency perspective, the project was being seen as a useful vehicle for introducing into the curriculum those habits and skills that would prepare students for their occupational roles in society. From a pedagogical or, more specifically, a developmentalist point of view, the introduction of the project held out the much grander prospect of reconstructing the curriculum around the real and immediate interests of the students.

ii

Paradoxically, it was one of the major leaders of the social efficiency movement, David Snedden, who, almost casually, may have been the first to make note of the fact that the project could be seen not simply as an addendum to the course of study but as a new unit with potential for replacing the subject as the basic building block of the curriculum. The subject matter that comprises the curriculum, he said, is subdivided into convenient packages we call subjects, and "the primary purpose of making all these divisions and subdivisions is, of course, some form of efficiency – efficiency of organization, of accessibility, of mastery" (Snedden, 1916, p. 419). Just as "cantaloups" are packed in crates, wheat in sacks, and sermons packaged within a certain time frame – all because particular conditions needed to be satisfied – so is what we teach packaged for various purposes. The large packages we call subjects are subdivided into lesser units, lectures, exercises and the smallest of the packages, the question and answer (pp. 419–20). Within the past few years, he noted, a new package, the project, had emerged in the field of vocational agriculture. Snedden acknowledged that a "logical sequence of a series of projects might be hard to find," but he nevertheless noted that since 1912 "the project as a pedagogic unit of organization in practical arts and in vocational education had found a place, if not always a welcome" (p. 422). Perhaps, with the introduction of what he called "modifiers" to describe different types of projects, it would emerge as a useful unit of curriculum organization transcending its original locus, vocational agriculture.

Within a month after Snedden published these observations, a new journal, *General Science Quarterly*, was launched with almost the express purpose of reorganizing the teaching of science around projects. The editors chose as the lead article for the first issue the transcript of an address that John Dewey had given to the National Education Association three months earlier. Dewey (1916b) proceeded from the assumption that "the end of science teaching is to make us aware of what constitutes the most effective use of mind, of intelligence" (p. 3). Since the achievement of such an aim must begin in the elementary school, the curriculum of nature study at that level should be reoriented with a view "to arouse interest in the discovery of causes, dynamic processes, operating forces" rather than its present emphasis – a static, miscellaneous accumulation of "a certain store of information" (p. 4). Dewey urged even those who have a sophisticated understanding of science to forget "the conventional divisions of the sciences" and try to see science from "the standpoint of pupil's experience of natural forces together with their ordinary useful applications" (p. 5). He deplored the teaching of science in "definitely segregated areas, concepts and terms which are found in books under the heads of physics, chemistry, etc." and urged instead that the teacher remember "that there is no material in existence which is physical or chemical or botanical, but that a certain ordinary subject-matter *becomes* physical or chemical or botanical when certain questions are raised, and when it is subjected to certain modes of inquiry" (p. 7). While Dewey's view of the teaching of science was consistent with certain principles associated with the project method, it was not an endorsement of the project as a substitute for a subject. For Dewey, an appropriate organization of the curriculum in science would not be built around "specialized technicalities of a highly matured science" (p. 5), but it would still be science. Beginning with concrete experience, the child's curiosity about the natural world and daily occupations was simply a surer path to sophisticated and intellectually respectable scientific knowledge because Dewey felt that even many promising future scientists, to say nothing of ordinary students, were "repelled by a premature diet of abstract scientific propositions" (p. 8).

In its first years of existence, *General Science Quarterly* remained dedicated to the promotion of the project as the way to reform the teaching of science. A persistent theme was the one that Dewey had sounded – science, as ordinarily taught in schools, was being presented to the child in a manner inappropriate to the child's level of development and understanding. Just as the home-project in vocational agriculture succeeded because it grew out of issues of immediate importance to farming, so projects in science could grow out of the natural interest of students in the world around them. One principal of a high school in Bridgeport, Connecticut, for example, attributed the failure of science in the public schools to the fact that "the subject matter and the method are not vitally connected with the needs and interests of individual students" (Moore, 1916, p. 15). Science projects should arise, he felt, out of spontaneous questions that students raise such as "Why does a crust form inside a teakettle?" or "Why do boilers explode?" (p. 15). The central thrust of this article as well as the numerous articles and editorials in subsequent volumes of *General Science Quarterly* was not the substitution of practical skills for science in the curriculum. In fact, in his keynote article, Dewey had urged that science be studied for the full four years of high school. The central point of the campaign was that, through a project organization, science could be made not only more interesting and vital to the student but a more intellectually stimulating subject in the curriculum of elementary and secondary schools.

iii

Without doubt, the single most dramatic event in the evolution of the movement to reform the curriculum through projects was the appearance in the September 1918 issue of *Teachers College Record* of an article with the unpretentious title, "The Project Method" (1918b). Written by a faculty member at Teachers College, William Heard Kilpatrick, the article caused such an immediate sensation that the Teachers College Bureau of Publications was obliged to distribute an astounding 60,000 reprints. Exactly why that particular article aroused such an explosion of interest was not exactly clear at the outset. The extension of the project idea beyond the field of vocational agriculture had, after all, been going on for several years, and educators of the prominence of David Snedden had previously published articles on the subject. Kilpatrick, already in his late forties and having some difficulty in getting promoted to full professor, was probably himself unprepared for such a reception.

Part of the answer, to be sure, lay in Kilpatrick's unusually felicitous style, an inspiring way with words that ultimately helped him become the most popular professor in Teachers College history. But beyond the easy cadence of his writing, Kilpatrick was able to rekindle the diminishing hope that the developmentalists had once ignited – that somewhere in the child lay the key to a revitalized curriculum. G. Stanley Hall, who once epitomized that position and whose leadership of the child-study movement had been so stirring and seemingly full of promise, had met with some sharp reversals as the new century began (Ross, 1972, pp. 341–67). Hall's pseudo-scientific approach to the study of the child had been more or less exposed, and his mystical belief in race recapitulation as a basis for an orderly curriculum built on natural law had fallen out of favor. William James's 1899 series of lectures on the relationship between psychology and school practice seemed at times almost a direct attack on the claims that Hall had once boldly set forth for the redirection of the curriculum through the psychological study of the child. In what appears to be a direct reference to Hall, James felt that there was "a certain fatality of mystification laid upon the teachers of our day" (James, 1899, p. 6), even going so far as to say that in his "humble opinion there *is* no 'new psychology' worthy of the name" (p. 7). Emphasizing that teaching is an art and not a science, James was wary of Hall's optimism about turning psychological laws into pedagogical recipes:

> I say moreover that you make a great, a very great mistake, if
> you think that psychology, being the science of the mind's laws,
> is something from which you can deduce definite programmes
> and schemes and methods of instruction for immediate
> schoolroom use. (p. 7)

With someone of the immense stature of James joining other major critics in the psychological world, such as Hugo Munsterberg (1899), Hall's prominence among psychologists and child-centered educators rapidly diminished. E. L. Thorndike, who emerged in the twentieth century as America's leading psychologist of education was openly critical of the assumptions that guided Hall and the child-study movement. "What development *is* can never teach us what it *ought to be*," Thorndike declared. "No word perhaps is a poorer synonym for 'the good' than 'the natural' " (Thorndike, 1901, p. 136). A once promising cause needed a new leader and

some new ideas, and "The Project Method" quickly cata-
pulted Kilpatrick, a philosopher rather than a psychologist,
into that role.

Kilpatrick's first contribution to the growing body of literature in the area of the project method appeared, naturally
enough, in *General Science Quarterly*. Actually, it was not an
article per se but a compilation of notes taken by various
people who had heard him speak on the subject. While
lacking a certain coherence, "Project Teaching" (1917)
sounded certain themes that were to stir the imagination of
one group of educational reformers for several decades. First,
there was the contrast between the logical and the psychological organization of the curriculum. In some sense, this was a
rough extrapolation of Dewey's position expressed a year
earlier in the same journal where he claimed that adult
(logical) versions of science were being inappropriately imposed on children's (psychological) understanding of natural
phenomena. As Kilpatrick put it, "we too generally take the
child at the beginning stage of experience and try to give him
the most complete adult formulation" (p. 68), a theme that
Dewey had been sounding for at least twenty years (Dewey
1897c). Kilpatrick, an avowed disciple of Dewey's, also incorporated into the project method a definition of thinking
that Dewey had set forth in his *How We Think* (1910).
Thinking was basically problem-solving. "The primary purpose of thinking," Kilpatrick (1917) said, "is to get out of a
difficulty," although he also recognized that a "secondary
purpose" of thinking could simply be to satisfy curiosity (p.
69).

When the Committee on Economy of Time reported at the
Atlantic City meeting of the National Education Association
on February 28, 1918, there appeared, smuggled in among
reports on progress in defining minimum essentials for a large
number of elementary school subjects, a brief report by
Kilpatrick from what he described as "a subordinate committee to study the problem of so modifying school practices as to
utilize the child and the child's resources more effectively
than has been done in our customary practice" (Kilpatrick,

1918a, p. 528). As its name implies, the Committee on Economy of Time had been almost exclusively efficiency-oriented, emphasizing, according to one of its principal figures, two major concerns: "the thoroughgoing acceptance of the point of view of social utility in curriculum making" and "the substitution of scientific method for mere opinion in the actual selection of the content of the course of study" (Horn, 1918, p. 526). Those two "concerns" could easily serve as a most apt and concise explication of the implications of the social efficiency movement for the curriculum. Minimum essentials were simply the educational counterpart to production standards or quotas where fixed amounts of learning, presumably determined by scientific means such as questionnaires and frequency studies of errors made by children, were presented as the factual and skill requirements in various subjects. Except, perhaps, for an oblique reference to "laws of learning," Kilpatrick's "subordinate" committee report made no allusion to those central concerns. Instead, Kilpatrick expounded on the theme of using children's purposes as the basis for organizing the curriculum, indeed proposing the child's own "purposeful act" as the "typical unit" not only of school life but of the "worthy life" in general (p. 528).

When "The Project Method" (1918b) appeared a few months later, any nominal association with the Committee on Economy of Time was no longer in evidence, and, if anything, what Kilpatrick was proposing was a clear alternative to the reforms being promoted by the social efficiency interest group. He seems to have struck in his proposal a deep wellspring of opposition to the scientific curriculum-makers whose hardline efficiency and scientifically determined standards represented newly dominant ideals in curriculum matters. Although Kilpatrick was usually careful to indicate that the project method of curriculum organization was consistent with what he continued to call the "laws of learning," his primary emphasis was that "education be considered as life itself and not as a mere preparation for later living" (p. 323), a position fundamentally opposed to what scientific curriculum-makers like Bobbitt and Charters were espousing. Instead of a curriculum broken into its most minute units and then reassembled into the most efficient arrangement possible, Kilpatrick boldly proposed "the conception of wholehearted purposeful activity proceeding in a social environment," or, in short, "the hearty purposeful act" as the basis around which a curriculum could be built (p. 320). Moreover, since what Kilpatirck called "the worthy life" also consisted of purposeful acts, the life of the school could be made consistent with worthy living. Worthy living, however, was not something you got ready for; it was something you did now. "We of America," Kilpatrick affirmed, "have for years increasingly desired that education be considered as life itself and not as a mere preparation for later living" (p. 323). Kilpatrick was thus taking advantage of the immediacy that the home-project had presented as a way of tying education to life and proposing it as the model for all of the curriculum. What he was at least implicitly rejecting was the idea that facts and skills ought to be presented to children and youth in schools in the hope that they would be of practical value in the years ahead.

Kilpatrick (1918b) managed to obfuscate some of the issues by referring to different "types" of projects including type 4, "where the purpose is to obtain some item or degree of skill or knowledge, as learning to write grade 14 on the Thorndike Scale, learning the irregular verbs in French" (p. 333), a type of project that would make project organization indistinguishable from anything else. The type 1 project, "where the purpose is to embody some idea or plan in external form," (p. 332) however, was clearly where his sympathies lay. It was for that type of project that he proposed four steps as a kind of problem-solving procedure: "purposing, planning, executing, and judging" (p. 333). As to type 4, he simply asserted that "planning had perhaps best come from the psychologist" (p. 334), admitting, along the way, that it was to the "purposeful act with the emphasis on the word purpose that I myself apply the term 'project' " (p. 320).

Kilpatrick's timing was evidently propitious. Within a short time, the project method became the major alternative to scientific curriculum-making for those reformers who saw the school's traditional curriculum as sadly irrelevant to modern times. Kilpatrick's accomplishment was to take a successful curriculum reform in a restricted area, vocational agriculture, and to recast it so as to make it plausible as a way of reconstructing the entire curriculum. Moreover, his position at Teachers College, which had by the second decade of the twentieth century become the national center of the study of education, put Kilpatrick in a position to spread his ideas to a wide audience. In that galaxy of star faculty that Dean James Earl Russell had assembled, Kilpatrick was the brightest in terms of overall popularity. By the time his career ended, it was estimated that he had taught approximately 35,000 students, many of whom went on to positions of prominence and influence in the educational world. So rapid was the rise in popularity of the project method that, by 1922, Charters felt compelled to issue a few words of caution. Referring to the fact that the "history of American education is a chronicle of fads" (p. 245), he warned of the project's many limitations. In particular, he felt that the project method simply did not teach future citizens what they needed to know. Without recommending the abolition of projects altogether, Charters urged that projects at least "be accompanied by a systematic study of subjects, by drills, and by exercises" (p. 246).

Despite these criticisms, the project method continued to attract unprecedented loyalty in the educational world. When the National Conference on Educational Method was held in Atlantic City on March 1, 1921 with the express purpose of reforming education along project method lines, the high school auditorium, seating 600, was not only filled to capacity, but many educators had to be turned away and this despite the fact that the star attraction, Kilpatrick, could not be present because of illness ("As reported," 1921, p. 37). The rapid growth of the project idea after 1918 was further stimulated by the founding of a journal with what amounted to an avowed intention of spreading and developing the idea. Three years after the appearance of "The Project Method," a devoted disciple of Kilpatrick's, James Fleming Hosic, founded the *Journal of Educational Method*, with the purpose of presenting the project "as a serious and consistent point of view, likely to have far-reaching effects in bringing about a reorganization of the curriculum" (Hosic, 1921a, p. 2). Indicating that no apology was necessary for devoting all that attention to the project method, he pointed out that there were already misconceptions developing as to the real meaning of projects, including one version that considered projects to be simply a new subject of study (p. 2). Hosic directed the new journal primarily to an audience of practicing school supervisors, hoping thereby to bring the use of the project as a new unit in the curriculum from its newly prominent place in the debates among leaders of various reform groups to the classrooms of elementary and secondary schools across the country. One month after launching the journal, Hosic was able to report that every elementary school principal in one large city and the entire faculty "of one of the two best-known state normal schools in the United States" had subscribed to it (Hosic, 1921b, p. 11).

In the second year of its existence, *The Journal of Educational Method* became the vehicle for an ambitious effort by Kilpatrick to explore the project method in its various ramifications. Central to Kilpatrick's endeavor was a redefinition of subject matter. Rather than minimum essentials or something set out to be learned, he saw subject matter as a rich reconstruction of the child's experience, one that "results in uplifting insight, inclination, and power" (Kilpatrick, 1922, p. 96). Arguing that the traditional conceptions of subject matter were merely being "reenforced by current conceptions of efficiency" (p. 231), Kilpatrick (1923) tried to make the case for subject matter as functioning "when some activity of the person is held up, hindered, or thwarted, and some new way of behaving is needed in order to get the balked activity going again satisfactorily" (p. 368), thus putting forward a kind of homeostatic view of thinking in which subject matter serves to restore balance in the organism once its purposes are thwarted. Kilpatrick was in this way seeking to reintegrate subject matter (knowledge) into the sphere of human action.

Subject matter, under these circumstances, was not simply there to be learned but was to function directly in accomplishing human purposes. It was in that context that Kilpatrick thought it should appear in the school curriculum.

iv

Almost from the time that William Torrey Harris focused national attention to the curriculum, debate had turned largely on the question of curriculum content. The opposition between the traditional humanists and the social efficiency educators had been framed in terms of what knowledge was most appropriate for the curriculum, with the social efficiency position being that the traditional curriculum consisted largely of dead wood, which had to be summarily lopped off. What they were proposing was the substitution of content that had a much more utilitarian and less academic character. Kilpatrick and his followers were dramatically changing the terms of that debate. They were not merely saying that one kind of content was somehow better than another; they were, in effect, arguing that selection of content was a matter of secondary importance at best. Knowledge was not simply there to be mastered; it was an instrument for accomplishing human purposes. As such, the child's own purposes should provide the basis for the development of the curriculum with subject matter employed instrumentally as it bore on the accomplishment of those purposes. Attacking what he liked to call the "cold storage" view of knowledge, in which facts and skills were stored up for future use, Kilpatrick proposed instead a currriculum which deemphasized the acquisition of knowledge in favor of a curriculum which was synonymous with purposeful activity. As Kilpatrick redefined it, the project was now not simply a way of reorganizing the teaching of, say, science; it became, contrary to Dewey's position, a substitute for science.

Kilpatrick (1924) began one of his major statements on this subject, an address before the Department of Superintendence, with the declaration that "The curriculum question is not so simple as to some it seems" (p. 3). Acknowledging that subject matter and curriculum are "intimately related," he went on to reverse what had been seen as the common relationship between subject matter and life. The curriculum was usually arranged in terms of appropriate subject matter with the expectation that it would have some beneficial effect in later life. Kilpatrick proposed that curriculum planning start with life (or at least what was increasingly being called the problems of living) with subject matter brought in only incidentally as it bears on those problems. "Subject matter," he boldly declared, "is primarily means, not primarily end" (p. 3). Kilpatrick was, in effect, reconstructing what we mean by a curriculum, and an interesting side effect of that redefinition was that the project *method* had become a curriculum. "Read," Kilpatrick urged in his customarily impassioned tone, "Ellsworth Collings, *An Experiment with a Project Curriculum.* . . Read and see. It has worked. It can work" (p. 9).

Collings's book (1923), described in Kilpatrick's introduction as a "pioneer work" (Collings, p. xvii)), was a glowing account of how three rural schools in Missouri had successfully implemented the project curriculum. Actually that book was only one of the incredible spate of books written in the 1920s on the subject. These included not only Kilpatrick's own most influential book, *Foundations of Method* (1925), but those of his growing number of disciples and like-minded contemporaries such as James L. Stockton's *Project Work in Education* (1920), Junius L. Meriam's *Child Life and the Curriculum* (1920), Margaret Wells's *A Project Curriculum* (1921), John A. Stevenson's *The Project Method of Teaching* (1921), E. A. Hotchkiss's *The Project Method in Classroom Work* (1924), James F. Hosic and Sara E. Chase's *Brief Guide to the Project Method* (1926) and Mary H. Lewis's *An Adventure with Children* (1928). With such discipleship, it was inevitable that the impact of the project curriculum should be felt in school practice, albeit not always in its purest form.

Initially, the project organization of the curriculum, as

would be expected, attracted the greatest enthusiasm from private and university-associated schools. The Lincoln School of Teachers College, for example, compiled a volume designed to report on the fruits of their experimentation with the project organization of the curriculum (Columbia University, 1927). Their units, usually referred to as "centers of interest," however, involved rather prolonged activities organized around a central theme presumably reflecting the children's interests. In "A Study of City Life" in the second grade, children began with a study of the city's transportation, one boy making a model of Grand Central Station while others made trains, trucks, buses, taxis and boats (p. 89). Next they constructed buildings – a wholesale market, a bakery, a post office, a fire station, a bank and so on (pp. 89–90). Rooms were rented in the buildings and "protests and arguments were numerous between landlords or landladies and tenants over the high costs of rooms or apartments, whether or not the rent should be paid in advance, or whether rental charges should or should not cover the price of electricity and various other details" (pp. 90–91). Eventually the project led to a six-week study of foods where various foodstuffs were prepared and sold at market prices. "These large units of work," it was reported, "become the core of the elementary-school curriculum" (p. 29). Kilpatrick (1928) himself had some reservations about such large units of work, suggesting that the smaller units employed by Collings were preferable, but he deemed them "far superior to the traditional assignment-in-order-to-cover-specified-subject-matter" (p. 87).

By the 1930s, the movement had grown to such proportions that it outgrew its original identification with the project *per se* and came to be more grandly advertised as the activity curriculum or the experience curriculum. Like its immediate ancestor, the home-project, the experience curriculum was built on the importance of child and adolescent interests, their sense of purpose, as a guide to what to study, and on activity, usually overt, replacing what was conventionally seen as the appalling passivity that characterized most school programs. According to its proponents who assembled the Thirty-Third Yearbook of the National Society for the Study of Education (Part II), entitled, *The Activity Movement* (Whipple, 1934), the greatest progress had been made in elementary schools. The principal of two elementary schools in Montclair, New Jersey, for example, reported having "changed rather abruptly . . . to an activity-experience type of teaching" (Hartman, 1934, p. 110). In a third-grade class, the activity was a post office unit, which involved the children writing to the postmaster requesting permission to visit the local post office. In a fourth-grade class, children building a feudal castle found "a need to deal with fractions" (p. 111), exhibiting great interest in that most tedious of arithmetic operations. Thus, in the context of the students' purposive activity were such conventional skills as writing and arithmetic incorporated successfully into an activity organization of the curriculum.

The superintendent of schools in Houston, Texas, reported on a major study designed to test the activity curriculum against a matched control group in the fourth and fifth grades. Responding to the frequent criticism that the activity curriculum would leave young pupils without the basic skills usually taught in elementary schools, he reported that the average gain as measured by the new Stanford Achievement Tests for two experimental groups was 13.3 months while the control group's average gain was 12.3 months. Teachers in the activity program devoted significantly less time to drill and devoted more to "creative self expression" (Oberholtzer, 1934, p. 138). Pupils in the two experimental groups, he reported, read an average of 27.9 and 31.9 books per year while the control group average was only 21.6 (p. 140). Even the quality of teaching was improved in the groups using the activity curriculum, with teachers reporting more enthusiasm in their teaching and planning their work more carefully (p. 141).

One reason for the relative success of the activity or experience curriculum in the elementary school *vis-à-vis* the high school was undoubtedly the elementary school's greater organizational flexibility. High schools, with virtually immutable class periods and with teachers trained specifically in subject areas, were much more difficult to penetrate. The most successful attempt to bring the experience curriculum to the high school was launched at the annual meeting of the National Council of Teachers of English by John DeBoer in 1935. Sounding a theme long cherished by curriculum reformers, DeBoer called for the high school curriculum consisting not of isolated compartments, but an integrated curriculum organized around four major divisions: English, science, social studies and the arts. He challenged teachers of English to make their subject the center of the curriculum and to take the lead in building a curriculum that would "provide the learner with an opportunity to discover significant relations between the facts that come within his experience" (DeBoer, 1936, p. 249). Essentially, DeBoer was proposing that the project organization of the curriculum be integrated into the conventional subject divisions that comprise the high school curriculum. The familiar subject labels would be retained, but the curriculum would be built around the life activities of the learners rather than around traditional subject matter.

At the same time that DeBoer was issuing his challenge, the National Council of Teachers of English already had in preparation a volume entitled, *An Experience Curriculum in English* (Hatfield, 1935), which substantially embodied the reforms that he was advocating. The proposed curriculum, in preparation since 1929, sounded its theme in the opening sentence, "Experience is the best of all schools" (p. 3). The curriculum itself was divided into "experience strands" (p. 6). In Literature Experiences, Grades 7–12, for example, the experience strands were listed in the following sequence: Enjoying Action, Exploring the Physical World, Exploring the Social World, Studying Human Nature, Sharing Lyric Emotion, Giving Fancy Rein, Solving Puzzles, Listening to Radio Broadcasts, and Enjoying Photoplays (p. xvii). The program for the seventh to twelfth grades in Speech Experiences under "Communication" included Social Conversation, Telephone Conversation, Interviews and Conferences,

Discussion, Questions and Answers, Organizations, and Special Occasion Speeches (p. xix). The effort to tie the teaching of English in high schools to the life experiences of adolescents met with what amounted almost to adulation from a wide spectrum of curriculum reformers. Within a year of *An Experience Curriculum in English* being published, the National Education Association's Department of Supervisors and Directors of Instruction devoted its Ninth Yearbook to *The Development of the Modern Program in English* (1936), a volume which largely supported and extended the principles enunciated in *An Experience Curriculum*. For several years thereafter, *The English Journal* continued to publish accounts by high school teachers of successful implementation of the recommendations that Hatfield's report had set forth.

Reaction on the part of leaders in the curriculum field was basically positive, but a bit mixed. L. Thomas Hopkins (1937), a professor of curriculum at Teachers College, and one of the new second generation of curriculum leaders, seemed a bit disappointed that the *Correlated Curriculum* report had not gone far enough. He complained about the fact that the terms "correlation," "fusion," and "integration" were used interchangeably in the volume even though they represented, in his view, differentiated psychological and philosophical concepts. Although he applauded the emphasis on unity and wholeness that pervaded the volume, he felt that the unity may not become evident to the learners unless they were part of the process of curriculum development themselves. "A closer synergism among the parts can occur," he said, "only when the wholeness or the unity appears first, and the parts differentiated therefrom" (p. 418). Hopkins was always suspicious of curricula developed without the active participation of the learners themselves.

Bobbitt's reservations were, of course, of a quite different order. He derived some comfort in the fact that "a significant phase of the study was the attempt to secure authoritative statements of the objectives of education from outstanding specialists in the fields of the several physical, biological, social, and philosophical sciences, and the fine arts" (Bob-bitt, 1937, p. 419). Bobbitt was never one to undervalue the importance of stating precise objectives in advance of the curriculum planning process. He was forced to conclude, in fact, that the committee "has not yet formulated its objectives with sufficient exactness" (p. 420). Beyond even that, the committee had simply not gone far enough in ridding itself of the remnants of the old academic curriculum. They exhibited, in his view, "a departmental bias that has grown up as the essence of the specialization in English" (p. 420). For Bobbitt, nothing but strictly functional categories in curriculum development would do. Correlation among subjects or between academic subjects and life experiences was simply too tame. "We believe," he concluded, "that the department of English must take care of matters much more fundamental than correlation before it can be ready to prepare anything more than a merely descriptive account of relatively unevaluated practices, such as the present yearbook" (p. 420). For reformers leaning toward the developmentalist as well as the social efficiency orientations, the position taken by the National Council of Teachers of English was a step in the right direction, but one that was simply too timid.

v

In spite of such reservations in terms of implementation, within a few years, the home-project, a promising approach to the teaching of vocational agriculture, had evolved into a messianic curriculum movement replete not only with a high priest but with a successful journal to promote its ideas, an army of followers, a particularly devoted set of energetic disciples, and even some satellite movements. Its influence was felt first and most directly in nonpublic elementary schools of an experimental bent, but extended later to public elementary and even secondary schools. The project curriculum (or, as it came to be called in the 1930s, the activity or experience curriculum), however, was not by any means supreme in the educational world. The developmentalist interest group, once a specific child-study movement rooted in genetic psychology but now a more broadly based group of child-centered educators with Kilpatrick at the helm, existed, after all, alongside other powerful interest groups with at least different and often contradictory conceptions of how a curriculum should be wrought. William C. Bagley, for example, Kilpatrick's colleague at Teachers College, was anything but enthusiastic about the idea. Bagley as early as 1921 insisted that many of the assumptions inherent in the project curriculum had "not as yet been established by thoroughgoing experimentation" (p. 289). He was skeptical, for example, of the claim that information mastered in very specific contexts would be successfully retained, indicating that the "transfer potency" inherent in the project organization of the curriculum was probably not as great as the proponents claimed (p. 290). The predominance of the instrumental role of knowledge, so central to Kilpatrick's conception of subject matter, was also a matter of concern:

> The prime function of education on the elementary level, and to a large extent on the secondary level, is to place the child in possession of his spiritual heritage, – the heritage of skill, knowledge, standard, and ideal which represents the gains that the race has made. Only a small fraction of this heritage is instrumental in the narrow meaning of the term. (p. 292)

Bagley also reminded his readers that much of learning is "of a non-purposive sort" and that adult purposes, in contrast to child purposes, should not always be regarded as an evil (p. 296).

Bagley's remarks were presented at a symposium on the project method and so his criticism (given his position in these matters) was almost demanded by the circumstances. On the whole, however, open debate between proponents of widely different positions in curriculum matters was not as common as would be expected, and this has served to obfuscate the complexity of what passed for curriculum reform efforts in this period. Although there were some notable exceptions, each interest group, by and large, spoke to its own constituency so that the truly profound differences, say, between the social efficiency educators and the proponents of child-centered education tended to get blurred in the eyes of an unsophisticated public. With critical cross-exchanges between contending groups held to a minimum, even latter-day commentators continue to see these widely divergent curriculum reform movements as all of one piece.

Easily the most trenchant and most remarkable exception to the absence of criticism of the proposed new reforms in curriculum was Boyd H. Bode's *Modern Educational Theories* (1927). In fact, his book presents not just his own educational ideas but represents a kind of catalog of what went wrong with the two rival reform thrusts that reached their zenith in the early 1920s. Like Kilpatrick, Bode drew much of his inspiration from Dewey, but unlike Kilpatrick, he was not prone to flamboyance and oversimplification. His approach tended to be more cautious and reasoned if not more politically sophisticated in its persistent attention to the social implications of the various proposed reforms of the curriculum. Bode never lost sight of the relationship between education and the vision of renewed society, and for him, an improved social order was not synonymous with efficiency or even with the creation of law-abiding citizens. Quoting Emerson, Bode held that "good men must not obey the laws too well" (p. 12), and that, rather than teaching adjustment to existing social conditions, democracy must be seen as "a progressive humanization of the social order" (p. 14).

As someone who believed that "our national safety lies in the general intelligence of our citizens" (Bode, 1927, p. 15), a position strongly reminiscent of Lester Frank Ward's, Bode naturally reserved his sharpest criticism for the social efficiency educators who were always skeptical about the ability of the masses to govern themselves and whose social ideas were mainly directed toward achieving social stability. In his book, Bode devoted a whole chapter to the ideas of each of the three major leaders of the movement, Bobbitt, Charters and Snedden, in each case attacking one major thrust of social efficiency doctrine. Unlike Dewey, Bode revealed a close familiarity with the work of social efficiency educators and an acute consciousness of their potency in the educational world.

In his chapter devoted to Bobbitt, Bode (1927) expressed some sharp reservations about the claims of scientific curriculum-making that were the hallmark of Bobbitt's position. Speaking of "our unbalanced enthusiasm for scientific method" (p. 78), Bode pointed out that those "scientific" methods that Bobbitt so freely espoused ignored "the ideal of a progressively changing social order" (p. 79). Not only did Bode believe that deriving ideals from the collection of facts is a delusion (p. 81), but that using Bobbitt's scientific method for the determination of curricular objectives resulted in "personal bias or preference being smuggled in under the guise of an objective, impersonal determination of fact" (p. 85). "When this happens," Bode argued, "educational objectives become once more, as in the past, an excuse for the perpetuation of tradition and the status quo" (p. 85).

Bode's chapter on Charters focused primarily on the method of job or activity analysis that had been borrowed from Taylorism in industry. He attacked the bricklayer analogy so prevalent in educational circles of the time, arguing that it was a case of applying what may seem reasonable in one situation to another situation that is hardly comparable:

> Theoretically, at any rate, we can analyze a case of "keen judgment" so as to show just what was done and what sorts of facts and circumstances were taken into account, in very much the same way that we can analyze bricklaying. But the analogy does not carry over to the next step. The bricklaying is analyzed in order that the novice may learn to repeat what has been done. The analysis of the case of "keen judgment," on the other hand, is made not to facilitate a simple repetition, but to improve the quality of subsequent judgments that are made under different conditions. (Bode, 1927, pp. 103–4)

Unless our lives follow a fixed pattern in which schooling becomes the setting for the rehearsal of specific responses to anticipated situations (which of course many social efficiency educators believed), the method of activity analysis as a means of discovering curricular objectives is useless or worse.

The chapter attacking Snedden's notion of the sociological determination of educational objectives elaborated on some of the criticism advanced in connection with Bobbitt and Charters. Again, the prevalence of activity analysis as the ultimate first step in curriculum development was treated with contempt. "There is no prospect of getting anywhere with this," Bode (1927) declared, "as long as we cling everlastingly to activity analysis 'like a sick kitten to a hot brick' " (p. 119). Instead of a technical formula by which curricula may be scientifically determined, Bode called for a process involving "historical perspective, for theory of mind, for insight into the educational significance of social institutions" (p. 119). In the end, he concluded that the unquenchable hope that Snedden held out for an objective determination of the curriculum through sociological analysis was nothing but a grand delusion (p. 139).

Nor was Kilpatrick's project method immune to Bode's keen critical eye. He was mindful of the numerous definitions of a project each with its own adherents and appeal. Kilpatrick's definition, "wholehearted purposeful activity," Bode (1927) found to be indistinguishable from simply interest (p. 142). While Bode was sympathetic to some of the criticism of the traditional curriculum that Kilpatrick and his followers had put forward, especially the dehumanizing of knowledge and the wide gap that had been created between school and life activities, he thought that learning that is limited to this method of project teaching is too discontinuous, too random and haphazard, too immediate in its function (p. 150). When the project method is simply "wholeheartedly purposeful activity in a social context," its defining characteristic is not to be found in "the organization of what is learned, but in the attitude of the learner toward his work" (p. 157). The emphasis Kilpatrick liked to place on the child constructing his or her own curriculum and on purposive activity without further direction ominously suggested to Bode "a mystic faith in a process of 'inner development' which requires nothing from the environment except to be let alone." He reminded his readers of Dewey's dictum that "There is no spontaneous germination in the mental life" (p. 163). If the child gets no direction from the teacher, he or she will simply get it from someone else. The whole thing smacked too much of Rousseau rather than a constructive approach to curriculum (p. 165). Bode, then, like Dewey, was profoundly skeptical of the fundamental developmentalist assumption that the key to the question of what to teach lay in the unfolding of natural forces within the child.

When Dewey delivered the Inglis Lecture at Harvard University in 1931, that skepticism was clearly evident although, of course, not as bluntly stated. His lecture, entitled "The Way Out of Educational Confusion," dealt with the two principal ways that had emerged for organizing a curriculum, by subject and by project. As would be expected from Dewey, he clearly endorsed neither. His criticism of the subject organization was similar to the position he presented in *General Science Quarterly* fifteen years earlier (1916b). Specifically he asked, "What is the value of the accepted and generally current classification of subjects?" (Dewey, 1931, p. 4). He pointed out that while old subject matter categories and labels tend to break down with the advance of scholarship, the old tags persist in the school curriculum. The appearance of new fields with hyphenated titles such as astro-physics and bio-chemistry, he said, is apt testimony "to the breaking down of dividing walls between subjects" (p. 15) and that this breaking down is indicative of the ways in which knowledge is interconnected and interdependent. The persistence of old subject matter labels and the absence of any attempt to integrate knowledge through the curriculum merely insures that students will get a fragmented and artificially isolated conception of what they are studying. The "subjects grow superficial," he said, and "their multiplication brings weariness to the spirit and the flesh" (p. 16). He summed up his objections to the traditionally conceived subject organization of the curriculum, not by rejecting it, but by pointing out that "in a situation where the skills or arts and the subject-matter of knowledge have become interwoven and inter-dependent," the persistence of a curriculum "on the basis of many isolated and independent subjects is bound to result in precisely the kind of confusion we have at present" (pp. 17–18). It was the traditional and outworn classifications and the absence of correlation among those classifications that Dewey objected to, not the subject organization itself, especially at the secondary and collegiate levels.

When Dewey (1931) turned to "the so-called 'project,' 'problem,' or 'situation' method," he warned his listeners immediately that he did not regard this as the only alternative to the present "confusion" in the curriculum (p. 30). While, like Bode, Dewey admitted that it "has certain characteristics which are significant for any plan for change" (pp. 30–1), he was anything but enthusiastic about the project as a mode of curriculum organization. For one thing, he felt that projects frequently involve too short a time span and are often casually arrived at. "In short," he said, "they are too trivial to be educative" (p. 31). The knowledge that is gained in that context, he thought, is commonly of "a merely technical sort, not a genuine carrying forward of theoretical knowledge" (p. 35). Just in case his point was lost on his listeners, Dewey stated flatly, "I do not urge it (the project method) as the sole way out of educational confusion, not even in the elementary school" (p. 36).

Instead, Dewey took the position that even when traditional titles of subjects are retained, it is possible to reorganize them so that the interdependence of knowledge and the relationship between knowledge and human purpose are made clear. Pointing to examples of such programs of study developed by Julian Huxley and H. G. Wells, he indicated that it was possible to cut across the traditional specialized divisions in science "yet not at the expense of scientific accuracy but in a way which increases both intellectual curiosity and understanding, while disclosing the world about us as a perennial source of esthetic delight" (Dewey, 1931, p. 37). As he had done fifteen years earlier, Dewey was endorsing science, not projects. What Dewey appeared to be advocating here most closely resembles what has come to be called the "broad fields" organization of the curriculum, a modification of the subject curriculum which attempts to address the problem of the isolation of school subjects from one another by linking together those subjects that have some affinity. In this way, the interrelationships within science as a whole would be fostered through the curriculum, not the insulated, specialized subdivisions.

Dewey (1931), perhaps naively, looked to schools of education to lead the way in instituting those practices but warned that any attempt to refine existing practices "under the protective shield of 'scientific method' " would be "more likely to increase confusion" (pp. 39–40). What he hoped for instead was that the schools of education could "undertake consecutive study of the interrelation of subjects with one another and with social bearing and application" (p. 40). Dewey's "way out of educational confusion" required too much by way of reconstruction of the traditional subjects to appeal to the humanists; it did not lack the romantic appeal of a curriculum nourished by children's natural predilections, but it stopped short of the dramatic rejection of subjects that the advocates of the activity curriculum proposed; and its emphasis on intellectual inquiry and social regeneration at all levels and by all segments of the population made it too vague and imprecise, if not too dangerous, to the scientific curriculum-makers and social efficiency educators. His intellectual stature, his international reputation and his many honors notwithstanding, Dewey did not have enough of a true following in the world of educational practice to make his impact felt.

CHAPTER 7

THE HEYDAY OF SOCIAL MELIORISM

i

On the eve of the 1928 presidential election, John Dewey, now sixty-nine years old and a regular contributor to the left-wing journal, *New Republic*, threw his support squarely behind the Democratic candidate, Governor Alfred E. Smith of New York, in what proved to be a futile attempt to stem the landslide for Herbert Hoover. Hoover, trained as an engineer and with the reputation as an efficient administrator, was in the minds of most Americans a symbol of the new breed of managers, a man above the hurly-burly of practical politics. While recognizing that Hoover's reputation for efficiency was well deserved, Dewey observed that "if he has any human insight, dictated by consciousness of social needs, into the policies called for by the day-to-day life of his fellow human beings, either in domestic or international affairs, I have never seen the signs of it" (Dewey, 1928b, p. 321). Lying just below the optimism, prosperity and gaiety that is our abiding image of the "roaring twenties," there seemed to be flowing a strong undercurrent of dissatisfaction ready to surface. Dewey, for example, argued that Hoover's "whole creed of complaisant capitalistic individualism and the right and duty of economic success commits him to the continuation of that hypocritical religion of 'prosperity' which is, in my judgment, the greatest force that exists at present in maintaining the unrealities of our social tone and temper" (p. 321). Dewey and a substantial number of intellectuals of the time were becoming increasingly vocal about what they perceived as a system riddled by social injustice. When that undercurrent of discord surfaced, it was to affect the course of curriculum reform in the first half of the twentieth century, but in the 1920s, the direction of that curriculum reform was still uncertain.

The general notion that the American curriculum needed a drastic overhaul reached its peak in 1926 when both volumes of the National Society for the Study of Education's *Twenty-Sixth Yearbook* were devoted to curriculum issues. Part I, called *Curriculum-Making: Past and Present*, attempted to catalog the principal trends that had emerged in the field of curriculum and contained a rather extensive review of specific experiments in curriculum in a large number of schools, almost all private or university-affiliated, across the country. Part II, *The Foundations of Curriculum-Making*, consisted mainly of statements on major curriculum issues by leaders in the field. Included, of course, were the twin stalwarts of scientific curriculum-making, Franklin Bobbitt and W. W. Charters, as well as those who had been arguing the case for the activity curriculum such as William Heard Kilpatrick and Frederick W. Bonser. Representing a different point of view from either the scientific curriculum-makers or the child-centered educators were George S. Counts of the University of Chicago and the man chosen to chair the committee that compiled the volumes, Harold O. Rugg of Teachers College, Columbia University. The inclusion of Counts and Rugg among the stars of the curriculum world invited to contribute to the two volumes marked the emergence of yet another force in the drive for curriculum reform, a force reflecting the social concern just beginning to gain momentum in the latter part of the 1920s.

The announced purpose of the *Twenty-Sixth Yearbook* was to reach a consensus as to what would comprise the new curriculum. For a quarter of a century or more, there had been a vigorous drive to replace what was commonly regarded as a curriculum unsuited for the new industrial age and for the new population of students entering both elementary and secondary schools in larger numbers. But the nature of the change was anything but clear, and the Yearbook Committee, beginning in 1924 under Rugg's direction, made a concerted effort to bring some kind of coherence to the welter of reform that continued to flow from several quarters. The "Composite Statement" that was finally hammered out was not so much a reconstruction or reformulation of the different strains of curriculum reform that had emerged since the 1890s as it was a glossing over of the profound differences as to the direction the curriculum should take. On the question, for example, of whether the curriculum should be directed toward efficient participation in adult life through activity analysis, as the scientific curriculum-makers maintained, or whether the curriculum should derive from the present needs and interests of children, as the experience curriculum advocates proposed, the committee boldly declared that education involves "participation in social life by providing a present life of experiences which increasingly identifies the child with the aims of activities derived from analysis of social life as a whole" (Whipple, 1926b, p. 14). With similar bravado, the Committee announced that "Curriculum-study should not only be carried on continuously; it should also be comprehensive" (p. 24) and that "The Committee believes that curriculum-makers should seek on every occasion to develop sympathetic, broad views of the world" (p. 24).

More interesting than the bland "Composite Statement" are the individual statements by curriculum leaders in the pages that follow. Most made a modest gesture of approval of the general statement, but then went on to present their own positions. Charters, for example, in the briefest of the supplementary statements, barely half a page, expressed his concern that the group might give its stamp of approval to "the position that the curriculum should be based entirely upon a study of the needs and interests of the learners" (Charters, 1926b, p, 71). Apparently satisfied that it did not, he pronounced the conference a success. Kilpatrick, alluding to the "extreme divergence" of opinion on the Committee, announced that "he may fairly claim the honor – or ignominy – of consistently deviating most from the present practice" (Kilpatrick, 1926, p. 119). In the most elaborate of the supplementary statements, actually more than twice the length of the "Composite Statement," he reiterated much of the position that he had heretofore enunciated.

By far the most startling of the statements was Bobbitt's. Inexplicably, he repudiated his earlier central position that education represents a preparation for adult living and declared instead that "Education is not primarily to prepare for life at some future time. Quite the reverse; it purposes to hold high the current living. . . . Life cannot be 'prepared for.' It can only be lived" (Bobbitt, 1926, p. 43). One can only conclude that Kilpatrick succeeded in completely mesmerizing him. The avowed intent of the yearbook, to reach a consensus among the broad spectrum of curriculum reformers that had emerged during the first quarter of the twentieth century, was completely unrealized. In fact, a careful reading of the statements by the foremost curriculum leaders of the time leads one to quite the opposite conclusion. Three seemingly irreconcilable reform thrusts were represented. One derived its impetus from the standards of adult living, as Bobbitt had long insisted, and sought to reorient the curriculum in the direction of preparing children and youth for a distinct adult role. A second took the immediate life of the child as the starting point, essentially discarded subject matter whether traditional or directly utilitarian, and conceived of the curriculum as the forum whereby the child could realize his or her own purposes. And with the emergence of Rugg and Counts on the curriculum scene, we begin to see the beginning of a third curriculum movement deriving its central thrust from the undercurrent of discontent about the American economic and social system. That last movement, establishing itself under the banner of social reconstructionism by the 1930s, saw the curriculum as the vehicle by which social injustice would be redressed and the evils of capitalism corrected.

Dissatisfaction with what Dewey called "the religion of

prosperity" in America had been gathering momentum among a small group of literati for some time and had expressed itself in the novels of Sinclair Lewis and the muckraking of Upton Sinclair. The Russian Revolution had attracted the admiration of a number of American intellectuals unhappy with the direction that capitalism was taking. Some of this dissent had even begun to express itself in the larger electorate with Eugene Victor Debs, the Socialist candidate running for president for the fifth time in 1920, receiving 919,000 votes. His vote total was all the more remarkable since he was at the time serving a ten-year sentence in prison, having been arrested under the Espionage Act in 1918 after delivering an anti-war speech. (President Warren G. Harding ordered him released on Christmas Day in 1921 and greeted him in the White House.)

Counts was one of the first among leaders in education to reflect that undercurrent of uneasiness about the American social structure and to direct that malaise to a critical examination of American schools. His earliest major work (1922) sounded the theme that American education, despite its claims, had been serving "the selected few, whether by birth or by talent" (p. 3). Essentially, he argued that, although the tax structure required schools to be supported by all, the American school system was serving a rather narrow and privileged segment of the population. Counts chose four cities, Seattle (Washington), St Louis (Missouri), Bridgeport (Connecticut) and Mt Vernon (New York) from which to secure his data. On the basis of his analysis of the social classes represented in the elementary and secondary schools of those cities, he concluded that secondary education differed from elementary education not simply by virtue of the age of their populations but in terms of the selectivity by social class that existed at the secondary level. "Misfortune, as well as fortune," Counts concluded, "passes from generation to generation" (p. 148). The rhetoric of democracy notwithstanding, access to secondary education, he found, was contingent on social and economic standing (p. 149).

Four years later, Counts (1926) published his *The Senior*

High School Curriculum, which investigated the secondary school curricula in fifteen American cities. In the 1923–4 school year when the data were being collected, he found that "secondary education has been radically altered in the immediate past" and that in "rapid succession new curriculums are appearing, and old curriculums are disappearing" (p. 144). While the pace of change represented some source of satisfaction to Counts, he was disappointed to find that "nowhere has a program been developed in the light of the needs of American civilization" (p. 146). Interestingly, he found that traditional subjects were now being defended in terms of "the great human interests of health, family life, industry, citizenship, and recreation, but the materials of instruction which they are thus defending were not introduced into the program for these purposes" (p. 146), a reflection perhaps of the recommendation of the Cardinal Principles Committee (National Education Association, 1918) that the old subjects reorient themselves in terms of the seven aims they enunciated. In the following year, Counts (1927) returned to the theme of the counter-democratic tendencies in American schools, this time by analyzing the social composition of boards of education. From the 1,654 school boards in the sample, Counts was able to draw a picture of the typical school board in rural, city, and statewide boards. Although there were differences, with three farmers serving on the typical six-member country board as opposed to business and professional men serving on city boards, Counts concluded that school board members were "drawn from the more favored economic and social classes" (p. 82) and that composition therefore reflected a bias in the control of American educational policy. "Only as the conditioning agencies and forces are won to the support of a liberal and creative type of education," he concluded, "will the school ever be able to make positive contributions toward the regeneration of the individual or the reconstruction of society" (p. 82). Counts's work in the 1920s called attention to what he saw as an American school system oriented not to a new and better social order, but to preserving and stratifying existing social conditions. And it was with a curriculum directed toward social reconstruction that Counts became identified with once the Great Depression struck.

ii

Whatever may have been the uneasiness expressed during the 1920s about American life in such novels as *Babbitt* and *Main Street* or in earlier exposés like *The Jungle* or even in the evidence being brought forward by dissenting educators like Counts over the course of American education, the business of America, in the words of Hoover's predecessor President Calvin Coolidge, remained business. Although unemployment began to rise markedly in 1926 and certain industries, such as coal mining and textiles as well as farming, seemed to be in trouble, Americans in general remained as optimistic as ever about America's future. Both public and private debt was growing rapidly as stock market investors continued their buying spree, often buying stocks and bonds with as little as 25 percent in cash. "Black Thursday," the twenty-fourth of October 1929, hit like a thunderbolt, with stocks continuing to drop dramatically. By the following Tuesday, stocks were being sold so fast that the ticker ran two and a half hours behind. By the end of October, some fifteen billion dollars in paper profits on the stock market had disappeared, and by the end of 1929 the loss had reached about forty billion. Within three years, about ninety billion dollars, three-fourths of the total worth of securities on the stock exchange, was wiped out. The vista of endless prosperity had suddenly vanished.

President Hoover, in response, tried to increase federal spending and urged state and local governments to do the same. He pleaded with business leaders not to cut their workers' wages, an appeal they heeded, by and large, until the United States Steel Corporation cut wages by 10 percent in October 1931, an action quickly followed by other leading manufacturers such as General Motors and United States

Rubber. Hoover appealed to bankers in 1931 to combine their resources in an effort to save banks that, in increasing numbers, were failing. His advice was ignored. In 1931, the effects of the depression struck Europe, and it was becoming clear that a worldwide crisis existed. By 1932, teachers' salaries had been cut dramatically all across the country, and Chicago teachers had gone unpaid for months. The president of the National Association of Manufacturers attributed the mass unemployment to the laziness of the workers, but leftist American leaders such as Charles A. Beard and Rexford Tugwell were calling for drastic action including a much larger measure of control over business and for more governmental planning.

The seed of social reconstructionism in education that Counts had planted in the mid and late 1920s flowered. By the early 1930s, his sentiments were being echoed by educational leaders throughout the country. Even some of those who had championed the child-centered movement, like Kilpatrick, were drawn wholeheartedly into the new orbit. Somehow the long unemployment lines and the soup kitchens dampened the spirit of optimism that had earlier prevailed, not only about the future of capitalism, but with respect to romantic ideas about the natural development of the child in the school setting. Both social efficiency, fitting the individual into the right niche in the existing social order, and developmentalism, with its emphasis on freedom and individuality for children and adolescents, gave ground to the feeling that the schools had to address ongoing social and economic problems by raising up a new generation critically attuned to the defects of the social system and prepared to do something about it.

In a book published in 1930 and dedicated to John Dewey, Counts deplored the social conformity, "the standardization of life" as he called it (p. 121), that had taken hold in modern industrial America. At the same time that the individual was being freed "from the coercive influence of the small family or community group" (p. 123), industrial civilization was imposing a new conformity. "The way in which the principle of social conformity finds expression in American Education," he claimed, "is perhaps best illustrated by the methods of curriculum-making which have come into vogue in recent years" (p. 124). In an obvious reference to the technique of activity analysis being promoted by such major leaders in the curriculum field as Bobbitt and Charters, Counts noted that this "interest in curriculum-making happened to be very intimately associated with the movement for the application of the scientific method to the study of education" (p. 124). Reflecting Bode's (1927) earlier criticism, he rejected the idea that a curriculum could be derived from an objective analysis of the activities that people engage in since "no amount of purely objective study of life activities will produce standards whereby the good may be distinguished from the bad, or the better from the worse" (p. 125). It was obvious to Counts that the critical point in so-called scientific curriculum-making was the selection of the judges who were to draw the inferences from the data, and these judges, almost invariably, would reflect dominant interests in American culture. The óbvious result would be the preservation of the status quo. As Counts put it, "The inevitable consequence is that the school will become an instrument for the perpetuation of the existing social order rather than a creative force in society" (p. 126).

Counts (1930) also attacked the supreme criterion of success to emerge from the social efficiency movement, efficiency itself. Referring to the dominant conception of efficiency, Counts called it "an efficiency without purpose, an efficiency of motion" (p. 137). He was not surprised that "this idolatry of efficiency should impress itself upon the schools" since the entire country had been influenced by the dominant "machine culture;" but "an efficiency of management," he declared, "should never be the ideal of education" (p. 138). He deplored the easy classification of students in the name of individualization and the division of the curriculum into "minute units of work" as his colleague Snedden so insistently demanded. He included in his criticism of American schools the widely heralded platoon system of Gary, Indiana, as merely a mechanical device to increase efficiency. Even "the accurate measurement of school products" in the name of efficiency was not spared (p. 146). While conceding some scientific value to the "orgy of testing that swept through the entire country," Counts argued that "the feverish and uncritical fashioning of tests in terms of the existing curriculum and in the name of efficiency has undoubtedly served to fasten upon the schools an archaic program of instruction and a false theory of the nature of learning" (pp. 147–8). As long as these approaches to curriculum development remained dominant, Counts maintained, only social drift would result. Counts's opposition to the social efficiency interest group and all that it stood for could not have been more evident. Clearly, much of what had passed for curriculum reform in the previous generation only served to perpetuate the very defects that he perceived in the American social fabric.

iii

Beginning in the 1930s, there appeared to be a resonance developing between leftist political and social leaders and certain educational reformers. Heretofore, with the exception of a handful of socially progressive leaders, such as Dewey and Bode, the dominant strains of educational reform had been tied specifically to hard efficiency and the maintenance of the existing social order on one hand and a sentimental belief in the natural unfolding of children's natural propensities on the other. The opposition between the social reconstructionists and the social efficiency educators was clear and well-defined. But a bitter opposition developed between those social meliorists and the developmentalists as well. The arena for that battle turned out to be the Progressive Education Association.

The Progressive Education Association was probably born in the mind of Marietta Johnson whose Organic School in Fairhope, Alabama, represented a model of a school based strictly on developmentalist principles. Founded by Johnson in a Henry George single-tax community in 1907, the school eliminated strict sorting of children by age as well as any kind of evaluation of their work that would produce competition among the children. Activities grew basically out of the spontaneous interests of the children themselves with strong emphasis on storytelling, singing and dancing in the early years. Like Hall, Johnson set great store by fairy tales and folklore and postponed the actual teaching of reading until about the age of eight or nine in line with what she believed to be the natural period for such training. Formal school subjects were postponed until the junior high school years. In the opening lines of her brief contribution to the National Society for the Study of Education's *Twenty-Sixth Yearbook* (Part I), she proclaimed her creed: "We believe the educational program should aim to meet the needs of the growing child. We believe that childhood is for itself and not a preparation for adult life" (Johnson, 1926, p. 349).

It was with ideas such as these that she approached Stanwood Cobb with a proposal to start a national organization to promote school experimentation. Cobb had founded an experimental school, the Chevy Chase Country Day School in Chevy Chase, Maryland. After Cobb finally agreed, the organization was founded in 1919 under the name, Association for the Advancement of Experimental Schools, which was changed shortly thereafter to the Association for the Advancement of Progressive Education and then to the Progressive Education Association. The first president was Arthur E. Morgan, himself a headmaster of an experimental school, the Morraine Park School of Dayton, Ohio, but who became president of Antioch College a year after the organization was founded. Actually, president emeritus of Harvard University and architect of the Committee of Ten report, Charles W. Eliot had been asked to be the first president, but at the age of eighty-five he declined, serving instead as honorary president (Graham, 1967, p. 23). With the exception of such an illustrious figure as Eliot, the organization was attractive mainly to a small coterie of teachers and administrators associated with private experimental schools and lay persons interested in school reform along developmental lines.

Whatever its modest beginnings, membership grew rapidly from the eighty-six members in 1919 to its peak of 7,400 in the 1930s. The person who took the lead in developing a platform for the new organization was Eugene Randolph Smith, the headmaster of the Beaver Country Day School of Chestnut Hill, Masschusetts. The Seven Principles of Progressive Education, representing the central creed of the organization, were adopted in 1920. Appearing on the inside cover of every issue of *Progressive Education* for about a five-year period in the 1920s, the prologue stated:

> The aim of Progressive Education is the freest and fullest development of the individual, based upon the scientific study of his physical, mental, spiritual, and social characteristics and needs.

The Seven Principles that followed provided a clear indication of the child-centered orientation that the organization was trying to promote: I. Freedom to Develop Naturally; II. Interest, the Motive of All Work; III. The Teacher a Guide, Not a Taskmaster; IV. Scientific Study of Pupil Development; V. Greater Attention to All that Affects the Child's Physical Development; VI. Co-operation Between School and Home to Meet the Needs of Child-life; VII. The Progressive School a Leader in Educational Movements. It was a platform that Hall could easily have written.

It was this extreme developmentalist position that became a fierce point of dispute once the Progressive Education Association achieved national recognition. Not coincidently, it was Dewey (1928a) who, in his speech upon accepting the position of honorary president (succeeding Eliot), raised some doubts about the direction the Association was taking. He began his address simply by asking the question, "What is Progressive Education?" and by attempting, "to raise the intellectual, the theoretical problem of the relation of the progressive movement to the art and philosophy of education"

(p. 197). Was a school progressive simply because it displayed "a certain atmosphere of informality" or because there was an emphasis on activity? (p. 198). While these characteristics obviously existed, Dewey took them to be merely superficial. The methods and the results obtained in progressive schools marked them off from the traditional ones. The "traditional schools," he said, "set great store by tests and measurements" (p. 199). The use of IQs and of test scores were merely ways of making the traditional schools more efficient. "At all events," Dewey said, "*quality* of activity and of consequence is more important . . . than any quantitative element" (p. 200). Dewey seemed to be deliberately rejecting the reforms introduced by the social efficiency educators with their emphasis on precise measurement as a way of reforming schools. In an obvious reference to determining curricular objectives through activity analysis, Dewey took the position that "the attempt to determine objectives and select subject-matter of studies by wide collection and accurate measurement of data" would only be appropriate "if we are satisfied upon the whole with the aims and processes of existing society" (p. 200). He urged his listeners not to become complacent about "what already exists" (p. 200). Dewey thus was recommending that the nine-year-old organization not associate itself with reforms that emphasize achievement standards, precise measurement, and the collection of data while ignoring the social impact of education.

He also took the occasion to try to disassociate the position of the organization from the emphasis on individuality and natural development that had been the basis for its founding. He suggested that this emphasis on removing traditional and artificial restrictions on the child in school had served a useful purpose, but, he said, "freedom is no end in itself" (Dewey, 1928a, p. 200). "I wonder," he told the membership, "whether this earlier and more negative phase of progressive education has not upon the whole run its course" (p. 201). Although he noted that progressive schools set great store by individuality, he suggested that this was not antagonistic to the orderly organization of subject matter. He even chastised those in the Association who felt that the curriculum ought to flow strictly from the individual impulses and predilections of children. "Thus," he said, "much of the energy that sometimes goes to thinking about individual children might better be devoted to discovering some worthwhile activity and to arranging the conditions under which it can be carried forward" (pp. 201–2). He rejected the position taken by many in the child-centered movement that the curriculum ought not to be imposed from without by adults, but ought to be designed with the full participation of the children themselves. A mere succession of unrelated activities, he argued, not only fails to present organized subject matter in some coherent form, it also fails to "provide for the development of a coherent and integrated self" (p. 202). He concluded this critique by declaring that "bare doing, no matter how active, is not enough" (p. 202). He recommended instead that teachers have "not only the right but the duty to suggest lines of activity, and to show that there need not be any fear of adult imposition" (p. 203). Dewey was thus rejecting two of the reform thrusts that had prevailed in the first quarter-century. It was obvious that he had little use for the efficiency reformers, particularly their tacit acceptance of the social status quo. He felt that the child-movement had had positive impact through their rejection of traditional and unnecessary restraints on the child, but that they were essentially at a dead end through a kind of self-imposed restriction on adult imposition in curriculum matters. Dewey clearly thought that the Progressive Education Association ought to move beyond its developmentalist origins.

iv

If there was a counterpart in the social reconstructionist movement to the stunning impact that Kilpatrick's "The Project Method" had on the educational world, it was the speech that Counts delivered at the twelfth annual meeting of the Progessive Education Association in February of 1932. In that address, "Dare Progressive Education Be Progressive?" Counts reiterated the theme of an organization lacking direction that Dewey had sounded a few years earlier, but delivered his criticism in much blunter and sterner terms. "The great weakness of Progressive Education," he asserted, "lies in the fact that it has elaborated no theory of social welfare, unless it be that of anarchy or extreme individualism" (p. 258). By "anarchy," Counts was, of course, not implying that the members were allied with political anarchists; he was attacking the long-standing belief of most of its members that any sort of curriculum that did not derive directly from the learners themselves represented an unwarranted intrusion on the child's distinctive individuality. Although he conceded that the members of the Association are basically tolerant and liberal-minded, he castigated them as people who

> have no deep and abiding loyalties, who possess no convictions for which they would sacrifice over-much, who would find it hard to live without their customary material comforts, who are rather insensitive to the accepted forms of social injustice, who are content to play the role of interested spectator in the drama of human history, who refuse to see reality in its harsher and more disagreeable forms, and who, in the day of severe trial, will follow the lead of the most powerful and respectable forces in society, and, at the same time, find good reasons for so doing. (p. 258)

Such verbal flagellation somehow struck home at a time when the effects of the Great Depression were already openly visible. Counts berated his audience for "at heart feeling themselves members of a superior breed [who] do not want their children to mix too freely with the children of the poor or of the less fortunate races" (pp. 258–9), a reference, no doubt, to the preponderance of private and usually very exclusive schools that were represented in the Association.

Counts (1932a) challenged the organization to meet the social issues of the day head on, unafraid of "the bogeys of *imposition* and *indoctrination*" (p. 259). He advocated fundamental changes in the economic system alluding to "capitalism, with its deification of the principle of selfishness, its reliance upon the forces of competition, its placing of property above human rights, and its exaltation of the profit motive . . ." (p. 261). Instead he called for a "coordinated, planned, and socialized economy" (p. 261) that would redress the evils rampant in the present system. One of those present on this occasion reported years later that Counts's speech was greeted with a stunned silence that spoke "more eloquently than applause" (Redefer, p. 188). The rest of the program for the day was virtually abandoned, and the Board of Directors felt it necessary to call a special meeting in order to discuss Counts's challenge.

Not a professed Marxist, Counts believed that democratic traditions were consistent with a much stronger measure of control over capitalism gone wild. His message held out the intriguing prospect that the evils so evident in the America of the Great Depression could be corrected not by revolution but by school programs that directed the new generation to changing the fundamental values undergirding the capitalist economy. Counts's call to arms was so enthusiastically received that later that year he issued a new manifesto that included even more radical proposals, *Dare the School Build a New Social Order?* (1932). He took the view there that the school could act as critic with respect to other social agencies and could undertake new tasks when those social institutions were not functioning successfully. In this respect, he favored an indefinite expansion of the scope of the curriculum much beyond the traditional subjects of study. Moreover, if teachers could mobilize themselves into a militant force, they could serve to correct some of the evils that the society imposed. Counts continued to sound the theme of an extreme individualism as the dominant value in American schooling, a value system that had to be replaced with an educational doctrine that emphasized social justice and social reform. After 1932, the Progressive Education Association was never the same. The child-centered position that had held sway in its early years diminished in popularity, and Counts's new radical social policy was in the ascendancy. Well-known professors, drawn largely from Teachers College, Columbia University, began to take over the reins of the organization from the headmasters of private schools and interested lay people who had founded the Association, and they succeeded in giving it a different character. In a sense, one interest group wrested control of the organization from the other. Stanwood Cobb, the Progressive Education Association's founder, was once asked why he resigned the presidency in 1930. He replied that, "They took it away from us." "They," he explained, were "the people at Teachers College, Columbia University" (Cremin, 1961, p. 250).

Counts's achievement in stirring the imagination not only of the membership of the Progressive Education Association but of educational leaders everywhere cannot be underestimated. Just as President Franklin D. Roosevelt's New Deal programs were bringing some hope to the American public, so Counts's message was bringing encouragement to a dispirited educational leadership. A new journal, *Social Frontier*, soon made its appearance in 1934 and over the few years of its existence served as a lively forum for debate on social reconstructionism generally and on the schools' role in creating a new social order in particular. The "Teachers College crowd" was, of course, prominently represented, with the works of John L. Childs, William Heard Kilpatrick, Bruce Raup, Harold Rugg and Goodwin Watson featured. Dewey remained a regular contributor throughout most of the journal's existence, joined frequently by one of his ablest disciples from Ohio State University, Boyd Bode. A persistent theme running through the articles and editorials was the evils of laissez-faire capitalism and rampant individualism. Although there were differences between "gradualists" and "antigradualists" on such issues as the efficacy of the class struggle as a basis for social change or on the merits of indoctrination in schools as a means of bringing about a better society, in its pages, *Social Frontier* remained a consistent voice for the reconstruction of American life through the intervention of the schools. By 1937, however, the magazine began to falter, and in 1939 was taken over by the Progressive Education

Association in an effort to save it. Renamed *Frontiers of Democracy*, it continued its struggle for existence until 1943 when it died amid severe financial problems and some acrimony among the remaining leadership.

If lively debate and the support of major American intellectuals such as the eminent historian Charles A. Beard were to be the decisive factors in response to Counts's challenge, then certainly social reconstructionism was a resounding success. Beard, for example, was one of the principal figures responsible for the final report of the Commission on the Social Studies in the Schools of the American Historical Association. That report clearly embraced the reconstructionism that Counts (who was himself a member of the Commission) had been advocating. The report declared unequivocally that "Cumulative evidence supports the conclusion that, in the United States as in other countries, the age of individualism and *laissez faire* in economy and government is closing and that a new age of collectivism is emerging" (American Historical Association, 1934, p. 16). Teachers were charged with overcoming their traditional silence in political matters and encouraged to strike out boldly in the interest of a new society, much as Counts had urged. "Today," the Commission reported, "because of . . . the timidity and weakness of the profession and the power of vested interests and privileged groups, the teacher seldom dares to introduce his pupils to the truth about American society and the forces that drive it onward" (pp. 75–6).

So politically charged was the report that it elicited a number of extremely hostile reviews. As would be expected, Bobbitt was outraged. He strongly implied that the Commission was deliberately vague about the kind of collectivism it was trying to promote. He accused the "integrators" of a desire "to think and to plan for the masses" (Bobbitt, 1934, p. 295). Sounding an ominous note, Bobbitt suggested that the members of the Commission used "the slogans of democracy as a mere protective smoke-screen for a communistic offensive" (p. 205). Alluding to "the revolutionary hysteria that grips all the collectivizing nations" (p. 208), he called upon

the American Historical Association either to clarify the
ambiguities in the report or to repudiate it. Even Bode
(1934), generally sympathetic to social reconstructionism,
wrote a stinging editorial which declared at the outset, "The
cynic who said that teaching is the art of taking advantage of
defenseless childhood will find confirmation for his pessimistic view in the recent Report of the Commission on the
Teaching of the Social Studies" (p. 1). Reflecting somewhat
Dewey's position on the issue of social reconstructionism,
Bode proceeded to castigate the Commission for appearing to
impose a predetermined social ideal on the child while ignoring "the vital importance of freedom in thinking" (p. 1). For
both Dewey and Bode, the road to social progress was much
more closely tied to the ability of the schools to teach independent thinking and to the ability of students to analyze
social problems than it was to an organized effort designed to
redress specific social evils.

Counts himself continued his rise to preeminence in the
curriculum world through his prolific writings and many
speeches to professional organizations, sounding the theme
that the curriculum should be directed toward correcting
social and economic ills. Dissenting voices, however, continued to be heard. Snedden, for example, as would be
expected, was anything but enthusiastic about Counts's drive
to remake the curriculum along social reconstructionist
lines. He did acknowledge that beneath the "romantic nonsense" that had been uttered on the subject of social reconstructionism, there was a genuine problem to be addressed.
"The times" he admitted, "are out of joint. America is sick"
(Snedden, 1935, p. 48). He was skeptical, however, about the
prospect of the million schoolteachers in the nation uniting
behind specific social or political programs. Even beyond
that, he felt that "dreams of having our schools share directly
in the furthering of any plans of social reconstruction are not
only visionary, but also subversive of civic decency" (p. 51).
What he proposed instead were "really functional civic
educations" based on sound sociological principles. He continued to rail against subject matter specialists "including

those that had become infected with Utopian radicalism" (p. 53).

More important, however, than the occasional resistance to social meliorism being thrown up by opposing interest groups, like the social efficiency educators, was the seeming impenetrability of the schools themselves to ideas being put forth by Counts and his allies. There appeared to be more than a superficial disparity in political outlook between the "frontier thinkers" who articulated their views in the pages of *New Republic* and *Social Frontier* and the practical educational administrators who actually ran the schools of the nation. One reporter observed, for example, that when the Department of Superintendence met in Cleveland in 1934, "the Progressive Education Association moved onto the scene before the superintendents had packed their grips, poked fun at the resolutions the superintendents had adopted, and by voicing 'advanced' ideas ran off with the headlines" (Boutwell, 1934, p. 297). Apparently, the Eastern establishment was tolerated but not wholly welcome. Although the reporter at the Cleveland convention admitted that its tone was "outwardly . . . distinctly pink," and that the assembled superintendents appeared willing to undertake some changes in school practice, they remained "averse to joining the Columbia torch-bearers at the barricades" (p. 297). One superintendent, sympathetic to social reconstructionism and writing in *Progressive Education*, observed later that, in general, there were just too many speeches on the subject and not enough grass roots efforts to work with the teachers themselves. His overall assessment of the movement four years after Counts's clarion call to the teachers of the nation was pessimistic. "The stream of words and books about a new social order which has poured over teachers in the last few years," he observed, "seems very much like the proverbial water on a duck's back" (Moseley, 1936, p. 337).

v

If there was one major success that the social reconstructionists achieved at the school level, it was the large-scale adop-
tion by school districts of a series of social studies textbooks
written by Counts's colleague at Teachers College, Harold
Rugg. Rugg came to Teachers College from the University of
Chicago in 1920 as a staff member at the Lincoln School, an
experimental school conceived of as a laboratory for testing
educational ideas. The school, founded three years earlier,
was created when the General Education Board agreed to
sponsor it in part with funds supplied by Mr and Mrs John D.
Rockefeller. Following his earlier inclinations and training,
Rugg embarked almost immediately on a testing program to
determine the abilities of the children enrolled in the school
apparently concerned that a school founded on child-
centered principles would not give sufficient attention to
achievement in the area of "social needs" (Rugg, 1941, p.
188).

But Rugg's interests turned quickly to the social studies as a
particular area in the curriculum. As an associate professor at
Teachers College, he taught a course called, "The Scientific
Method in the Reconstruction of Elementary and Secondary
School Subjects", and this led him to consider alternatives to
the conventional organization of school studies. In one of his
earliest articles on the subject of the reconstruction of the
social studies, he seemed to have been pondering the notion
that a course could be developed around the "great principles
or generalizations in history, economics, politics, industry,
geography, etc." (Rugg, 1921b, p. 692). In envisioning such a
course, he proposed that the conventional subject matter be
swept away and that a new curriculum be developed strictly
on the criterion of "social worth" (p. 697). For Rugg, the social
studies were a prime example of curriculum fragmentation
and unnecessary compartmentalization. What he proposed
was a unified social studies built on the laws and generalizations as enunciated by the finest practitioners in the various
social disciplines:

Rather than have teachers attempt the almost impossible task of "correlating" history, geography, civics, economics and sociology (taught as separate subjects), we postulate that more effective outcomes will be secured by weaving together lesson by lesson the facts, movements, conditions, principles and social, economic and political "laws" that depend upon one another *and that can be fully comprehended only when they are woven together*. (Rugg, 1921a, p. 188)

Rugg saw this approach not only in terms of "social worth" but as a way to encourage independent thinking on the part of the students. From a psychological point of view, he saw a curriculum organized around real social problems as having the potential for replacing the passivity that characterized not only social studies classrooms but schooling generally with an active concern for social justice.

Rugg had been influenced at least to some degree by all of the curriculum reform movements of the twentieth century. He had earlier expressed great faith in the power of science to transform what was taught in school; his first book, for example, considered the experimental evidence on the question of mental discipline (Rugg, 1916), and he later published a statistics textbook for teachers (Rugg, 1925). In the late 1920s, he wrote *The Child-Centered School* (with Ann Shumaker, 1928), generally regarded as contributing to the new popularity of schools built around the activity principles that Kilpatrick and his followers were promoting. But throughout the twenties, he also expressed a persistent concern for the social role of the schools. Indeed, he became one of the first in the Progressive Education Association to view with alarm the continued tendency of that organization as late as 1930 to align itself with child-centered experimental schools while neglecting what he regarded as a social crisis. Looking back on that period, he once recalled the Board meetings where few directors took his warning seriously, some referring to his persistent calls for an organized effort by the Progressive Education Association in the arena of social action as "Harold's annual crisis speech" (Rugg, 1947, p. 576). Once the Great Depression struck, Rugg's allegiance to the social reconstructionists was unequivocal. Increasingly, he saw social regeneration as a worldwide problem. In 1932, for example, Rugg declared dramatically, "The world is on fire, and the youth of the world must be equipped to combat the conflagration" (p. 11). Much of the social unrest he saw in countries like England, France, Germany, Japan, China and the Philippines he attributed to "the dangerous social effects of a lopsided academic education" or the "phenomenon of hyperintellectual education" (p. 12). Only through a fundamental reconstruction of the educational system could the current drift toward disaster be stemmed. Rugg was in no doubt as to how to proceed: "The first step is the building of a new program of work, a new content for the curriculum, directly out of the problems, issues, and characteristics of our changing society" (p. 13).

Rugg was actually expressing here his hopes for the monumental effort he had undertaken a decade earlier to reconstruct the social studies curriculum through the introduction of an avant-garde series of social studies textbooks. His primary emphasis, of course, was on calling attention to the critical social problems that America faced, but he also wanted his books to embody scientific respectability. Activity analysis, the allegedly scientific approach to curriculum development advocated by the social efficiency educators, was clearly out of the question since Rugg undoubtedly foresaw that using present activities as the basis for a curriculum would only serve to promote the existing social structure. Rugg, with an able and dedicated research staff at his command at the Lincoln School, embarked on an effort in 1921–22 to build the program of studies, not on a catalog of ongoing life activities, but on fundamental problems faced by American society and on generalizations set forth by leading social scientists. In a bold move to get his work into the schools, Rugg wrote to over three hundred school administrators who had been in his classes at the University of Chicago and Teachers College inviting them to subscribe to the new social science pamphlets "sight unseen" (Rugg, 1941, p. 207), and by June 1922, some four thousand orders for each of the twelve pamphlets had been received. In this way, the experimental edition of *Social Science Pamphlets* was underwritten in advance. By the end of the summer of 1922, the first seventh-grade pamphlet, *America and Her Immigrants*, was shipped. Over the first nine-year period, 750,000 experimental pamphlets were distributed to subscribing school systems.

The program of research that Rugg undertook in connection with his series was enormous. One significant step in the process was the identification by one member of the research team of three thousand important problems facing American society (later reduced to three hundred) which were to be the backbone of the social studies program (Hockett, 1927). Another staff member worked with students from the third through the twelfth grades, determining their ability to deal with the concepts critical to those problems (Meltzer, 1925). Still another key step in the development of the series was the work of Rugg's doctoral student at Teachers College, Neal Billings, in developing a list of generalizations central to the social sciences. The list of generalizations was drawn from the group of books written between 1915 and 1922 by scholars that Rugg called "frontier thinkers" (Billings, 1929, pp. 68–70). Billings systematically combed 61 books written by "frontier thinkers" such as Charles A. Beard, Van Wyck Brooks, John Dewey, Harold J. Laski, W. F. Ogburn, James Harvey Robinson, Thorsten Veblen, Sidney and Beatrice Webb, and Clark Wissler carefully cataloging and categorizing the social science generalizations he found there. Ultimately, 888 generalizations were compiled (pp. 99–209). Many had a distinct political orientation: "Fortunes sometimes originate in fraud and corruption" (p. 146); "The economic and social advance of women is not favorable to a high birth rate" (p. 151); "Militarism opposes democracy" (p. 161); and "Specialized industry in the factory system has divided society into capitalists and laborers" (p. 180). It would be difficult to establish the extent to which all of these generalizations found their way into the Rugg textbooks, but certainly some of them did. Even the difficulty levels of various materials, written and pictorial, were scrupulously studied before they were incorporated into the final version of the *Social Science Pamphlets* (Mathews, 1926; Shaffer, 1930).

Within a few years, the commercial possibilities of the series became apparent, and in 1926, Rugg signed a contract with Ginn and Company to market the series under a new format and the new title, *Man and His Changing Society*. Three months before the stock market crash, in August of 1929, the first volume in the series was ready. By the end of that year alone, 20,000 copies had already been sold. By 1930 that figure reached almost 60,000. Between 1929 and 1939, 1,317,960 copies in the series were sold along with an additional 2,687,000 workbooks (Winters, 1968, p. 91). Especially considering that these sales were achieved in a period of declining school resources as a result of the depression, the sales figures are indeed astounding. But beyond that, Rugg's individual achievement represents the single greatest victory in the attempt by the social reconstructionists to reform the school curriculum in line with their social ideals.

The commercial series was divided into a "First Course" consisting of eight volumes and a "Second Course" consisting of six. Volume One in the junior high school, to take one example, tackled the question of what is an American. The emphasis was on America as a nation of immigrants, including an effort to break down stereotypes of various nationalities and stressing the contributions of various immigrant groups. Included as well were "African immigrants" brought to the country as slaves. Rugg presented, particularly in its time, an unusually candid account of the slave trade. The story of James Morley, a gunner on one of the slave ships, for example, was quoted:

> I have seen them under great difficulty of breathing. The women, particularly, often got upon the beams to get air, but they are generally driven down, because they were taking the air from the rest. I have seen rice held to the mouths of sea-sick slaves until they were about strangled. I have seen medicine

thrown over them in such a way that not half of it went into their mouths. The poor wretches were wallowing in their blood, hardly having life, and this with blows from a whip, the cat-o'-nine-tails. (Rugg, 1938, p. 117).

In another volume, the disparity between rich and poor was emphasized. One set of pictures showed two neighborhoods in Washington, D.C. Under one, the heading ran, "This is one of the fine residential neighborhoods in Washington, D.C. Notice the wide, well-kept cement boulevard, the trees, the neat hedges, the large, well-built houses, and the automobile" (Rugg, 1931, p. 53). The heading under the second said, "This is another neighborhood in Washington, D.C. Notice the broken pavement in the alley, the lack of trees, the old tenements, and the carts" (p. 53). The changing role of women in society was also included. One photograph showing a woman wearing a white coat and conducting a scientific experiment had the heading, "Many women find that their housework does not keep them sufficiently occupied, so they enter industry, business, or the professions" (p. 132). A photograph on the opposite page showed a man and woman at the kitchen sink doing the dishes together. The text appearing below the photograph read, "This was a rare sight in 1890. It is not unusual today" (p. 133). Another unusual facet of the series was the inclusion in the social studies textbooks of one of Rugg's major interests, the arts. Architect Frank Lloyd Wright, poet Carl Sandburg, novelists Sinclair Lewis and Theodore Dreiser, as well as prominent figures in theater and music, were included. The central theme of the series, however, was probably best captured in the caption of the last section in the concluding chapter of the volume on problems of American culture: BUT AMERICA IS NOW ENTERING A NEW AGE OF SOCIAL PLANNING (p. 596). Like Counts, Rugg was not calling for revolution, but for a much stronger measure of restraint on the free enterprise system.

It was this anti-capitalist theme that eventually brought on the demise of the series. As early as 1934, Rugg's name appeared in a publication by Elizabeth Dilling designed as a

"Who's Who and Handbook of Radicalism for Patriots." But it was not until about 1940 that truly organized opposition to the textbooks began to appear. A turning point was the appointment to the Englewood, New Jersey, school board of Bertie C. Forbes, a Hearst newspaper columnist and owner of *Forbes*, a business journal. Using his own journal as a vehicle for his attacks, Forbes declared, "I plan to insist that this anti-American educator's text books be cast out" (1939, p. 8). Rugg eventually accepted an invitation from the Parent-Teacher Association at Englewood to debate his opponents, but Forbes did not appear at the meeting. Despite further attacks in his magazine, Forbes eventually lost that battle after the mayor did not reappoint him to the board.

Later similar criticisms of Rugg's series as un-American and subversive began to appear in such cities as Bronxville (New York), Binghampton (New York), Atlanta (Georgia), and Philadelphia (Pennsylvania). In Philadelphia, an official of the Daughters of Colonial Wars attacked the textbooks because they "tried to give the child an unbiased viewpoint instead of teaching him real Americanism" (Book Learning, 1940, p. 65), although these local attacks were not especially successful. At the national level, the campaign was joined by the National Association of Manufacturers whose objections received wide publicity through George Sokolsky, the widely read Hearst columnist. Later, the American Legion made the Rugg textbooks a cause célèbre, with the most vigorous attack being launched by Orlen K. Armstrong, long a Rugg opponent, in an article entitled, "Treason in the Textbooks." Armstrong's analysis of the textbooks led him to conclude that the real purposes of the books were:

1. To present a new interpretation of history in order to "debunk" our heroes and cast doubt upon their motives, their patriotism and their service to mankind.
2. To cast aspersions upon our Constitution and our form of government, and shape opinions favorable to replacing them with socialistic control.
3. To condemn the American system of private ownership and enterprise, and form opinions favorable to collectivism.

The heyday of social meliorism / 207

4. To mould opinions against traditional religious faiths and ideas or morality, as being parts of an outgrown system. (Armstrong, 1940, pp. 51–70)

A defense on Rugg's behalf was quickly organized which included some of the "frontier thinkers" whose ideas had been incorporated into his books as well as his colleagues on *Frontiers of Democracy*. Rugg's own *That Men May Understand* (1941) is largely a spirited defense of his work. Some retractions of the most damaging charges were eventually wrested from Rugg's accusers, but the series was never completely revised and, after 1940, it diminished rapidly in popularity.

Lester Frank Ward, the great anti-Social Darwinist sociologist of the 1880s and 1890s has been called by Henry Steele Commager (1964) "the philosophical architect of the welfare state" (p. xxxviii). Indeed, Ward saw the emerging problems of the twentieth century not simply in the maldistribution of real wealth in the society but in the unequal distribution of the cultural capital through the schools. The maldistribution, he felt, could be corrected by intelligent intervention, not by letting raw social and economic forces play themselves out. Insofar as curriculum reform was concerned, those ideas remained largely dormant for years. Roughly half a century after Ward first enunciated these ideas, however, educational leaders like Counts and Rugg managed to reinvigorate them and bring them first to an elite group of mainly eastern intellectuals but, ultimately in the Rugg textbooks, to hundreds of thousands of school children. What seems to account for the reemergence of this subterranean stream of American curriculum reform is the interplay of the ideas themselves with social and economic conditions favorable to its survival. Once the prospect of a world conflict loomed on the horizon, however, and criticism of American social conditions was no longer in vogue, social meliorism as a force for curriculum change gave way to curriculum thinking more in tune with the times. Those times were no longer right for social reconstructionism. With America's entry into

World War Two imminent, criticism of American society slipped out of vogue in favor of a wave of patriotism occasioned by an external threat of aggression.

Curriculum fashions, it has long been noted, are subject to wide pendulum swings. While this metaphor conveys something of the shifting positions that are constantly occurring in the educational world, the phenomenon might best be seen as a stream with several currents, one stronger than others. None ever completely dries up. When the weather and other conditions are right, a weak or insignificant current assumes more force and prominence only to decline when conditions particularly conducive to its newfound strength no longer prevail.

CHAPTER 8

HYBRIDIZATION OF THE CURRICULUM

i

At roughly the same time that the social reconstructionists were mounting their offensive in the struggle for the American curriculum, another even more powerful force was affecting the course of curriculum change in the United States. It was not so much a new antagonist emerging as it was a blending of what were once clear-cut ideological positions into new amalgams of curriculum reform. Rather than a distinctive alternative to the existing contenders, it was a sometimes intentional, sometimes unintentional, potpourri of all of them.

By the 1930s, curriculum reform had become a national preoccupation. Change had definitely permeated the curriculum atmosphere. When the joint committee of the Department of Supervisors and Directors of Instruction of the National Education Association and the Society for Curriculum Study (a committee that was the precursor of the Association for Supervision and Curriculum Development of the National Education Association) issued a volume on the state of the curriculum, their opening sentence announced, "Curriculum development is definitely and markedly on the increase, and interest in this movement is nationwide" (Hand and French, 1937, p. 1). The authors went on to point out that well over 70 percent of cities with populations of 25,000 or more, according to their survey, were engaging in organized curriculum development. Not necessarily a particular curriculum doctrine but curriculum change itself was becoming a popular and widespread phenomenon. In the light of that phenomenon, it should not be surprising that some, probably a great many, school districts should undertake programs of curriculum change, not out of any deeply held conviction that the curriculum ought to be revised in a given direction, but so as not to appear out of step with what had become a major national trend. High status and even national recognition were being accorded to those school systems that had achieved or were in the process of engaging in curriculum revision of whatever sort. It was just not in the best interest of school administrators and school boards simply to stand pat. In the minds of more and more Americans, the traditional academic curriculum was becoming increasingly obsolete. Accordingly, many of the curriculum reforms that were emerging in the decade of the 1930s represented not so much a victory for one position over the other as a hybridization of what were once distinct and easily recognizable curriculum positions.

Even before the advent of the 1930s, some school districts had experimented with curriculum plans that were considered innovative. Of these the Dalton plan of Helen Parkhurst and E. D. Jackman, the Winnetka plan of Carleton Washburne, and the Denver project of Jesse Newlon and A. L. Threlkeld were probably the best known. Each was initiated at the local level and adopted by school systems eager to depart from conventional curricular practices. The direction of the departure in each of these cases, however, is unclear. Ultimately, these plans achieved wide accclaim although none of these curricular innovations was particularly long-lived. Both the Dalton plan and the Winnetka plan seemed to be prompted by an effort to get away from recitation as the primary form of classroom instruction. What was substituted (although not exclusively) was a kind of contract plan in which students undertook to accomplish a certain amount of school work on their own. Under the Dalton plan of Dalton, Massachusetts, each student was issued an individual monthly card with the assignments for the month. Students maintained their own records of their progress, and, upon completing the assigned work, could elect to be examined on the subject matter. The subject matter itself, however, departed little from the traditional curriculum. What was most important was that "cut-and-dried recitations were altogether to be dispensed with as being forced and artificial" (Jackman, 1920, p. 691). Recitations, the familiar question and answer format of most classrooms, had come to be associated with traditional education, and this lent credence to reforms that promised its abolition even when the subject matter remained relatively unchanged.

The Winnetka plan in Winnetka, Illinois, even more closely resembled what came to be known later as programmed instruction. Although the plan was strongly identified with individualized instruction, it was individualized in the sense of children working individually on assigned material, not of children's expression of their own individuality. If anything, the individualization at Winnetka was infused with social efficiency ideas. Reflecting Bobbitt's position, Superintendent Carleton Washburne once declared that, "It is a comparatively simple matter to determine what knowledge and skills are commonly needed" (Washburne, 1926, p. 219). While the Dalton plan was geared mainly toward the student individually completing a large body of material often culminating in a report, the Winnetka plan concentrated on specific skill attainment, with promotion being based on individual subject achievement rather than by grade placement (Washburne, 1924). Kilpatrick, understandably, was critical of both the Dalton plan and the Winnetka system, declaring that "both assume that education mainly and properly consists of learning certain prearranged subject matter for examination purposes" ("Individualizing Instruction," 1925, p. 177). Of the Winnetka plan in particular he said, that "it carries its mechanized work too far." Washburne, in turn, questioned some of the basic assumptions of the project method, arguing that it tends "to give children a random, unscientific training and to ignore the wide differences which exist among individuals" (Washburn, 1928, p. 187). Terms like individualization and individuality in the curriculum were operating not so much as precise descriptions of a particular way to reorganize instruction as they did a kind of slogan attracting allegiances but meaning quite different things to different groups. To some in the 1920s, individuality meant building the curriculum around the individual child's spontaneous creative interests; to others, individuality meant adapting the pace of instruction to the differences in individual learning capacities. By the 1930s, the social reconstructionists had converted individuality into "rugged individualism," the enemy of cooperation and restraint on the free enterprise system.

The Denver, Colorado, program was initiated in 1922 with an appropriation of $31,500 from the school board for curriculum revision. Elimination of waste seems to have been one of the main considerations. Superintendent Jesse Newlon's recommendation to the school board, for example, pointed out that, in view of the size of the school budget in Denver, if it turned out that as little as "10 percent of teacher's time is spent on non-essential and misplaced materials in courses of study," that would represent an "annual waste to the Denver taxpayers of $315,000" (Newlon and Threlkeld, 1926, p. 230). For the most part, the money appropriated was for the purpose of releasing teachers to work on curriculum revision projects with prominent leaders in the curriculum field, such as Thomas Briggs, W. W. Charters and Harold Rugg brought in from time to time to review their work. Again, there was no clear ideological direction, although some of Newlon's early pronouncements on curriculum were strongly tinged with social efficiency ideas. (Later, as a Professor of Educational Administration at Teachers College, he became more closely associated with social reconstructionism.) The most lasting legacy of the Denver program was the emphasis given to active teacher participation in curriculum reform. In fact, what came to be known as "process" in the curriculum world, the emphasis on active participation by school personnel in curriculum change and the group processes associated with it, became a favorite theme of the Association for Supervision and Curriculum Development. Established as a branch of the National Education Association in 1943 as a result of a merger between the Society of Curriculum Study and the Department of Supervision and Directors of Instruction, the Association through its journal, *Educational Leadership*, and its yearbooks lobbied ceaselessly for "democratic" as opposed to "authoritarian" curriculum change.

ii

Emphasis on locally initiated curriculum change continued to gain momentum in the 1930s. Probably the most ambitious of the efforts to stimulate curriculum reform at the local level was undertaken by the Progressive Education Association in what came to be known as the Eight-Year Study. For years, members of the organization had been expressing dismay at the slow pace of curriculum change, particularly at the secondary school level. The source of this problem in the minds of most of the leadership was the imposition of entrance requirements by the colleges, and this, they believed, was the prop that held up the traditional academic subjects. As far back as the Committee of Ten report (National Education Association, 1893), complaints were being voiced about alleged domination of the high school curriculum by the colleges, and, by the early 1930s, the conviction became firmly implanted in the minds of curriculum reformers that the colleges were the principal impediment to curriculum reform at the secondary school level. As an initial step to break the logjam, the Progressive Education Association on the motion by Harold Rugg appointed a Committee on the Relation of School and College (although variations in the name of the committee appeared occasionally in official documents), with Wilford M. Aikin, headmaster of the John Burroughs School of St Louis, Missouri, in charge. Aikin (1931b) was generally sanguine about the revolutionary changes that had been accomplished in the elementary school curriculum, but expressed the view that college domination had created a situation where "there are no truly progressive secondary schools, in spite of many attempts to create them" (Aikin, 1931a, p. 275).

Beginning in 1932, grants were secured from the Carnegie Foundation and the General Education Board (eventually amounting to $70,000 and $622,500 respectively – munificent sums for their day), and a plan was developed whereby colleges would accept students from a select group of secondary schools without reference to the particular subjects they had taken and without examination in those subjects. The basic idea was to free the secondary schools in the experimental group from the shackles of college domination and then to demonstrate that the graduates of these "unshackled schools" were at least the equal of students who had completed a traditional program of college-entrance subjects. The key test would be to see how the experimental group of students compared with a matched group in terms of success in college. Eventually 30 high schools (later reduced to 29 by one withdrawal) were selected, and approximately 3,600 students in "matched pairs" were included in the sample.

To be research director of this massive undertaking, the Committee brought Ralph Tyler from the Bureau of Educational Research of Ohio State University. Tyler had earned his doctorate in 1934 at the University of Chicago under Charles Hubbard Judd, a highly esteemed educational psychologist, who had earned a reputation for bringing scientific respectability to the study of education. Tyler had had some previous experience with the Extension Division of the University of North Carolina, and while at Ohio State University, his own reputation as a scientific student of education grew rapidly. Early in his long career, he allied himself with the advocates of activity analysis, defending the study by Charters and Douglas Waples that attempted to derive a curriculum in teacher-training through an exhaustive study of the activities that teachers actually performed (Tyler, 1930). In particular, Tyler's expertise in the measurement of educational outcomes attracted the Committee on the Relation of Secondary School and College. In that respect, Tyler may have been the first to argue that "the first step in improving validity is to define clearly the types of behavior which we are trying to teach" (Tyler, 1931, p. 327), thus providing a portent of what was to become a massive behavioral objectives movement in later years.

One problem that emerged early in the study was the actual drawing of the sample that would comprise the "thirty unshackled schools." Schools had to demonstrate their willingness to experiment with their curricula to be eligible, and this tended to skew the sample strongly toward the prestigious private schools whose headmasters still constituted a significant element in the Progressive Education Association. Of the twenty-nine schools in the final sample, fifteen were private schools, among them the most exclusive and expensive in the United States. Typical of those schools chosen were the Baldwin School of Bryn Mawr (Pennsylvania), the Beaver Country Day School of Chestnut Hill (Massachusetts), the Dalton Schools and the Fieldston School (New York City), and Aikin's own John Burroughs School of Clayton (Missouri). Also included were four university-affiliated schools such as the Lincoln School of Teachers College, the University School of Ohio State University, and Wisconsin High School of the University of Wisconsin. Of the remaining ten public high schools, four were drawn from wealthy suburban communities such as Bronxville High School of Bronxville (New York) and New Trier Township High School of Winnetka (Illinios). The others could reasonably be described as typical American high schools (Lancelot, 1943).

No particular curriculum pattern was imposed on the experimental schools. In line with the growing emphasis on locally initiated curriculum reform, the schools themselves were given free rein to change the existing curriculum. From 1932 to 1934, the schools with the aid of curriculum consultants developed and implemented the changes. The extent to which the schools chose to depart from traditional curriculum patterns was enormous. With some satisfaction, Aikin (1942) cited one report indicating that the North Shore Country Day School of Winnetka, Illinois, had eliminated from its Latin program "such stupid material as the Catiline Orations" and substituted twenty to twenty-five of Cicero's letters as well as about an equal number from Pliny (p. 47). At the Baldwin School, the five-year Latin program was revised to reduce the amount of Caesar studied in the second year, and in the fifth year, readings from Plautus, Terence, Catullus and Horace were introduced (Spring, 1936). New Trier Township High School reported that, among other innovations, it had introduced into the senior year in English an eight-week study of the drama, working back chronologically from the modern play to Shakespeare and finally to the Greek dramatists. Both comedy and tragedy were studied beginning with a modern tragedy, Eugene O'Neill's *Emperor Jones*, and then moving to Shakespeare's *Macbeth* ("Thirty Schools", 1943, p. 514).

Wisconsin High School on the University of Wisconsin campus, on the other hand, struck out boldly in removing their "shackles." H. H. Ryan, the principal, had long been an advocate of a supremely functional curriculum. Once commenting on the persistent cries for the elimination of "frills" in the curriculum, he urged that "if the tax payer insists on paring the curriculum down to the essentials, it is the educators who must determine what the essentials are" (Ryan, 1933, p. 143). What are the frills, he asked rhetorically, "Algebra or speech training? Latin or home economics? Ancient history or music?" (p. 142). Given his freedom from college domination under the Eight-Year Study, Ryan developed a special experimental curriculum at Wisconsin for a segment of the high school population that was instituted in 1933. Pointing out that a whole series of prestigious commissions from the Cardinal Principles Committee (National Education Association, 1918) had "declared that the school's job is to help orient and adjust boys and girls in certain 'areas of living,' such as work, leisure, citizenship, family membership, health, and the like" ("Thirty Schools", 1943, p. 780), he argued that the school curriculum ought to reflect more directly these vital social functions. Whereas Kingsley, in the Cardinal Principles Report, had stated such areas of living as aims of the curriculum, he stopped short of dispensing with the traditional subjects, recommending instead that the existing subjects reorient themselves toward the accomplishment of those functional aims. By the 1930s, the conviction was growing among certain educators that the aims representing areas of living ought to become the subjects. Accordingly, the experimental Wisconsin curriculum was organized around four "constants": community living, health, vocations and leisure time. These constants, Ryan (1935) reported, made up approximately two-thirds of the school day. In time, this organization of the curriculum became identified as the core curriculum or more specifically as the social functions or life functions core. In a portent of what was to come, Ryan associated the core curriculum with life adjustment. "This universal problem of adjustment," he declared, "is logically the guiding principle for the development of the core-curriculum" (Ryan, 1937, p. 15).

In Tulsa, Oklahoma, a select group of "accelerated" ninth and tenth grade students was required to enroll in a two-hour a week "Social Relations" program along with either a physical education program or a "creative activity" to form a three-hour "block" also described as a "Core program" ("Thirty Schools", 1943, pp. 643–5). "The Tulsa teachers believe," said one report, that the core portion of the program "should be based upon functional needs and significant life problems" (Hanna, 1939, p. 350). As always, the announced intention was "to meet the needs and interests" (p. 351) of the students, and this meant giving a less prominent role to the traditional subjects of study and more to such problems as health, safe driving, consumer economics and personal finance. Another strong emphasis was on teacher–pupil planning of the curriculum usually assigned to a regularly scheduled "conference hour" (Hanna, 1940, p. 66). In one seventh-grade class, for example, joint planning of the curriculum resulted in a year's study on the question, "How Can the Family Spend Their Leisure Time?" (p. 66).

At the Denver high schools, some modest curricular changes were introduced such as the establishment of a correlated curriculum combining social studies and English, but, after four years of experimentation, a core curriculum was also developed "to provide more effectively for the individual interests and needs of pupils as well as to provide for common concerns of all high school pupils" ("Thirty Schools," 1943, p. 167). The heart of the program was four "areas of living": "Personal Living, Immediate Personal-Social Relationships, Social-Civic Relationships, and Economic Relationships" (p. 169). Among the problems considered in these areas were "learning how to make the most of ourselves in appearance, poise, and social adequacy, through emphasis upon health, grooming, cleanliness, order, and fitness" (p. 173); "preparation for marriage, eugenics, inheritance, the problem of divorce, and the care of children" (p. 174), "the setting up of criteria for the choosing of friends" (p. 147), and "exploring vocational opportunities in the community and the nation and studying the individual's special abilities and capacities in terms of vocation" (p. 176). In a strong expression of social efficiency doctrine, one participant at Denver observed that "the subject matter of the core course will be related to those matters which society expects schools to present to youth. No attempt will be made to classify this subject matter under the usual subject-matter headings" (Rice, 1938, pp. 201–2). In the tenth grade, emphasis was placed on the relationship between school, home and civic affairs. In the eleventh, special consideration was given to "larger social, political, and economic relationships," and in the twelfth, the problems and issues of modern life were the focal point of the curriculum "with attention to personal adjustment to these problems" (p. 202).

Although some of the "unshackled schools" were clearly making only modest changes in their traditional academic programs, others, under the general rubric of a core curriculum, were experimenting with directly functional courses that, although they had strong social efficiency overtones, were being justified in terms of the needs and interests of the adolescents involved. What society needed and expected of its youth was becoming indistinguishable from what the youth themselves needed. The so-called core curriculum, one of the most abiding outcomes of the Eight-Year Study, was emerging as a fusion of the social efficiency concern that the schools prepare directly and specifically for the duties of life and the activity curriculum's overriding emphasis on the needs and interests of the learner as the basis of the curriculum.

For years, social efficiency educators had been making the case for trimming the deadwood off the traditional academic curriculum. To teach history, algebra and foreign languages to people who would never use them was an inexcusable waste. Their campaign, to a large extent, consisted of the effort to cast off those wasteful and inert subjects and to replace them (for most students) with subjects that bore a direct relationship to life, of which vocational education was a prime example. Under the aegis of the Eight-Year Study, at least some schools were able not only to introduce directly functional subjects like Personal Development and Immediate Social-Personal Relationships to the existing curricula, they made them the core of the curriculum. In part, acceptance of that drastic change in curricular pratice was made possible not simply by force of the old slogans of effficiency and functionalism but because they appeared to blend smoothly with the claims of the developmentalists that the curriculum ought to meet the common and individual needs of children and youth. Needs, then, or the needs curriculum, provided a convenient meeting ground where two interest groups could converge. Whatever would be the outcome of the matched-pair race between the students in the experimental "unshackled" schools and their counterparts from the traditional ones, the popularization of the core curriculum as a resilient hybrid was to emerge as one of the long-term outcomes of the Eight-Year Study.

A second development to which the Eight-Year Study gave strong impetus was the infusion of behaviorism in curriculum thinking. Volume Three of the report on the study was concerned with evaluation and declared flatly, "it was assumed that education is a process which seeks to change the behavior patterns of human beings" (Smith and Tyler, 1942, p. 11). From that assumption, it was only a small step to link these behaviorist principles to the stating of objectives as the crucial first step in the development of a curriculum, a position that Tyler had been advocating for some years. "The kinds of changes in behavior patterns in human beings which the school seeks to bring about," according to Tyler (in the part of the book that he wrote), "are its educational objectives" (p. 11). Objectives, in other words, should not be stated in vague terms such as knowing, appreciating and understanding, but in terms that would describe in rather precise terms how the student would behave after a period of study. Moreover, the success of the program would be determined by the extent to which the behaviors embodied in the objectives would be achieved. "An educational program," Tyler asserted, "is appraised by finding out how far the objectives of the program are actually being realized" (p. 12). These objectives, furthermore, had to be stated as a preamble to other curriculum development activities for the "unshackled schools." "As the first step," he declared, "each school faculty was asked to formulate a statement of its educational objectives" (p. 15). In a portent of what later became widely celebrated as "the Tyler Rationale," the objectives would represent "a compromise" based on evidence derived from "the demands of society, the characteristics of students, the potential contributions which various fields of learning may make, the social and educational philosophy of the school or college, and what we know from the psychology of learning as to the attainability of various types of objectives" (p. 16).

Since the framers of the Eight-Year Study specifically declined to promote any particular curriculum ideology, except perhaps change itself, they wound up at least partially supporting all of them. Putting their imprimatur, however, on the stating of objectives in behavioral terms as a first step in the curriculum planning process was to have a lasting and profound effect on the future course of curriculum development. It is one indication that in the stew that became the

American curriculum in the twentieth century, social efficiency emerged as the principal ingredient. The idea that, in curriculum development, exact specifications ought to be drawn up in advance and that success would be measured in terms of the extent to which those blueprints were followed is derived from the root metaphor of social efficiency, production, by which educational products are manufactured by the school-factory according to the particulars demanded by a modern industrial society.

Early results of the experiment began to trickle through in the 1939–40 academic year, and the final reports were published in 1942 and 1943 in a five-volume series under the general rubric of "Adventure in American Education." The actual result was something of an anticlimax. Of the graduates of the "thirty unshackled schools," 1,475 who had been admitted to college under the agreed-upon relaxed entrance requirements were selected for the final study. Given the wide diversity of programs in the experimental schools, the final report indicated that some in that sample were "fairly close to the orthodox program, but many of them almost wildly heterodox" (Chamberlain, Chamberlain, Drought and Scott, 1942, p. xx). Using common criteria of success in college such as grade-point average, the graduates of the experimental schools neither "set the colleges on fire" (p. xx) nor did they compare unfavorably with their counterparts from traditional secondary school programs. Some consolation was derived from the fact that the experimental group came out *"a little ahead"* (p.xxi). Put in its best light, the Progressive Education Association could claim that the traditional college-entrance curriculum was no surer road to success in college than any other one. "Is the traditional program the only safe and sane plan?" they asked. "The answer is, NO – with no more if's and but's about it" (p. xxi). When student grade averages were compared in English, Humanities, Foreign Languages, Social Studies, Physical Science, Mathematics and other subjects, there appeared, if anything, a very slight advantage accruing to the experimental group (pp. 27–8). The experimental group, in other words, had acquitted themselves creditably but not spectacularly. In a secondary analysis, the graduates of the six schools judged to be most experimental were compared to their counterparts in traditional programs, and their success in college was said to be greater than the graduates of the six schools judged to be least experimental. Although some of the leaders of the Progressive Education Association appeared jubilant by their apparent success in breaking the back of college domination on the secondary school curriculum, the overall reaction of the educational world and of the general public was strangely muted. What amounted to a tie between the experimental and the control group was not exactly charged with high drama, and the fact that the experimental variable was no particular curriculum pattern, but experimentation itself, made the results difficult to interpret. Much was also made of the fact that the final reports were published shortly after America's entry into World War Two, a time when the niceties of curriculum reform were far from the public consciousness.

iii

Throughout the 1930s, eclecticism in curriculum development continued as a major force alongside social reconstructionism. On their side, the social reconstructionists had the stars of the educational world and the more dramatic message, but it was the eclecticists who attracted a strong following among practicing school administrators. The school rank and file were a mixed lot politically and only sporadically responded to the vision of a new social order that the social reconstructionists were advancing. Eclecticism, on the other hand, was not nearly as politically sensitive, and the public appeal of a curriculum tied directly to the needs of children as well as the duties of life made it a much safer course for school administrators to follow. Americans had always been suspicious of elitism in schooling, and a curriculum that proposed to replace what they perceived to be an elitist curriculum useful only as an admissions ticket to college with one that was directly functional in terms of actual life activities seemed to be a definite step in the right direction. Moreover, although "meeting the needs and interests of children and youth" became an almost universal commonplace when curriculum affairs were being discussed, the longstanding social efficiency appeal of a curriculum tied to the needs of a modern industrial society and a population that was being fitted neatly and efficiently into a stable social order never seemed to lose its efficacy.

One of the mechanisms of change emerging in the 1930s was curriculum revision as a statewide enterprise. For about two decades, educational luminaries such as Ellwood P. Cubberly, Judd, Franklin Bobbitt and George Strayer had been hired by school systems to conduct what came to be known as school surveys in which the condition of a particular school system was assessed and recommendations made, usually along social efficiency lines, to improve the system (Sears, 1925). In some cases, such as in Mississippi (O'Shea, 1927), such surveys were conducted on a statewide basis. By the 1930s, influenced by the increasingly popular notion that curriculum revision should be undertaken by the participants who would be called upon to implement the innovations, some states initiated major programs of change built substantially on the Denver model.

By far the most famous of these was the Virginia Curriculum Program initiated in 1931. To head this mammoth enterprise, Hollis P. Caswell, fresh from similar projects in Florida and Alabama, was brought in as curriculum advisor by State Superintendent Sidney B. Hall from his faculty position at George Peabody University. It was Caswell who was most instrumental in the effort to direct the creation of a new and radically different statewide course of study in elementary schools. Initially, all 17,000 teachers in the State were invited to join in a curriculum study program, and according to Superintendent Hall's account, an incredible 15,000 joined the study committees that were formed and held in 1931–2. Hall (1933) claimed that "there was no compulsion; it was entirely voluntary" (p. 341). In systematic fashion, the program proceeded through what became a familiar series of steps in curriculum-making, beginning, of course, with the stating of objectives.

In the second year of the program, the various committees undertook the second step in the process, the preparation of the materials to carry out the objectives. Then the programs were introduced on a trial basis, and after appropriate modifications were made the curriculum was ready. In substance, it closely resembled what was becoming familiar as the core curriculum. In fact, under Caswell's direction, a new curriculum device, the scope and sequence chart, was developed, a kind of deliberate cross-hatching of two approaches to organizing the curriculum: one, the "major functions of social life" curriculum drawn from longstanding social efficiency ideas, provided the scope, the actual subject matter of study; the second, centers of interest, provided the sequence of these activities by attending to the interests that children presumably exhibited as they proceeded from early childhood to later maturity. The social functions in the elementary school curriculum, listed vertically on the scope and sequence chart, consisted of such functions as Consumption of Goods and Services, Communication and Transportation of Goods and People, and Recreation. Listed horizontally across the chart were the centers of interest according to sequential grade level. In Grade I , for example, the center of interest was Home and School Life, in Grade II, Community Life, and in Grade III, Adaptation of Life to Environmental Forces of Nature. The vertically listed social functions and the horizontally listed centers of interest formed cells in the body of the scope and sequence chart which would be filled with appropriate subject matter. Thus, where Recreation (a social function) met Home and School Life (a center of interest), the appropriate subject matter would become "How can we have an enjoyable time at home and school?" (Virginia State Board of Education, 1934, p. 16). Whether the centers of interest ranging from Effects of Machine Production upon our Living in Grade VI to Social Provision for Cooperative

Living in Grade VII actually represented interests of children in anything like the sense that Kilpatrick and the activity curriculum exponents meant is open to question, but the social functions that formed the scope of the Virginia curriculum, in the main, did in fact closely resemble the areas of living that the social efficiency interest group felt ought to replace the traditional academic subjects.

The same technique was used in extending the curriculum to the secondary level, although the subject designations in English, social studies, science and mathematics were maintained whereas in the elementary school curriculum, an attempt was made to integrate all subject areas. The thirteen major functions of social life chosen for the social studies at the high school level were: Protection and conservation of life, property, and natural resources; Production of goods and services; Distribution of the returns of production; Consumption of goods and services; Transportation of goods and people; Communication; Exploration; Recreation; Education; Extension of Freedom; Expression of Aesthetic Impulses; Expression of religious impulses; and Integration of the Individual (Alexander, 1934, p. 76). The centers of interest for the four years were: First year – Adaptation of our living through nature, social and mechanical discoveries, and inventions; Second year – Industrialism and agrarianism and their effects upon our living; Third year – Effects of changing culture and changing social institutions upon our living; and Fourth year – Effects of a continuously planning democratic social order upon our living (p. 77). Although it might be stretching a point to think of these as centers of adolescent interest, the latter two indicate that at least some social meliorism made its way into the Virginia curriculum along with developmentalism and social efficiency; for example, where production and distribution of goods and services as a social function intersected with the center of interest on the effects of changing culture (third year), the central theme of the content became, "How can we improve production, establish an economic balance between production and consumption, and provide for the more equitable distribution of the returns of production?" (p. 79). Where the social function, Extension of Freedom, crossed with the fourth-year center of interest, Effects of a Continuously Planning Democratic Social Order Upon Our Living, the central topic became, "How can a planning society extend political, economic, intellectual, and social freedom to all people?" (p. 79).

In attempting to evaluate the success of the Virginia State curriculum, particular attention was given to the extent of teacher participation, since, like the Denver program, one of the main outcomes was perceived to be wider participation by the teachers themselves in the process of curriculum development. One questionnaire study reported on the basis of 4,356 replies that 85 percent of Virginia elementary school teachers were actually using the course. Some 55 percent were helping develop units of work, and 49 percent were adding to the course of study. Six percent of the teachers were reported to be using the textbook only and 9 percent were described as "disinterested and unwilling to change teaching" (Leonard, 1937, p. 69). While no data had been gathered on the children or children's achievement, the wide acceptance of the program and the extensive participation of the teachers in curriculum development activities were a source of great satisfaction to the Virginia curriculum's promoters. It also was widely discussed on a national level not only as an ideal case of "process" but as a prime example of the core curriculum. Like Tyler and the Eight-Year Study, Caswell's work on the Virginia curriculum put him in the forefront of the second generation of curriculum leaders, succeeding the Bobbitts, Charters's and Sneddens of an earlier era. In fact, Caswell was brought to Teachers College in 1937 by Dean Russell to direct a reorganization of its departmental structure, and a year later became head of the first Department of Curriculum and Teaching.

iv

The word "progressive" had been applied to some practices in education as early as Joseph Mayer Rice's series of articles on American schools in the 1890s. For the most part, it was used synonymously with adjectives like "modern" and "new" to designate something other than traditional practice or in some cases simply as a positive term. But with the Progressive Education Association growing in size and visibility in the 1930s, more and more concern was expressed as to what progressive education actually was. For years, the inside track had been held by the developmentalists and epitomized by the activity curriculum, but as reconstructionists bolted into the limelight and attracted adherents like Newlon and Caswell, the picture became positively perplexing. Those sympathetic to reform of the curriculum strove mightily to bring some coherence to the medley of doctrines that had begun to claim some affinity to progressivism as articles and books began to appear addressing the question, what is progressive education? What emerged from these efforts was sometimes a hodge-podge of incompatible practices laid side by side or an attempt to reconstruct the concept of progressive education along particular lines. In fact, what was known as progressive education became analogous to a chemical mixture in which different elements are thrown together but still retain their own characteristics. The tenuous common cause that held them together was their disillusionment and in some cases outright antagonism to the traditional course of study. The source of the opposition, however, varied. By some, the traditional curriculum was seen as ignoring the natural course of development in children and youth as well as their interests and penchant for activity; by others, it was regarded as supremely non-functional, dangerously ignoring the actual roles that adults are called upon to play in our society, leaving society bereft of the trained individuals that would make it work; and by still others, it was clearly lacking in social direction, particularly irrelevant to issues of social justice and social renewal.

The chaos that surrounded what was called progressive education increasingly made it an easy target for criticism. Here and there, cries of alarm were heard from academicians such as the youthful president of the University of Chicago, Robert Maynard Hutchins, who sought to revive the humanistic ideal of a liberal education at least at the higher education level (Hutchins, 1936). Other humanist scholars, such as Irving Babbitt speaking from his perch at Harvard University, consistently deplored the state of decay into which American scholarship had fallen. But apart from the eternal complaint that students were arriving at the great centers of learning with ever weaker preparation for the rigors of scholarly endeavor, academicians in the 1930s rarely bothered to intervene in the internal affairs of elementary and secondary schools.

Ultimately, a movement began to evolve within the professional education establishment as a counterforce to the curricular practices that were being promoted under the hazy rubric of progressive education. For the most part, these attacks were directed at the activity movement, which in the minds of many of the critics was considered identical with progressive education. The pivotal figure in this growing opposition was William Chandler Bagley of Teachers College. Bagley's overall position is not easily characterized. He was one of the first to hold up social efficiency as the supreme educational ideal (Bagley, 1905), and was a longtime admirer of Ross L. Finney, one of the major figures in the social efficiency movement. As early as the *Twenty-Sixth Yearbook*, Bagley (1926) suggested the "unwisdom" of adjusting the elementary curriculum to the needs of the local community (pp. 31–2), arguing that there ought to be a "reasonable degree of uniformity" (p. 33) in certain crucial subjects in the elementary school curriculum. The most common charge among its detractors was that the activity program lacked rigor, and, as a result, the children of America were simply not learning what they needed to know. Bagley was critical, for example, of what he called the "freedom-theory," reminding his listeners, "I told you sixteen years ago that we could not build our democratic structure on the shifting sands of soft pedagogy," proposing instead his own motto, *"Through discipline to freedom"* (Bagley, 1929b, p. 146). Bagley, like Hall before him, consistently deplored the progressive feminization of the schools, linking it to weakness, and he looked to the day when "a more virile and less elusive educational theory" would replace the currently popular effeminate one, at the same time praising the "rugged masculinity" of Henry C. Morrison's work, especially his concept of "mastery" (Bagley, 1929a, p. 573). Although Bagley deplored the flaccidity of the activity curriculum, he also endorsed much of what social reconstructionism stood for, arguing that if a proper investment in education were made, there would flow a "significant amelioration of social ills" as well as a "diminution of corruption in public office . . . [and] a diminution of religious and racial intolerance" (Bagley, 1930, p. 224). Although almost every educational leader in the post-depression period felt impelled to pay at least lip service to the idea that education could respond to social ills, in Bagley's case the commitment to a fully realized democracy through education seemed genuine. He had, after all, been one of the very few leaders in education to see significant anti-democratic tendencies in the mental measurement movement that swept the country following World War One (Bagley, 1925). Bagley's quarrel was not so much with the political progressives who saw education as a potent instrument of social regeneration, but with the weak and effeminate project curriculum that robbed American children of their common cultural heritage.

By 1933, Bagley was joined in his criticism by a powerful ally, a young émigré from Russia, Michael John Demiashkevich who helped sharpen the attack on the child-centered school. Demiashkevich received a classical education at the Imperial Historico-Philological Archaeological Institute in Petrograd before coming to Teachers College for his doctorate which was awarded in 1926. As against a project method deriving from children's natural impulses, he proposed, much like Harris, a "directed and controlled mastery of systematic, consecutive, and continuous curricula" (Demiashkevich, 1933, p. 170). It was in Demiashkevich's book, *An Introduction to the Philosophy of Education* (1935) that the term essentialism was first used as a direct contrast to progressive education. The "first meaning of the term 'education,' " he argued, "implies systematic, that is, sequential curricula (adequately covering the subject) and definite, distinctly shaped procedures or methods of study" (p. 5). It was also Demiashkevich who along with Fred Alden Shaw, the headmaster of the Detroit Country Day school, first conceived of building a national organization around the idea of essentialism as a counterpoint to the doctrines that were issuing forth under the name of progressive education. Ultimately, however, Bagley became by far the most prominent member in the group and emerged as its acknowledged leader.

Their manifesto was issued at the annual meeting of the American Association of School Administrators in Atlantic City, New Jersey, on February 26, 1938. Almost from the outset, Bagley (1938a) sounded the theme of American education being "appallingly weak and ineffective" (p. 241), epecially when compared with the levels of achievement in other countries. The most direct attack on the new education in America appeared in Section II of the manifesto "THE CAUSES: B. EDUCATIONAL THEORIES THAT ARE ESSENTIALLY ENFEEBLING" (pp. 244–50), and it was almost exclusively against the activity curriculum that the attack was directed. The history of education, Bagley claimed, could be summed up by pairs of opposites: freedom versus discipline, interest versus effort, individual versus society, play versus work, and in more recent times, immediate needs versus remote goals and psychological organization versus subject organization. (There were dualisms, of course, that Dewey spent a lifetime trying to dispel.) Under the press of mass education, Bagley argued, there was a "loosening of standards . . . [and] the theories which emphasized interest, freedom, immediate needs, personal experience, psychological organization, and pupil initiative . . . naturally made a powerful appeal" (p. 245). Rigorous attention to academic achievement was abandoned, systematic and organized learning was discredited, and the activity movement came into vogue.

Bagley claimed that many of the subjects that required the most exacting study had been virtually abandoned because of the decline of mental discipline under the influence of the psychological experiments such as those conducted by Thorndike and Woodworth (1901) where the evidence, he claimed, was generalized more than the experiments warranted. A concomitant of the discrediting of mathematics and other exacting studies was the rise of social studies, "the primrose path of least resistance," essentially nothing but "an educational pablum" (Bagley, 1938a, p. 248). It was unfortunate, according to Bagley, that all this should be happening when the situation at home and abroad was so critical. The ideals of democracy, he declared, "are among the first essentials in the platform of the Essentialist" (p. 250). With democracy on trial, however, it became all the more important that in relation to totalitarian states there is developed "a democratic discipline that will give strength and solidarity to the democratic purpose and ideal" (p. 251). "An effective democracy," he insisted, "demands a community of culture" (p. 252), emphasizing that for democracy to survive, it was necessary that a common core be developed in the curriculum that would help create that community. He was bemused by the fact, for example, that in 1933 he found more than 30,000 courses of study in the Teachers College curriculum library. To Bagley, the elements of this common culture and therefore the essentials in the curriculum were really self-evident: reading, arithmetic, "at least a speaking acquaintance with man's past," art, "health instruction and the inculcation of health practices," along with basic instruction in the natural sciences (p. 253). He concluded by sounding one of his favorite themes – that American educational enterprise needed a theory that was "strong, virile, and positive not feeble, effeminate, and vague," declaring that the theories that had dominated American education had been "distinctly of the latter type" (p. 256).

The Essentialist Committee for the Advancement of American Education was from the beginning an isolated group, and, apart from Bagley himself, Demiashkevich, Isaac Kandel and one or two others, never elicited the sympathies of major figures of the educational world. Bagley's was increasingly a lonely voice. Demiashkevich, a young and extremely promising scholar, fell severely ill in April of 1938 and, unable to continue his teaching in the spring quarter at Peabody College, took his own life in August at the age of forty-seven. Bagley found some solace in his isolation. He said once that "It will not be a new experience" (Bagley, 1938b, p. 565), recalling that in his criticism of the determini-sim of the IQ tests he basically stood alone. "I had no companions then," he said; "As regards my anti-determinism, I seem now to be travelling with real quality folks". "It is better," he concluded, "to be right than re-spectable" (p. 565).

Essentialism is sometimes seen as the intellectual alterna-tive to the naive sentimentalism of the activity curriculum, but its own claims notwithstanding, it never quite asserted the primacy of the intellect that the early humanists made their linchpin. More often than not, essentialism took the form of insisting that there are certain things that future citizens need to know and these elements ought to be the heart of the curriculum. One defender of essentialism, for example, argued that "the true Essentialist believes that only those things that are vitally important should be taught . . ." and took the position that public money should not be spent on courses "unless they can be justified on the grounds of essentiality" (Tonne, 1941, p. 312). That position is much more consistent with social efficiency than with traditional humanism. Bagley himself implied that mass education was inconsistent with quality education. The upward expansion of education, he felt, was "not guarding itself against the most fatal pitfall of democracy," "leveling down rather than level-ing up" (Bagley, 1939a, p. 248). Unlike humanists such as Eliot, Bagley regarded this lowering of standards as inevit-able. "Rigorous requirements," he said, "simply had to be relaxed, and they have been progressively relaxed over a period now of more than thirty years" (Bagley, 1939b, p. 330). It was, Bagley claimed, almost as if educationists had actually welcomed and supported the softening of the American curriculum. But hard, "masculine," rigorous education should not be taken as synonymous with a classical liberal education or an education designed for intellectual mastery of the modern world. It can merely mean including in the curriculum the everyday things that people need to function in their society and making absolutely sure that every child masters them. There was much said by the essentialists about the importance of a common cultural heritage, but there were also easily recognizable elements of social efficiency doctrine. The 1930s was an era where previously clear-cut ideological distinctions were obfuscated, and essentialism may have been a case where the established lines between traditional humanism and social efficiency became difficult to delineate.

v

In the same year that the Essentialist Committee for the Advancement of American Education issued its platform, two short books appeared, each written by a highly respected leader in what had become known as progressive education. Both Boyd H. Bode's *Progressive Education at the Cross-roads* (1938) and John Dewey's last book on education, *Experience and Education* (1938) attempted to give definition and direction to what had become a loose collection of reform ideas beset by drift, internal dissension and external threat. Both books, although written by sympathetic critics, painted a somewhat somber picture about the current state of affairs in educational reform and sounded an ominous note about the survival of the miscellany of reforms that had become associated with progressive education.

Bode reemphasized the absence of social direction that bedeviled the Progressive Education Association since its founding. Pointing to the "grim events" (Bode, 1938, p. 4) that were occupying the world stage, he felt that, without a guiding social philosophy, the movement was facing a major crisis. In much the same manner that Dewey had taken his cue from the nature of democracy as a way of life (Dewey, 1916a), Bode insisted that, to survive, progressive education had to evolve a democratic education as a way of life, not as a sentimental concern for children. "Progressive education," he said, "must either become a challenge to all the basic beliefs and attitudes which have been dominant for so long in every important domain of human interest, or else retreat to the nursery" (p. 5). He pointed especially to the fact that a so-called progressive school has no real defining characteristics. To be sure, there might be more of an atmosphere of freedom than in a traditional school and perhaps more active participation by the children, but a progressive school was also full of contradictions that made it impossible to define precisely. There was freedom, but there was also guidance and direction. Individualism was emphasized, yet the competitive nature of contemporary society was constantly being criticized. The colleges were regarded as the "citadel of the enemy," yet the private schools that constituted an important part of the movement and "are generally the more prosperous element in society" make preparation for college their "chief business" (p. 10). Bode urged that progressive education rather than engaging in such shilly-shallying become "an avowed exponent of democracy" (p. 26), arguing that, if democracy is to prevail, it must evolve its own distinctive educational system.

In Bode's terms, the enemy was absolutism. That kind of aristocratic education he attributed to Hutchins, who, according to Bode, would base his educational system on "basic principles, which are valid at all times and in all places for every manner and condition of men" (Bode, 1938, p. 31). As against that conception, he presented the ideal of modern science where "our tests and standards are not derived from elsewhere but are constructed as we go along" (p. 35). It was out of this rejection of absolutism that Bode felt a democratic system of education could be based. Laws and truths in a democratic society are not handed over to us, but are constructed and discovered as we go along. The problem was, however, that progressivism was in danger of becoming its own absolutism, with Rousseau's doctrines being the most notable example. "Over and against the absolutes of the social order," Bode said, Rousseau "placed the alleged absolute of human nature" (p. 38). The education that had once been directed by so-called immutable truths was now being controlled by immutable laws of child development. "This," claimed Bode, "is absolutism all over again" (p. 39).

Bode's critique was a last-ditch effort to expunge what had been the child-centered origins of the Progressive Education Association, and, before that, the developmentalist notion that the curriculum ought to spring spontaneously from the interests of children. The immediate interests of children may have their place, Bode felt, but they must spring from a larger social interest and from a continuity in trying to achieve it. "To interpret the doctrine of interest as meaning that all activity must be motivated by immediate and spontaneous interest," he claimed, "is to misrepresent it" (Bode, 1938, p. 53). The answer that Bode proposed is to center an educational system not on submission to authority, but on the cultivation of intelligence. Democracy, Bode insisted, is a system that relies on intelligence, for when interests collide, they are not resolved by an appeal to some final truth but by social adjustments arrived at in relation to some common end.

Bode also reiterated his earlier skepticism (Bode, 1927) about the power of science to determine the curriculum, particularly in this case attacking the notion that a curriculum could be derived from an objective study of needs, especially what had come to be called "felt needs," as definitive expressions of the objectives of the curriculum "since a need may be a real need without being felt at all" (Bode, 1938, pp. 65–6). Bode's contention, however, was that the problem of finding the key to determining the difference between real and spurious needs was something like the problem of finding the key to the difference between good and bad desires. Bode did not object to studies of child and adolescent development, but "it is misleading to call them studies of needs, because the needs still remain to be determined after the investigation is completed" (p. 67). To try to discover needs through scientific investigation was not science, but "academic bootlegging" (p. 67). The answer to the dilemma of creating a curriculum, he argued, "will not be revealed by any educational microscope" (p. 68). Bode even claimed that the extraordinary attention that was being lavished on the "needs" of childhood and adolescence had "bred a spirit of anti-intellectualism" and "indiscriminate tirades against 'subjects' in the absurdities of pupil planning, and in the lack of continuity in the educational program" (p. 70).

Bode, one of the great exponents of what had come to be called progressive education, was thus rejecting the two ingredients most commonly associated with it. In the effort to make education a direct and supremely functional preparation for life, some reformers dreamed of a scientifically determined catalog of human activity as the basis for the curriculum. In the effort to champion the child's freedom and to bring the curriculum in line with the child's true nature, other reformers turned to the laws of child growth and development. Each approach in its own way rejected the logical organization of subject matter and attempted to substitute something more scientifically valid. But, said Bode (1938), "if we may assume that the purpose of teaching is to liberate the intelligence of the pupil, it appears that we must go into 'logical organization' and beyond it" (p. 94). He even added a dictum that did not gain currency until about a quarter of a century later: "The pupil must acquire some capacity for thinking as the specialist thinks" (p. 94). The traditional subjects, Bode continued, are something "we neglect at our own peril" (p. 96). The problem with organized subject matter is not that it is organized subject matter but that it has become trivialized. "Tinkering in a laboratory," he argued, "becomes training in the scientific attitude, just as any splotching of colors and any flubdub in written composition can pass as creative self-expression" (p. 97). If the freedom that progressives seek is ever to be achieved, Bode concluded, it is to be achieved through intelligence, not the other way around. For Bode, then, it was not the promise of a scientific curriculum or a course of study attuned to the real interests of children that constituted progressive education, but the freeing of intelligence as a way to make democracy work.

When Dewey's *Experience and Education* (1938) appeared, it was taken by many to be a repudiation of the things he had stood for since the turn of the century. Actually, however, it is more accurately described as simply a summing up of what he had been saying all along. Like Bode, Dewey was dismayed by the apparent rejection by the new education of organized subject matter. Just because "external authority is rejected, it does not follow that all authority should be rejected, but rather that there is need to search for a more effective source of authority" (p. 8). One should not assume, said Dewey, that "the knowledge and skill of the mature person has no directive value for the experience of the immature" (p. 8). One of the major problems of the "newer schools," as Dewey called them, is that they "tend to make little or nothing of organized subject-matter of study" (p. 9). What was needed was not a rejection of organized subject matter but a reconstruction of it.

Chapter VII of *Experience and Education* gave a name to the curriculum theory that Dewey had been expounding since the days of the Dewey School, Progressive Organization of Subject-Matter (Dewey, 1938, p. 86). A central principle, enunciated as early as *The Child and the Curriculum* (1902), was that the disciplines of knowledge, whatever their current lofty status, had their origins in basic human activity. "Anything which can be called a study," he said, "whether arithmetic, history, geography, or one of the natural sciences, must be derived from materials which at the outset fall within the scope of ordinary life experience" (Dewey, 1938, pp. 86-7). The problem of the traditional curriculum was that these basic origins in human experience were ignored, and hence knowledge was merely being heaped indiscriminately upon unwilling and uninterested children and youth. Dewey's concept of "occupations" was, he hoped, a way of restoring organized knowledge to its human origins. "But," he said, "finding the material for learning within experience is only the first step" (p. 87). That is the step that many of the newer schools have accomplished. But the curriculum remains meaningless without the next step. "The next step is the progressive development of what is already experienced into a fuller and richer and also more organized form, a form that gradually approximates that in which subject-matter is presented to the skilled, mature person" (p. 87). As with Bode, the direction the curriculum should be taking is one in which the learner progressively approximates the intellectual processes exhibited by the mature scholar. "It is a ground for legitimate criticism," said Dewey, "when the ongoing movement of progressive education fails to recognize that the problem of selection and organization of subject-matter for study and learning is fundamental" (pp. 95–6). Moreover, subject matter in its organized and logical form cannot simply be picked up in a cursory manner. While logically organized subject matter cannot provide the starting point of the curriculum, it must be the deliberate direction in which the curriculum must move.

The 1930s were ending in chaos as far as the curriculum and, as it turned out, the whole world, were concerned. Essentialists had mounted a highly visible but somewhat confused and feeble attack on the trend that American education had been taking since the 1890s. The Progressive Education Association was becoming moribund. Bode, one of the major stalwarts of the progressive movement, and Dewey, its living symbol, had rejected in unequivocal terms doctrines that many had assumed to be part and parcel of the new education. Curriculum revision was unquestionably in vogue, but local school districts and, in some cases, statewide systems of education were adopting curricula of uncertain pedigree and direction. Even the common front that curriculum reformers had once made against their old enemy, academic subject matter, had developed some cracks. What would be salvaged from a half century of struggle to remake the American curriculum was very much an open question.

CHAPTER 9

LIFE ADJUSTMENT EDUCATION AND THE END OF AN ERA

i

When the United States officially became an active belligerent in World War Two on December 8, 1941, it was obviously an important event in world history, but the course that the American curriculum had been taking over the previous half century was not so much significantly altered as accelerated. Leaders in education insisted, of course, that American schools would not stand idly by in a time of crisis. Although United States soil was not the site of active battle nor was the country the victim of massive bombardment, American schools would play their part on the home front. When the Conference on War Problems and Responsibilities of Illinois Schools and Teacher Colleges was held on December 17, 1941, on the University of Illinois campus, a comprehensive outline of the schools' role in the war ahead was outlined. First there was their part in "helping to create and maintain a democratic moral" (Smith, 1942, p. 113). The contrast between the democratic way of life and that of our totalitarian enemies must be made clear. Youth must participate in scrap metal and paper collection drives, Red Cross work, and receive training in first aid. Schools must also do what they can to counteract wartime propaganda directed against people of German, Italian and Japanese descent, and the contributions of different racial and cultural groups should be emphasized. Additionally, in times of shortages, consumer education must be strengthened. Vocational training and the subject matter of such courses as physics and mathematics should be reoriented so as to place "greater stress upon aeromechanics, aeronautics, auto mechanics, navigation, gunnery, and other aspects of modern warfare" (p. 115). Subjects like biology and home economics should be redirected toward training in nursing and first aid. With the noble exception of undertaking to preach tolerance toward the descendants of the enemies of the United States, these are the kinds of measures that one might expect schools to take as a country entered into a major war. Later publications recommended similar efforts (Educational Policies Commission, 1943; National Education Association, 1943).

The course that the curriculum took was generally in the direction of those recommendations. Aviation and navigation were given special attention in the context of several subjects, and social studies emphasized war aims. Industrial arts courses were revised to take into account armament needs. Consumer economics and home management also received increased attention in order to assist the citizenry to live under wartime conditions. Some teachers whose subjects were seen as not contributing to the war effort were shifted to teaching subjects of more immediately practical value. One source of pride to educators was that whereas only 20 percent of the armed forces in World War One had completed an eighth-grade education, that figure was close to 70 percent in World War Two.

As the hostilities wore on, more and more attention was given not so much to the school's contribution to the war effort, but to what changes ought to be wrought in the postwar system of American schooling. In wartime, when criticism of the American social structure, such as that advanced by the social reconstructionists, could be construed as unpatriotic, and with child-centered education increasingly being attacked on all sides as lacking in social commitment, it was once more social efficiency that moved to center stage. It was, after all, the curriculum doctrine that promised the most directly functional return for schooling, and with the country

fighting a war for democracy, the reordering of the curriculum to accommodate the mass of students was equated with
the democratization of the curriculum. As the trend toward
the mixing of curriculum ideas persisted, however, social
efficiency became increasingly more difficult to recognize in
its once pure form. In a period when curriculum concoctions
were being brewed on every side, it was life adjustment
education that emerged in the mid-1940s as the sauce that
captured the attention of the professional education community.

There is no question, however, that social efficiency was its
most potent ingredient. The origins of social efficiency as a
curriculum ideal go back, of course, to the period shortly after
the turn of the century when such leaders as David Snedden,
Charles C. Peters and Ross Finney began to articulate its
major premises, but its powerful reemergence in the 1940s
had more immediate antecedents. Probably the most significant by-product of the war insofar as school leaders were
concerned was the steep decline in high school enrollments.
From a high of 6.7 million in 1940–41, enrollments fell to 5.5
million in 1943–4. Some of this may have been due to a
declining birth rate during the depression, but early enlist-
ments in the military service and the lure of lucrative work in
defense industries were probably also contributing factors.
Once more the holding power of the high school arose as a
signficant issue, and, inevitably, this led to calls for a complete reordering of the high school studies in the direction of a
much more functional and work-oriented curriculum.

One portent was a report of a Special Committee on the
Secondary School Curriculum prepared for the American
Youth Commission in 1940, *What the High Schools Ought to
Teach*. The superintendent of schools of Pittsburgh, Pennsyl-
vania, Ben G. Graham, headed the special committee that
included three Teachers College professors, Thomas Briggs
in secondary education and Will French and George D.
Strayer in educational administration, but also including
Charles A. Prosser, the key figure in the promotion of the
Smith–Hughes Act twenty-three years earlier, and Ralph W.

Tyler, now Chairman of the Department of Education of the University of Chicago. *What the High Schools Ought to Teach* began with an historical account of the growth of American schools tracing the appearance of useful subjects in what had been a system patterned after the elite schools of Europe. The committee touched on the Douglas Commission Report (1906) and how it led to the establishment of trade schools in Massachusetts and finally to the creation by Congress of the Board for Vocational Education in 1917. This, they acknowledged, was an important advance, but vocational education tended "to cultivate highly specialized skills" and much of it "fails to meet the needs of pupils because it is quite as specialized as were the traditional preprofessional courses" (p. 10). (Academic subjects in this sense were considered vocational; they were vocational preparation for the professions.) It was also unfortunate in the eyes of the committee that so much of vocational education consisted actually in the "preparation for so-called 'white collar' jobs" because, given the state of the economy as they saw it, many "are sure to be disappointed" (p. 10). While the "preprofessional" courses were appropriate to one small segment of the school population and the vocational courses to another, the majority of students were left with a curriculum that was inappropriate "in preparing young people to take their place in adult society" (p. 10). The answer did not lie in adding a new course here and another there; "the complete curriculum must be described as inappropriate because of its emphasis on items that do not accord with the ability or the outlook on the future of the majority of pupils" (p. 11).

There was, almost inevitably, a recommendation that reading instruction be improved, but the most persistent theme in the report was the emphasis on the schools' role in the world of work. "Labor is the lot of man," the report announced, "and it has not been recognized as it should have been in arranging an educational institution" (American Council on Education, 1944, p. 15). Reading, by contrast, is easy to institutionalize. It can be taught to a class. "Productive manual work," on the other hand, cannot easily be carried forward in the classroom, and this has led American schools to neglect one of the major features of life. "Manual work," the report noted in sorrow, "is now no longer a part of the education of a great number of people" (p. 16). The strong emphasis on work, particularly manual labor, may have been prompted by certain of President Franklin D. Roosevelt's New Deal programs in the 1930s, such as the National Youth Administration and the Civilian Conservation Corps, programs which were designed to provide useful employment to youth in a period of economic crisis. These federal initiatives in the training of youth, once the exclusive domain of the schools, were a source of concern at least to some educational leaders, and federal intervention into what were once state or local prerogatives haunted many school officials (Krug, 1972). The report made specific mention of these federal work projects implying that the schools could perform the functions of these federal agencies. While vocational education had long been advocated and even accepted as a function of schooling, the role of the school in the development of worthwhile work habits as well as occupational skills had rarely been given such an overriding emphasis. Criticisms were also presented of what were called the "conventional subjects" (p. 27), but preparation for one's adult occupational role, professional, clerical or manual, was the central theme throughout the report.

The report singled out for the particular censure the "vicious aspects of the ninth grade" where an array of courses of no appeal are presented to adolescents most of whom are not "academically-minded" (p. 31). "The ninth grade," the committee announced in no uncertain terms, "puts an end to all general studies" (p. 31). With appropriate "exploratory" studies in the junior high school years, ninth-graders should be ready for more specific training. The report concluded with the general recommendation that schools take the same interest in their products that a good manufacturing company does in its "output" (p. 32). To do this, the schools needed to know "in perfectly explicit terms what a young person is capable of doing" and then be prepared to see to it that those potentialities are realized. Throughout the report the implications were clear that, insofar as the high school curriculum was concerned, the academic subjects were appropriate only for a narrow segment of the school population. That position *vis-à-vis* the conventional high school curriculum was not only one of the defining characteristics of life adjustment education once it became a full-blown movement but the source of the vehement charges of anti-intellectualism that were to be levelled against it.

In 1944 and 1945, two more major reports were issued attempting to delineate the future course of education in the United States – reports that pointed in quite different directions. The first of these was issued by the Educational Policies Commission, a standing body of the National Education Association, formed in 1935 to serve as a kind of unofficial school board for the nation. The Commission periodically issued pronouncements on the state of American education, making recommendations on what they considered matters of import. Of these reports, *Education for ALL American Youth* (1944) dealt most directly with the curriculum. In a rambling and rather far-fetched attempt at literary novelty, the Commission contrasted "THE HISTORY THAT SHOULD NOT HAPPEN" (p. 2) with two utopian conceptions of American education in postwar America, one a rural school system called Farmville and one urban, called American City. In the history that should not happen, the frightening picture of a National Bureau of Youth Service was conjured up as an outgrowth of federal experiments with youth programs in the decade preceding. By 1954, there would even be nationally prescribed courses in secondary schools, junior colleges and adult classes (p. 9). These drastic actions, according to the fictitious history, were made necessary by the shortsightedness of educators in meeting the common and individual needs of the youth of the nation. In the end, the few remaining local high schools had no recourse but to return "to their original function of preparing a selected minority of our youth for strictly cultural pursuits" (p. 9). The nightmare of federal control of the educational system presumably could be avoided if the schools could demonstrate their capacity to realign the curriculum along immediately functional lines.

In the ideal postwar school, the needs of youth would be met beginning, of course, by vocational preparation. In the tenth grade, only one-sixth of the typical student's program would be vocational, but in the eleventh and twelfth grades that would reach one-third. The common core of subjects would be designed "to help students grow in competence as citizens of the community and the nation; in understanding of economic processes and of their roles as producers and consumers; in cooperative living in family, school, and community; in appreciation of literature and the arts; and in use of the English language" (Educational Policies Commission, 1944, p. 244). But beyond these common learnings there would be particular attention paid to the diversity that exists within the school population with "the curriculum of Grades X through XIV . . . differentiated to suit the needs of individuals" (p. 36). The Commission listed ten Imperative Educational Needs of Youth, the first of which was the need "to develop salable skills" (pp. 225–6), with the abilities of each student dictating a differentiated course of study in relation to those needs. As in the case of *What the High Schools Ought to Teach* (American Council on Education, 1940), *Education for ALL American Youth* perceived academic subject matter as surviving in the high school curriculum mainly to serve the needs of the chosen few.

As would be expected, the Harvard faculty committee that produced *General Education in a Free Society* in 1945 (popularly known as the Redbook) was far more generous to academic subject matter. They did go out of their way, however, to strike a tone of moderation. American society, they admitted, had indeed changed since the late nineteenth century as had the nature of the secondary school population, leading them finally to endorse a differentiated curriculum. But even for those with "lower facility with ideas," the committee recommended a general education that included "the world, man's social life, the realm of imagination and ideal" (Harvard University, p. 95). Careful not to exclude the now ubiquitous concern with the school's role in developing occupational skills, they tried to balance that function with the school's role in general education. "The aim of education," the committee declared, "should be to prepare an individual to become an expert both in some particular vocation or art and in the general art of the free man and the citizen" (p. 54). The special education part of the curriculum would address itself to the former task and the general education part to the latter. And clearly their sympathies lay with the general education segment of the curriculum. The core of that curriculum they recommended was expressed in terms of year-long course-units: "three in English, three in science and mathematics, and two in the social studies" constituting half of the high school curriculum, a fraction they considered to be the "barest minimum" (p. 100). Although the Harvard committee report was a far cry from the report of Harvard's former illustrious president Charles W. Eliot (National Education Association, 1893) in terms of its academic recommendations, it did represent a cautious, almost timid, reemergence of the traditional humanist ideal.

Bagley (1945) thought the Harvard report was "one of the most important educational documents of recent years" (p. 69) and interpreted it as a repudiation of Eliot's elective system, citing Eliot as "the pioneer advocate in the higher institutions of what are now known as the 'Progressive' educational theories" (p. 70). Clearly, Bagley thought that the Harvard committee was on the side of the angels. Bobbitt, on the other hand, was appalled. Recognizing the distinction that the report had made between general and special education, he argued that "placing the strong emphasis on the training of specialists has not been a mistake. Quite the reverse, except for literacy, it is the finest thing that educational institutions have yet done" (Bobbitt, 1946, p. 327). But he was clearly dissatisfied with the way the Harvard faculty had defined general education. The general portion of the curriculum, he argued, is composed of very specific skills in all "ten areas that make up the layman's daily living" (p. 327).

These ten areas "call for as many different series of specific competencies" (p. 328). General education was quite as specific as specialized education. Rather than defining general education in terms of a set of subjects, as the Harvard Committee had done, he felt the ten areas of living that he had identified ought to be scientifically investigated in order to determine their precise components and what was necessary in order to perform them efficiently. Generally, he saw the Harvard Report as being built on obviously outmoded academic foundations "that have been patently and conclusively proved unsound" (p. 332). What was needed for American education was a curriculum guided "not by medieval misconceptions, but by *educational* science" (p. 332). Bobbitt, now a senior statesman in the curriculum world, was obviously concerned about the possible reintroduction of academic requirements in what ought to be supremely functional curriculum not just in the specialized segment of the curriculum, but in general education as well. For the immediate future, the world of curriculum was not moving in that direction.

ii

Life adjustment education actually has a semi-official birthday, June 1, 1945. The gestation period began in January of 1944 when the United States Office of Education commissioned a study called *Vocational Education in the Years Ahead*. Even with over 150 working on the project the report took about a year and a half to complete. Finally, the results of the study were presented at a conference in Washington, D.C. on May 31 and June 1, 1945. There was agreement that the youth of the nation were not being adequately served by the high school, but the direction that reform should take was not exactly clear. Finally, the participants turned to Charles A. Prosser, Director of the Dunwoody Institute of Minneapolis, Minnesota, and veteran of the battle over the Smith–Hughes legislation, to summarize the proceedings.

Responding to the challenge, Prosser delivered what has come to be known as the Prosser Resolution, the opening salvo in the campaign for what became life-adjustment education:

> It is the belief of this conference that, with the aid of this report in final form, the vocational school of a community will be able better to prepare 20 percent of its youth of secondary school age for entrance upon desirable skilled occupations; and that the high school will continue to prepare 20 percent of its students for entrance to college. We do not believe that the remaining 60 percent of our youth of secondary school age will receive the life adjustment training they need and to which they are entitled as American citizens – unless and until the administrators of public education with the assistance of the vocational education leaders formulate a comparable program for this group.
>
> We, therefore, request the U.S. Commissioner of Education and the Assistant Commissioner for Vocational Education to call at some early date a conference or a series of regional conferences between an equal number of representatives of general and of vocational education – to consider this problem and to take such initial steps as may be found advisable for its solution. (United States Office of Education, 1951, p. 29)

Without dissent, the Consulting Committee of the conference adopted the resolution. What is more, the idea of life adjustment education received the enthusiastic endorsement of the United States Office of Education and its official organ, *School Life*.

According to plan, the series of regional conferences seeking to implement the resolutions began in New York City on April 11th and 12th of 1946 (Broder, 1977, p. 12). The ever-present Prosser, a forceful and dynamic advocate, declared that:

> social and economic facts point to the failure of our total educational system to meet the real need of an efficient life adjustment training for America's young people. The vocational educational forces of the country have a potential service to the high schools of the Nation involved in the adjustment of these youth. The . . . sad tales of the social and economic

maladjustment of millions of America's citizens is evidence
enough of the failure of the education forces to render the service
they should. They also indicate unmistakably a failure on the part
of the general high school itself. Thus the tale constitutes a
general indictment of both services. All the evidence shows that
both of us are just poor sinners. (p. 13)

In the four regional conferences that followed the one in New
York City, Prosser preached essentially the same message.
The traditional humanist curriculum in secondary education
had failed the 60 percent that he had identified in his original
resolution. What was needed was a curriculum attuned to the
actual life functions of youth as a preparation for adulthood.
Actually, in time, the original percentages that Prosser had
enunciated (20 percent college-entrance, 20 percent vocational, 60 percent life adjustment) had become something of
an embarrassment since they implied that the curriculum had
to be reorganized for only a majority of the school population. Life adjustment education, in line with its most immediate ancestor, social efficiency education, had to be applied to
the total school curriculum.

Almost from the outset, life adjustment education faced a
problem of definition. Although support from most of the
professional educational community was enthusiastic from
the beginning, there was some question as to what it actually
implied. Kandel (1947) felt with some justification that "It
implies that all the contingencies which human beings are
likely to encounter in their lives must be anticipated and
education must be adjusted to them. Among these contingencies are dating, marriage, mating, rearing of children, work
experience, vocations, and all the social issues which make up
the day's headlines in the newspapers" (p. 372). Harl R.
Douglass, one of life adjustment's stalwart supporters,
associated life adjustment education with education in a
democracy, arguing that the 40 percent dropout rate across
the country indicated that American schools were failing to
serve a significant proportion of the school population. He
rejected what he regarded as the unsound theories that
preceded life adjustment, the "decorative" theory, the "dis-

ciplinary" theory and the "college preparation" theory as inappropriate to a democratic social order (Douglass, 1949, pp. 110–11). Like Bobbitt in his criticism of the Harvard Report, Douglass identified general education not with a core of basic disciplines, but with adequate preparation for various categories of life activities. "Reduced to its simplest terms," he said, life adjustment education "stands for *an adequate program of secondary education for fairly complete prepara- tion for all the areas of living in which life adjustment must be made, particularly home living, vocational life, civic life, leisure life, and physical and mental health*" (p. 114). In line with the definitions of life adjustment education advanced both by its detractors and its proponents, the guide to its implementation produced by the Illinois Secondary School Curriculum Program proceeded from a compilation of the needs of youth: "Tools of communication; Strong body, sound attitude toward it; Satisfactory Social Relationships; Competence in and appreciation of improved family living; Knowledge of, practice in, and zeal for democratic processes; Sensitiveness to importance of group action; Effectiveness as consumers; Adjustment to occupation; and Development of meaning for life" (Houston, Sanford and Trump, 1948, p. 23). These, rather than mathematics, history, English, science and so on, constituted the general education of youth, a position that bore some obvious indebtedness to the *Cardinal Principles of Secondary Education* (National Education Association, 1918). In its early years of existence, life adjust- ment education enjoyed unprecedented political support. United States Commissioner of Education, John W. Studebaker, was an enthusiastic advocate and quickly helped set in motion the two national conferences on life adjustment designed to spread its message.

The first Life Adjustment Conference was held in 1947 with Benjamin Willis, the superintendent of schools of Yonk- ers, New York, acting as chairman. Although no new drama- tic pronouncements were issued, the conference served to maintain the momentum initiated by the Prosser Resolution. It did, for example, recommend that "there be established a

National Commission on Life Adjustment Education for Youth" with members of various national education organizations serving as members (Basler, 1947, p. 6). Prosser, with his usual sense for high drama, concluded the meeting with a call to arms:

> Never was there such a meeting where people were so sincere in their belief that this was the golden opportunity to do something that would give to all American youth their education heritage so long denied. What you have planned is worth fighting for – it is worth dying for. (United States Office of Education, 1948, p. 20)

Enthusiasm for the program was so strong that Studebaker's successor, Commissioner of Education, Earl James McGrath, was moved to remark: "Terms such as 'flapdoodle' have been ruinous to certain educational projects, but I am confident that no incident of name calling can similarly endanger Life Adjustment Education. It is too well established in the public confidence" ("Life Adjustment," 1949, p. 40). By the time the Second National Commission met in 1951, however, some of the original zeal was lacking and much of the proceeding became bogged down in discussions of monetary problems (Broder, 1977).

One unfailing bastion of support was the National Association of Secondary-School Principals. Over the course of the twentieth century, the self-perception of school administrators had been evolving from that of educators to hard-headed business managers (Callahan, 1962), and an education attuned to the real business of life as opposed to the remote values of the academic curriculum must have had an enormous appeal. Besides, the threat of federal intrusion into the world of schools remained a source of concern, and the answer seemed to lie in demonstrating that school administrators were ready to transform secondary schools into a potent force in American social and economic life, not simply as preparatory institutions for the colleges. The Association sponsored several "discussion groups" on life adjustment education, and their *Bulletin* frequently ran articles extolling

its virtues. At one of the discussion groups, the Superintendent of Public Instruction of the State of Illinois identified life
adjustment education with the schools' concern for "real-life
problems." Accordingly, he could enunciate a test for
schools: "If the products of our schools turn out to be healthy
and patriotic citizens who are good husbands, good wives,
good fathers, good mothers, good neighbors, good workers,
good employers, wise spenders of income, wholesome users
of leisure time and so forth, we know that our schools are
good" (Nickell, 1949, p. 154).

One major feature of life adjustment education was its
emphasis on the indefinite expansion of the scope of the
curriculum. That position was echoed at the meeting of the
Association a year later. One speaker from the State Department of Education in Connecticut also emphasized the theme
of "real problems" and presented a similar conception of
what the real problems were: "preparation for post-
secondary education, preparation for work, doing an effective day's work in school, getting along well with other boys
and girls, understanding parents, driving a motor car, using
the English language, engaging in recreational activities, and
so on are representative areas encompassing real problems
faced by youth" (Collier, 1950, p. 125). It was this attention to
"real life" problems that was of such attraction to school
administrators, particularly the promise that a curriculum
drawn along those lines would have a dramatic effect on
reducing the drop-out rate.

Catholic educators were included in many of the regional
life adjustment conferences, and the impact of the new
movement was beginning to be felt in that quarter as well.
One Catholic educator saw in life adjustment education the
opportunity to stem "a steady and disastrous lowering of
purely academic standards which has made a joke of college
education" (Townsend, 1948, p. 363). He interpreted the
Prosser resolution as proposing to create "a vast network of
terminal high schools" (p. 364). Since few Catholic high
schools could justify their "prep school" status, he thought,
the obvious implication was that a similar pattern should be

followed in Catholic education. The Superintendent of Schools of the Archdiocese of Milwaukee was particularly sympathetic to the idea of preparation for living rather than simply a classical education. He felt that through "life situations we effect an intimate relationship between the curriculum and life experiences, between principles of Christian living and the 'profane' materials embodied in the curriculum" (Goebel, 1948, p. 377). Sister Mary Janet, one of life adjustment education's most vigorous supporters, saw in the movement a positive concern for "home and family living" and a much healthier attitude toward shop courses and vocational education (Sister Mary Janet, 1952, p. 344). In general, the rhetoric of life adjustment education was infused with a seemingly genuine concern for the mass of students not being served by contemporary secondary education, and this gave it a humanitarian appeal that reached into a variety of different quarters.

iii

Although life adjustment was receiving unprecedented support in professional educational journals and among highly placed school officials, it is difficult to establish the extent to which the "areas of living" curriculum which it was promoting was actually replacing the traditional curriculum built around subjects. As early as December of 1947, *Time* reported that schools in thirty-five of the forty-eight states were trying to implement at least some aspects of life adjustment education ("Get Adjusted," 1947, p. 64), but it would be easy to imagine reluctance on the part of the various state departments of education to report no initiatives in the direction of such a widely popular reform. On the same day that the *Time* article appeared, *Newsweek* made note of the alarming dropout rate in many areas of the country (Passaic, New Jersey, 45 percent; New York, 42 percent; Minneapolis, Minnesota, 31 percent) and commented favorably on the attempts by the United States Office of Education to implement the Prosser

Resolution as a response. *Newsweek* reported Commissioner Studebaker as feeling that "old standbys like Milton's 'Il Penseroso' and George Eliot's 'Silas Marner' would probably disappear from the schools" ("High School Overhaul," 1947, p. 86) as a result of the reforms.

Of the actual attempts to put life adjustment education into action, the two most prominent were the Illinois Secondary School Curriculum Program and Battle Creek High School of Battle Creek, Michigan (Broder, 1977). Illinois was clearly the hotbed of life adjustment education, enjoying not only the strong support of State Superintendent of Public Instruction Vernon L. Nickell, but some of the most prominent faculty in the College of Education at the University of Illinois such as Harold Hand and Charles W. Sanford. In line with the pattern set in Denver by Newlon and the support given to it by the Association for Supervision and Curriculum Development, teacher participation in curriculum development was central to the Illinois program. The program in Canton High School was built around a core of common learnings that included personality, etiquette, family living and vocations (p. 184). A high school in Peoria developed a program for high ability seniors including a course in "senior problems" (p. 185). Other life adjustment programs were developed in Crystal Lake, Decatur and Gillespie high schools.

A model of its kind was the life adjustment curriculum developed in Battle Creek, Michigan, organized around the central theme of "Basic Living" ("Cooperative Research," 1950, p. 408). Arising out of a 1944 study of dropouts, the program developed links with the Horace Mann–Lincoln Institute of Teachers College and with faculty there such as Hubert Evans, Stephen M. Corey and Arthur Jersild. In line with the now widely accepted idea that the teachers themselves should participate in curriculum planning, teachers were organized into committees dealing with various aspects of the Basic Living theme. The Health Committee, for example, investigated health hazards in the school such as "no soap" and "dirty erasers" (p. 413). Further investigation revealed that tenth graders were dropping out of school in disproportionate numbers and were responsible for most discipline problems. In response, the Health Committee organized a year-long course around units such as "the food we eat" and "understanding ourselves and getting along with others" (p. 416). The heart of the Basic Living curriculum was described as "the problem-centered group" (p. 438). The problems investigated were so-called personal-social problems such as "Basic Urges, Wants and Needs, and Making Friends and Keeping Them" (p. 443). As in the case of other life adjustment programs, the Basic Living curriculum developed at Battle Creek was considered to be the new general education. The intent, of course, was to dispense with the traditional subjects of study that the Harvard Committee had defined as general education and replace them with areas of living that were directly relevant to the needs of youth.

The extent to which the principles of life adjustment education that were enunciated at regional and national conferences as well as in a growing body of professional literature on the subject depended to a large degree on the commitment and energy of local school officials. Even what passed for life adjustment education varied considerably from the model established in Battle Creek. In Billings High School in Billings, Montana, for example, four years of English, one in American history, a half year of civics and one half year of another social science were retained as minimum requirements (*Life Adjustment Curriculum*, 1949, p. 2). Students were also expected to contribute, however, to the good of the community, and this was monitored through a system of "activity points" (pp. 3–12), with each student expected to amass at least 200. Losses of points were inflicted for antisocial behavior including violation of school regulations. Earning points in some areas such as "School and Life Planning" and "Growth Toward Maturity" (p. 5) were required, while other, such as "Learning to Work" (pp. 6–7), "Boy–Girl Relationships" (p. 10), and "Preparation for Marriage" (p. 10) were elective. Two to ten points could be earned by "participation in initiation of sophomores" (p. 11). An alternative to the life adjustment curriculum called "The Scholarship Plan for Graduation" was available, but stringent requirements such as 97 percent attendance were instituted. A severe warning was attached to the page in the student handbook describing the Scholarship Plan:

> The Scholarship Plan on the third cover page is a misnomer. It is better named a plan for recalcitrants. This is merely a protective device. Students and parents who have not accepted the Life Adjustment plan may graduate under the conditions of our old plan with the more stringent requirements to offset failure to do the work, develop the habits, and improve the attitudes inherent in the present program. Our reasoning is as follows: If students and their parents believe that the only value of the high school is in learning subject matter then the school will insist that they do more than a minimum standard. Our counseling is definitely pointed to Life Adjustment method of graduation for all students. (n.p.)

Clearly, the percentages that Prosser had orginally stated in his resolution were gradually being ignored.

Again and again, proponents of life adjustment education expressed their concern for the high dropout rate in particular and for the alienation of youth from school in general. The clear source of the problem as they saw it was a curriculum rooted in a discredited ideal of scholarship remote from the vast majority of the school population. This was a theme that had been heard at least since the Douglas Commission Report (Massachusetts 1906), but by the early 1950s it was no longer an isolated concern; it had become conventional wisdom in the educational world. In earlier periods, the problem had been addressed by providing special programs such as vocational education for those few not suited to the delights of scholarly endeavor, but as the momentum for change accelerated, the segment of the school population not inclined to such pursuits seemed to grow ever greater and greater. In fact, the group for whom the conventional curriculum was deemed appropriate had grown to such insignificant proportions that it constituted a kind of "college-preparatory" aberration within the schools. If there was a single defining characteristic in the morass of what passed for life adjustment education, it was the desire to transform general education from subjects representing common elements of the cultural heritage, as Harris had advocated before the turn of the century, to functional areas of living. In general, however, subjects proved to be more resilient than had been thought, and areas of living were more likely to be incorporated within existing subjects rather than replace them, although admittedly, *Silas Marner* and How to Make Friends and Keep Them must have seemed like strange bedfellows.

iv

Life adjustment education turned out to be the prod that awoke a slumbering giant. For about a half a century, ever since the major figures of traditional humanism like Charles W. Eliot and William Torrey Harris had retired from the scene, leaders in the academic world had given only sporadic attention to what was being taught in elementary and secondary schools. Hutchins was perhaps the most notable exception but his seemingly elitist proposals and his association with a rather far-fetched great books program attracted only a small coterie of followers. Jacques Maritain (1943) proposed similar platforms but, like Hutchins, his following was restricted on the whole to the elite of higher education institutions. As the proponents of life adjustment education increasingly promoted programs like Basic Living, not merely as an addendum to the traditional curriculum, but as a substitute for it, however, the wrath of academicians was aroused. After a period of neglect almost amounting to disdain, an intense interest began to develop among leading scholars in a variety of disciplines as to the state of the curriculum in the lower schools.

Some of the attacks on the state of schooling in America at mid-century were concentrated on Satan and alleged political radicalism in the public schools, and these campaigns achieved some success. Willard Goslin, for example, the superintendent of schools in Pasadena, California, was induced to resign his position by pressure groups inspired by Allen A. Zoll's National Council for American Education (Hulburd, 1951). Beleaguered educators sometimes failed to distinguish, however, that another sort of challenge was rapidly emerging as the more potent of the two. It was a frontal attack on the intellectual respectability of what passed for public education in America. Two books published in 1949 were portents of the floodtide of criticism to follow. Bernard Iddings Bell's *Crisis in Education* (1949) dwelt on the theme of godlessness and ethical relativism in the schools, but Mortimer Smith's *And Madly Teach* (1949) raised the issue of an anti-intellectual strain in the leadership of American education. He questioned the sheer scope of what was being included in the curriculum, ranging down to the most trivial, and argued that modern educators were unduly pessimistic about the ability of American youth to grapple with the higher reaches of scholarship.

But the most vitriolic of the criticisms were yet to follow. Harry J. Fuller, a professor of botany at the University of Illinois and retiring president of the local chapter of Phi Beta Kappa, delivered, at their annual banquet, a scathing attack on not just the state of education in America but on professors of education. Alluding to "the foe and his tactics," Fuller (1951) sounded four basic themes:

I. The falsity of the basic assumptions from which education professors commonly proceed in their anti-intellectual activities
II. The deterioration in the contemporary training of students, particularly in the high schools
III. The substitution of "societally significant" subjects for sound education in the humanities, the arts, and the sciences
IV. The confusions and inconsistencies that dominate the thinking (perhaps my use of this word is inexcusably charitable), the utterances, and the activities of many education professors. (p. 33)

Fuller cited some recent statements by "the foe" and then pronounced them to be "rubbish . . . consistent and colossal rubbish" (p. 34). That Fuller should sprinkle his address with anecdotes about deterioration in the use of English or high school graduates "who could not name the lake against which Chicago nestles" (p. 36) should not have been surprising. What was most striking was the sheer ferocity that his address exuded. Apparently, however, such resentment had been seething just below the surface in the academic world. *Scientific Monthly*, the journal that published the address, received 248 responses to Fuller's article, 226 of them favorable.

Almost without warning, the decade of the 1950s became a period of criticism of American education unequaled in modern times. Although some of the criticism was an offshoot of the infamous campaign of Senator Joseph McCarthy of Wisconsin to root out communists and subversives from a wide range of influential positions, the enduring assault was made by academics speaking from their platforms on university campuses. Probably the most persistent and effective of these critics was Arthur E. Bestor, Jr, a professor of history at the University of Illinois. Like Fuller, Bestor saw professors of education as largely responsible for the mess, but his most pervasive theme was that schools had been diverted from their central function, the development of the intellect. Bestor ridiculed the ten Imperative Educational Needs of Youth that had been included in *Education for ALL American Youth* and then became semi-official dogma in the National Association of Secondary-School Principals. He objected to the "vague inclusiveness" of any statement that attempts to define education in terms of the needs of youth. "It is *not* the job of the school," he insisted, "to meet the common and the specific individual needs of youth" (Bestor, 1952, p. 415). Instead he argued that the school is a particular kind of institution with a distinctive function to perform. It is not, as many professional educators claimed, the heir to functions that are not performed successfully by other social institutions. "Much of the cant about education for 'home and family living,' " he argued, "is a disguised way of saying that the school must take responsibility for things that the family today is supposedly failing to do" (p. 416). What was missing from statements by the supporters to life adjustment education was the central role of the school in intellectual training even for the "masses." Citing the 60 percent figure in the Prosser Resolution, Bestor interpreted it to be blatantly anti-democratic in that it assumed that a majority of people "are incapable of being benefited by intellectual training" (Bestor, 1953a, p. 12). Reminiscent of Eliot's (1905) defense of the Committee of Ten report, Bestor argued that such a division of the school population "enthrones once again the ancient doctrine that the majority of people are destined from birth to be hewers of wood and drawers of water to a select few who, by right of superior fitness, are to occupy the privileged places in society" (pp. 12–13). A first-rate polemicist, Bestor was reaching an ever larger portion of the intellectual community and even attracting some attention in the mass media.

Bestor capped his attacks in periodicals with a book, *Educational Wastelands* (1953), that set forth the striking contrast between his own ideal of education and that of the proponents of life adjustment education. Bestor was reluctant to associate life adjustment education with progressive education because progressive education was such a "vague and ambiguous" term that it tended to be applied to such a wide variety of programs toward many of which he felt "hearty sympathy" (p. 44). "I consider myself fortunate," he said, "to have received my high school training, from 1922 to 1926, in one of the most progressive schools in the country, the Lincoln School of Teachers College, Columbia University" (p. 45). Bestor seemed to realize what other critics did not – that life adjustment education was not a descendant of reforms that Dewey had advocated. In fact, he quoted a lengthy passage from Dewey's *Experience and Education* (1938) as illustrative of "the points I have been making" (Bestor, p. 51). As a student of the life adjustment literature, he was able to provide prime examples of the anti-intellectualism he perceived in the movement. Perhaps his favorite example, cited on several occasions, was from an article that had appeared in the *Bulletin* of the National Association of Secondary-School Principals:

When we come to the realization that not every child has to read, figure, write and spell . . . that many of them either cannot or will not master these chores . . . then we shall be on the road to improving the junior high curriculum.

Between this day and that a lot of selling must take place. But it's coming. We shall some day accept the thought that it is just as illogical to assume that every boy must be able to read as it is that each one must be able to perform on a violin, that it is no more reasonable to require that each girl shall spell well than it is that each one shall bake a good cherry pie.

When adults finally realize that fact, everyone will be happier . . . and schools will be nicer places in which to live. (Lauchner, 1951, p. 299)

An expert marksman like Bestor had little trouble hitting such a grossly inflated target.

Like other academic critics of American education in the 1950s, Bestor was prone to hyperbole, and his passion on the subject sometimes got in his way, but beyond that he was able to expose a serious problem that had been festering since life adjustment education and, before that, social efficiency education had captured the imagination of certain education-al reformers. In their effort to reach out to a new population of students and to attune the curriculum directly to the many activities that children and youth would need to perform as members of the society, these reformers had relegated the school's role in intellectual development to an inferior status or, in many instances, saw it as worth preserving only for a small college-going contingent.

Whether by design or default, Harold C. Hand, a professor of education at the University of Illinois, became the knight errant in the cause of life adjustment education. Early in the controversy, he and Harold W. Sanford, the associate dean of the College of Education of the University of Illinois (in collaboration with the Executive Committee of the National Association of Secondary-School Principals, the Curriculum Planning and Development Committee of that organization, the Executive Committee of the Illinois Curriculum Program and the National Commission on Life Adjustment Education for Youth), undertook a lengthy analysis of some of Bestor's initial attacks (Hand and Sanford, 1953). One response was that Bestor, while recognizing that public education had expanded, had failed to take into account significant differences in the learning ability of the new school population and, therefore his charges as to the decline in scholarly achievement over the course of the century could be attributed to that change, not to the innovations being implemented in the name of life adjustment. "The level of a pupil's innate intelligence," they insisted, "is a very real determinant of how much intellectual training he is capable of acquiring" as is "the pupil's family situation" (p. 464). Referring frequently to the report of the Harvard Committee (Harvard University, 1945) for support, Hand and Sanford interpreted their recommendations as endorsing the tripartite division of the school population that was embodied in the Prosser Resolution. Much of their argument revolved around Bestor's alleged propensity for taking quotations out of context as a way of dramatizing his charges. Bestor, for example, had used *The Schools and National Security* as one of his prime examples of life adjustment (Sanford, Hand and Spalding, 1951). In particular, he cited a reference to a proposed study of dating patterns. Hand and Sanford meticulously reviewed the entire context for this reference, arguing that it was but one of 66 suggestions for classroom practice and not necessarily indicative of the tone of the document as a whole. Hand, a dynamic, even inspiring speaker, somehow seemed overly cautious, relying on small detail to undermine the charges. Unable to mount a counterattack in sufficient force to overwhelm the enemy, life adjustment education quickly began to lose credibility first with the intellectual community and ultimately with the general public as well.

For one thing, the vision of life adjustment education was simply too grandiose. Instead of a reconstruction of the existing curriculum for general education, social efficiency reformers sought to replace it. Not satisfied with the new prominence given to vocational education or a subject realignment that gave greater attention to utilitarian outcomes, they sought to effect a victory over competing interest groups via a massive effort to substitute areas of living for the conventional subjects in the curriculum. Life adjustment education was a dramatic attempt to demonstrate the direct social value of a secondary education. That effort proved ill-timed. The sheer magnitude of the proposed changes was so great as to rouse the intellectual community into a spirited defense of academic subject matter. While there were attempts to dismiss their effort as representing the biases of the academic world as against the majority of schoolchildren, academicians stuck to their charge that intellectual development as the basic function of schooling was being undermined by the effort to install a new and supremely functional general education.

Surprisingly, the counterattack of the intellectual community reached a sympathetic public. The stature of the intellectual had been rising since the days of President Franklin D. Roosevelt's "brain trust," and, although there was some backtracking, the success of scientists in creating the atomic bomb and the context of a technological race with the Soviet Union had created a new respect for the intellectual. An "egghead" candidate, Adlai Stevenson, ran for the presidency in 1952 and 1956, and although he lost to a national hero, Dwight Eisenhower, a new admiration for intellectual prowess was emerging. This gave the critics of life adjustment education a fertile ground for denouncing the work of educational reformers who assumed that an academic curriculum was clearly unacceptable to the mass of American students. The road to prosperity, social reform, and even national security, it seemed, was tied not to adjustment to existing conditions but to intelligent action.

v

Life adjustment education was already in steep decline when on October 5, 1957, Sputnik, the world's first earth-orbiting satellite, was launched by the Soviet Union. Within a matter of days, American mass media had settled on a reason for the

Soviet technological success. Just as Prussian schools were widely believed to be the basis for the victory of the Prussians over the Austrians in the Battle of Konigratz in 1866, so, implausibly, did the Soviet technological feat become a victory of the Soviet educational system over the American. Quickly, life adjustment education was seen as the prime example of America's "soft" education in contrast to the rigorous Soviet system. While American schoolchildren were learning how to get along with their peers or how to bake a cherry pie, so the explanation went, Soviet children were being steeped in the hard sciences and mathematics needed to win the technological race that had become the centerpiece of the Cold War.

Some of the seeds for this interpretation of the Soviet success had been planted in a series of speeches delivered by Vice Admiral Hyman G. Rickover beginning around 1956 which were eventually published in book form (Rickover, 1959). Rickover, who was usually credited with the development of the atomic submarine, had acquired a reputation as an intellectual and carried considerable influence with many members of Congress. In his criticisms of American education, he consistently called attention to Soviet technological advances, emphasizing that "the greatest mistake a nation can make is to underestimate a potential enemy. Russian engineering and scientific development constitute a threat to out military power" (p. 50). As the core of this problem, he singled out the superiority of the Soviet system of education over that in the United States. As would be expected, life adjustment education was a favorite target, but he also indicted John Dewey as one whose ideas had led to an educational system gone soft. Rickover liked to compare the American curriculum not simply with that of the Soviet Union, but with European countries generally arguing that a misconceived notion of equality had led American schools to degenerate.

One of Rickover's major themes was that the gifted and talented of the country were neglected as part of the effort to increase the holding power of schools. He pointed out that 60 to 70 percent of the scientists who had been instrumental in developing the atomic bomb were foreign-born and educated (Rickover, 1959, p. 153). After making a count of Nobel prize winners in physics and chemistry through 1955, Rickover concluded that the combined "brain power" of Germany, England, France, Denmark and Italy was precisely "eleven times as rich as we" in those scientific fields (pp. 152–3). Reflecting a position that the academic critics had taken, Rickover argued that *"the school's concern is with the intellect alone"* (p. 154) and he was, like the others, a champion of the liberal arts, but his interest in developing the intellect was infused with his intense desire to outstrip the Soviet Union in scientific and technical areas. He decried "piecemeal attempts to toughen the schools," contending that these would be insufficient to "put our educational system in the forefront – at least ahead of the Russians" (p. 154). As such, there was, oddly enough, a distinct element of social efficiency thinking in Rickover's criticism. The development of the intellect was not so much a good in itself or for giving the individual a way of mastering the modern world but a direct avenue to victory in the Cold War. That, more than the standard humanist arguments, had strong popular appeal and helped convert what had been a rather limited battle between academicians and professional educators over control of the curriculum into a matter of urgent national concern.

Within a year after Sputnik, Congress reacted to the national clamor by passing the National Defense Education Act on September 2, 1958. The first paragraph in the Act made the intent clear:

> The Congress hereby finds and declares that the security of the Nation requires the fullest development of the mental resources and technical skills of its young men and women. The present emergency demands that additional and more adequate educational opportunities be made available. The defense of this Nation depends upon the mastery of modern techniques developed from complex scientific principles. (National Defense Education Act of 1958)

The main body of the act was concerned with curriculum revision in mathematics, science and foreign languages, with additional attention given to strengthening guidance services, an outgrowth of the increasing concern about identifying talented students. As in the case of the Smith–Hughes Act of 1917, Congress felt impelled to pass a specific measure designed to meet a national emergency. Unlike the Smith–Hughes Act, however, administrative control of the massive amount of money involved did not fall to professional educators. Their credibility impaired by the excesses of life adjustment education, professional educators were no longer to be given free rein in curriculum matters. Congress had clearly accepted the verdict of the academic critics that educators had foisted a soft and intellectually puerile curriculum on American schools.

Much of the money for curriculum revision was funneled through the National Science Foundation which had been established in 1950 as an agency of the executive branch of government for the support of science. Of the principal beneficiaries of Congress's largess were curriculum reform programs in science and mathematics that had been under way prior to the passage of the 1958 Act. The Physical Sciences Study Committee, for example, headed by Jerrold R. Zacharias, a professor of physics at the Massachusetts Institute of Technology, had gotten started in 1956 and subsequently received strong support in its effort to restructure the teaching of physical sciences. Over its first five years of existence, the Committee expended approximately six million dollars for that project including the production of teaching materials and another six million for the retraining of teachers in the use of those materials. The University of Illinois Committee on School Mathematics had been working on new mathematics curricula since 1952, but others such as the School Mathematics Study Group, the Chemical Education Material Study and the Biological Sciences Curriculum Study were not undertaken until after the passage of the National Defense Education Act. Unlike 1917, when the nation saw skilled workers as the key to prosperity and security, the mood had swung to the intellectual, particularly to scientists, mathematicians and engineers, as the key to world preeminence.

The burgeoning of these curriculum projects represented the end of an era in several respects. First, almost without exception, the directors of these major projects were drawn from academic departments in major universities. Control of curriculum change in other words had reverted from its traditional locus in the professional education community to specialists in the academic disciplines. Secondly, as would be expected, the effort to replace the academic subjects as the basic building blocks of the curriculum, going back about half a century, was brought to an abrupt end. No longer would projects or areas of living be actively promoted as substitutes for the subject. Thirdly, the longstanding emphasis on local efforts at curriculum change was replaced by a pattern of centrally controlled curriculum revision. Although the major revision projects of the National Science Foundation and related programs did not have the legal power to mandate the changes they were recommending, they did transform the process of curriculum change to one in which the curriculum would be developed first by experts at a center set up for that purpose with the local school systems perceived as consumers of external initiatives. The extent to which these highly significant changes would survive the immediate social and political climate in which they were born or their efficacy as ways of addressing curriculum issues remains to be determined.

The entry on a massive scale of the federal government in the battle for the curriculum of American schools dramatically altered the relative strength of the various interest groups. With huge sums of money available for changing the way school subjects were taught, the humanist position became dominant almost overnight. Efforts were directed not at replacing the academic subjects or reconstructing them to make them more functional, but to bringing them in line with the frontiers of scholarly endeavor. There remained, here and there, the feeling that the intellectual riches being purveyed should be available only for a select few, but by and large, there was an effort to raise the intellectual level for all – ultimately extending to the social sciences and the humanities as well as the natural sciences and mathematics. The other interest groups, however, were not exactly vanquished. For better or worse, the changes accruing from the new federal involvement in the curriculum did not obliterate the victories that had been achieved over the previous 65 years of curriculum reform. Developmentalists had partially succeeded in drawing attention to the nature of child life as a key element in curriculum thinking. Social efficiency educators had reinforced an instinctive belief on the part of Americans that education ought to be tied to tangible rewards. Social meliorists brought to the fore the issue of schooling in relation to social progress. The school, for example, more than any other social institution, became the focus of the civil rights struggle.

The one fortress that proved virtually impregnable was the school subject. The subject as the basic unit in the curriculum successfully resisted the more ambitious efforts to replace it with anything like functional areas of living or projects arising from student interest. If the success of the 65-year effort to reform the American curriculum is to be judged by the extent to which English, mathematics, science, history, geography and the like simply survived the assault against them, then the effort must be counted a failure. But subject labels alone may be misleading. Some of the reforms advanced by the various interest groups were accomplished within the overall context of the subject organization of the curriculum. To be sure, not all the changes may be regarded as signs of progress, but modest successes were achieved in restructuring, integrating and modernizing the subjects that comprise the curriculum. The subjects survived but in an altered form.

As the struggle proceeded, distinct indications of the efforts of all the various interest groups became evident in terms of what was taught under the subject labels. English, for example, had been affected by the experience curriculum movement, and social studies had absorbed significant elements of both social efficency and social reconstruction. In that sense, the outcome of the struggle for the American curriculum was an undeclared, almost unconscious, détente. At one and the same time, the curriculum in the twentieth century has come to represent a reasonably faithful reflection of the intellectual resources of our culture and its anti-intellectual tendencies as well; it serves to liberate the human spirit and also to confine it; it is attuned to the well-being of children and youth and also contributes to their disaffection and alienation from the mainstream of social life; and it represents a vehicle for social and political reform as well as a force for perpetuating existing class structures and for the reproduction of social inequality.

1   Charles W. Eliot, 1834–1926, c. 1891
(Courtesy Harvard University Archives)

2   G. Stanley Hall, 1844–1924, 1884
(Clark University Archives)

3   Lester Frank Ward, 1841–1913, 1886
(Brown University Library)

4   William Torrey Harris, 1835–1909, 1902
(Library of Congress)

5   Francis W. Parker, 1837–1902, *c.* 1883   6   John Dewey, 1859–1952, *c.* 1902

(University of Chicago Archives)   *(University of Chicago Archives)*

7   Children at the Laboratory School, University of Chicago, engaged in the famous 'clubhouse project', *c.* 1900

(Lander MacClintock Photographs, Morris Library, Southern Illinois University at Carbondale)

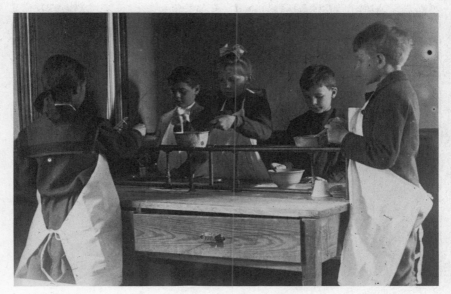

8 & 9 'Occupations' provided a focal point for the curriculum in Dewey's school. Above
Children preparing food. Below a boy spins wool on a spinning wheel, *c.* 1900

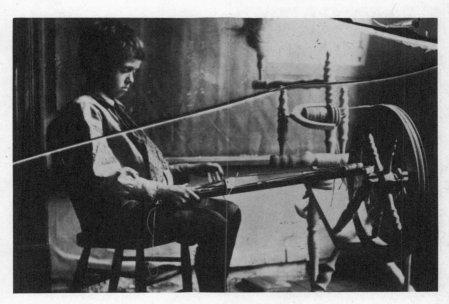

10　Franklin Bobbitt, 1876–1956, *c*. 1926
(State Historical Society of Wisconsin)

11　W. W. Charters, 1875–1952, 1920
(The Ohio State University Library)

12　David Snedden, 1868–1951, *c*. 1918
(State Historical Society of Wisconsin)

13　Charles Prosser, 1871–1952, 1933
(Dunwoodie Industrial Institute)

14 Typewriting class at Herman Ritter Junior High School (P.S. 98), The Bronx, New York City, 1934–5

(Archives of the Board of Education of the City of New York, Milbank Memorial Library, Teachers College, Columbia University)

15 Automobile mechanics class, Brooklyn High School of Automotive Trades, Brooklyn, New York City, 1956

(Archives of the Board of Education of the City of New York, Milbank Memorial Library, Teachers College, Columbia University)

16   William Heard Kilpatrick, 1871–1965,
c. 1925

(Milbank Memorial Library, Teachers College, Columbia University)

17   William Chandler Bagley, 1874–1946,
c 1930

(State Historical Society of Wisconsin)

18   Activity Program, Fourth grade store, University School

(The Ohio State University, 1948)

19   Rural one-room school, *c.* 1895

(Author's collection)

20   Urban school, *c.* 1910. As the twentieth century progressed ungraded schools like the one above became less common. Like the city school below, schools were increasingly grouped by age and were managed by a school principal

(Author's collection)

21 Boyd H. Bode, 1873–1953, 1926
(The Ohio State University Archives)

22 George S. Counts, 1889–1974, *c.* 1945
(The Ohio State University Archives)

23 Harold O. Rugg, 1886–1960, *c.* 1939
(Dartmouth College Library: photo by Mary Morris)

REFERENCES

Adams, C. F. (1879). *The New Departure in the Common Schools of Quincy and Other Papers on Educational Topics*. Boston: Estes & Lauriat.

Addams, J. (1907). Address. In *Bulletin No. 1 of the National Society for the Promotion of Industrial Education* (pp. 37–44). New York: The Society.

Addams, J. (1908). Discussions. In *Bulletin No. 5 of the National Society for the Promotion of Industrial Education* (pp. 92–97). New York: The Society.

Aikin, W. M. (1931a). Committee on the relation of school and college. *School and Society*, 33, 274–6.

Aikin, W. M. (1931b). Report of the committee on college entrance and secondary schools. *Progressive Education*, 8, 318–20.

Aikin, W. M. (1942). *The Story of the Eight-year Study, with Conclusions and Recommendations*. New York: Harper & Brothers.

Alexander, F. M. (1934). Social studies in Virginia. *The Clearing House*, 9, 76–81.

American Council on Education, American Youth Commission. (1940). *What the High Schools Ought to Teach: The Report of a Special Committee on the Secondary School Curriculum*. Washington, DC: The Council.

American Historical Association. (1934). *Conclusions and Recommendations of the Commission on the Social Studies*. New York: Charles Scribner's Sons.

Armstrong, O. K. (1940, September). Treason in the textbooks. *The American Legion Magazine*, 8–9, 51, 70–2.

As reported. (1921). *The Journal of Educational Method*, 1 (1), 37–41.

Author of "Preston Papers." (1894). The critic at sea, V. *Education*, 15, 149–57.

Author of "Preston Papers." (1895). The critic at sea, VII. *Education*, 15, 288–97.

Ayres, L. P. (1909). *Laggards in Our Schools: A Study of Retardation and Elimination in City School Systems*. New York: Charities Publication Committee.

Bagley, W. C. (1905). *The Educative Process*. New York: Macmillan.

Bagley, W. C. (1921). Projects and purposes in teaching and learning. *Teachers College Record*, 22, 288–97.

Bagley, W. C. (1925). *Determinism in Education: A Series of Papers on the Relative Influence of Inherited and Acquired Traits in Determining Intelligence, Achievement, and Character*. Baltimore: Warwick & York.

Bagley, W. C. (1926). Supplementary statement. In G. M. Whipple (ed.), *The Foundations and Technique of Curriculum-Construction, Part II. The Foundations of Curriculum-Making. The Twenty-Sixth Yearbook of the National Society for the Study of Education* (pp. 29–40). Bloomington, IL: Public School Publishing.

Bagley, W. C. (1929a). Discipline and dogma: A reply to Professor Scholtz. *Educational Administration and Supervision*, 15, 561–73.

Bagley, W. C. (1929b). Some handicaps of character education in the United States. In National Education Association, *Official Report of the Department of Superintendence, February 24–28, 1929* (pp. 140–46). Washington, D.C.: The Department.

Bagley, W. C. (1930). The future of education in America. *Proceedings of the Sixty-Eighth Annual Meeting of the National Education Association*, 68, 218–25.

Bagley, W. C. (1938a). An essentialist's platform for the advancement of American education. *Educational Administration and Supervision*, 24, 241–56.

Bagley, W. C. (1938b). Some relations of education to the status quo. *School and Society*, 47, 562–5.

Bagley, W. C. (1939a). An essentialist looks at the foreign languages. *Educational Administration and Supervision*, 25, 241–50.

Bagley, W. C. (1939b). The significance of the essentialist movement in educational theory. *The Classical Journal*, 34, 326–44.

Bagley, W. C. (1945). The Harvard University report on "General education in a free society." *School and Society*, 62, 69–70.

Bailey, L. H. (1908). *On the Training of Persons to Teach Agriculture in the Public Schools*. Washington, DC: US Government Printing Office.

Basler, R. (1947). Life adjustment education for youth: Commission to develop program for universal secondary education. *School Life* 30(2), 3–6.

Bell, B. I. (1949). *Crisis in Education: A Challenge to American Complacency*. New York: Whittlesey House.

Bestor, A. E. Jr (1952). "Life-adjustment" education: A critique. *Bulletin of the American Association of University Professors*, 38, 413–41.

Bestor, A. E. Jr (1953a). Anti-intellectualism in the schools. *New Republic*, 128(3), 11–13.

Bestor, A. E. (1953b). *Educational Wastelands: The Retreat from Learning in Our Public Schools*. Urbana: University of Illinois Press.

Billings, N. (1929). *A Determination of Generalizations Basic to the Social Studies Curriculum*. Baltimore: Warwick & York.

Bobbitt, F. (1912). The elimination of waste in education. *The Elementary School Teacher*, 12, 259–71.

Bobbitt, F. (1918). *The Curriculum*. Boston: Houghton Mifflin.

Bobbitt, F. (1922). *Curriculum-Making in Los Angeles*. Chicago: University of Chicago.

Bobbitt, F. (1924). *How to Make a Curriculum*. Boston: Houghton Mifflin.

Bobbitt, F. (1926). The orientation of the curriculum-maker. In G. M. Whipple (ed.), *The Foundations and Technique of Curriculum-Construction, Part II. The Foundations of Curriculum-Making. The Twenty-Sixth Yearbook of the National Society for the Study of Education* (pp. 41–55). Bloomington, IL: Public School Publishing.

Bobbitt, F. (1934). Questionable recommendations of the Commission on the Social Studies. *School and Society*, 40, 201–8.

Bobbitt, F. (1937). A correlated curriculum evaluated [Book review]. *The English Journal*, 26, 418–20.

Bobbitt, F. (1946). Harvard reaffirms the academic tradition. *The School Review*, 54, 326–33.

Bode, B. H. (1927). *Modern Education Theories*. New York: Macmillan.

Bode, B. H. (1934). Editorial comment. *The Phi Delta Kappan*, 17, 1, 7.

Bode, B. H. (1938). *Progressive Education at the Crossroads*. New York: Newson.

Book burnings. (1940, September 9). *Time*, pp. 64–5.

Boutwell, W. D. (1934). The Cleveland meeting. *School and Society*, 39, 296–305.

Boydston, J. A. (1969). A note on applied psychology. In J. A. Boydston (ed.)., *The Early Works of John Dewey, 1882–1898: Vol. 3. 1889–1892: Early Essays and Outlines of a Critical Theory of Ethics* (pp. xiii–xix). Carbondale: Southern Illinois University Press.

Boyer, E. L. (1983). *High School: A Report on Secondary Education in America*. New York: Harper & Row.

Brickman, W. W. and Lehrer, S. (eds). (1961). *John Dewey: Master Educator* (2nd ed.) New York: Society for the Advancement of Education.

Broder, D. E. (1977). *Life Adjustment Education: An Historical Study of a Program of the United States Office of Education, 1945–1954*. Unpublished Ed. D. report. Teachers College, Columbia University.

Brown, G. P., Hoose, J. H., Parr, S. S. and Harris, W. T. (1889). The educational value of manual training. *Journal of Proceedings and Addresses of the National Education Association, Session of the Year 1889*, 417–23.

Bullard, E. P. (1909). Industrial training through the apprenticeship system. In *Bulletin No. 9 of the National Society for the Promotion of Industrial Education* (pp. 51–63). New York: The Society.

Bunker, F. F. (1916). *Reorganization of the Public School System*. Washington, D.C.: US Government Printing Office.

Butler, N. M. (1888). *The Argument for Manual Training*. New York: E. L. Kellogg.

Callahan, R. E. (1962). *Education and the Cult of Efficiency: A Study of the Social Forces that have Shaped the Administration of the Public Schools*. Chicago: University of Chicago Press.

Chamberlain, D., Chamberlain, E., Drought, N. E. and Scott, W. E. (1942). *Did They Succeed in College? The Follow-up Study of the Graduates of the Thirty Schools*. New York: Harper & Brothers.

Charters, W. W. (1921). The reorganization of women's education. *Educational Review*, 62, 224–31.

Charters, W. W. (1922). Regulating the project. *Journal of Educational Research*, 5, 245–6.

Charters, W. W. (1926a). Curriculum for women. *Bulletin of the University of Illinois*, 23(27), 327–30.

Charters, W. W. (1926b). Statement. In G. M. Whipple (ed.), *The Foundations and Technique of Curriculum-Construction, Part II. The Foundations of Curriculum-Making. The Twenty-Sixth Yearbook of the National Society for the Study of Education* (p. 71). Bloomington, IL: Public School Publishing.

Charters, W. W. (1926c). The traits of homemakers. *Journal of Home Economics*, 18, 673–85.

Charters, W. W. and Waples, D. (1929). *The Commonwealth Teacher-Training Study*, Chicago: University of Chicago Press.

Charters, W. W. and Whitley, I. B. (1924). *Analysis of Secretarial Duties and Traits*. Baltimore: Williams & Wilkins.

Collier, P. D. (1950). What is education for life adjustment? *Bulletin of the National Association of Secondary-School Principals*, 34(169), 122–8.

Collings, E. (1923). *An Experiment with a Project Curriculum*. New York: Macmillan.

Columbia University. (1927). *Curriculum Making in an Elementary School, by the Staff of the Elementary Division of the Lincoln School of Teachers College, Columbia University*. Boston: Ginn.

Commager, H. S. (ed.). (1967). *Lester Ward and the Welfare State*. Indianapolis: Bobbs-Merrill.

Cooperative research and curriculum improvement. (1950). *Teachers College Record*, 51, 407–74.

Copley, F. B. (1923). *Frederick W. Taylor: Father of Scientific Management*, Vol. 1. New York: The American Society of Mechanical Engineers.

Counts, G. S. (1922). *The Selective Character of American Secondary Education*. Chicago: University of Chicago.

Counts, G. S. (1926). *The Senior High School Curriculum*, Chicago: University of Chicago.

Counts, G. S. (1927). *The Social Composition of Boards of Education: A Study in the Social Control of Public Education*. Chicago: University of Chicago.

Counts, G. S. (1930). *The American Road to Culture: A Social Interpretation of Education in the United States*. New York: John Day.

Counts, G. S. (1932a). Dare progressive education be progressive? *Progressive Education*, 9, 257–63.

Counts, G. S. (1932b). *Dare the School Build a New Social Order?* New York: John Day.

Courtis, S. A. (1913). The Courtis tests in arithmetic. In *Report on Educational Aspects of the Public School System of the City of New York to the Committee on School Inquiry of the Board of Estimate and Apportionment, Vol. 1* (pp. 391–546). New York: City of New York.

Cremin, L. A. (1961). *The Transformation of the School: Progressivism in American Education, 1876–1957*. New York: Alfred A. Knopf.

Curti, M. E. (1951). *The Growth of American Thought* (2nd ed.). New York: Harper.

Dean, A. D. (1908). Education of workers in the shoe industry. *Bulletin No. 8 of the National Society for the Promotion of Industrial Education* (pp. 7–110). New York: The Society.

DeBoer, J. J. (1936). Integration – a return to first principles. *School and Society*, 43, 246–53.

Deems, J. F. (1908). Trade instruction in large establishments. In *Bulletin No. 5 of the National Society for the Promotion of Industrial Education* (pp. 51–5). New York: The Society.

Demiashkevich, M. J. (1933). Some doubts about the activity movement. *Harvard Teachers Record*, 3, 170–8.

Demiashkevich, M. J. (1935). *An Introduction to the Philosophy of Education*. New York: American Book.

Dewey, J. (1895). Plan of organization of the university primary school. In J. A Boydston (ed.), *The Early Works of John Dewey, 1882–1898: Vol. 5 1895–1898: Early Essays* (pp. 223–43). Carbondale: Southern Illinois University Press, 1972.

Dewey, J. (1896a). Interest in relation to training of the will. In *Second supplement to the Herbart Yearbook for 1895* (pp. 209–46). Bloomington, IL: National Herbart Society. [Rev. ed., Chicago: The Society, 1899, pp. 5–38.]

Dewey, J. (1896b). Interpretation of the culture-epoch theory. *The Public School Journal*, 15, 233–6.

Dewey, J. (1896c). The university school. *University [of Chicago] Record*, 1, 417–19.

Dewey, J. (1897a). Criticisms wise and otherwise on modern child study. *Journal of Proceedings and Addresses of the Thirty-Sixth Annual Meeting of the National Education Association*, 867–8.

Dewey, J. (1897b). The interpretation side of child-study. *Transactions of the Illinois Society for Child-Study*, 2(2), 17–27.

Dewey, J. (1897c). The psychological aspect of the school curriculum. *Educational Review*, 13, 356–69.

Dewey, J. (1897d). The university elementary school: History and character. *University [of Chicago] Record*, 2, 72–5.

Dewey, J. (1898). The primary-education fetish. *The Forum*, 25, 315–28.

Dewey, J. (1899a). *Lectures in the Philosophy of Education.* R. D. Archambault (ed.), New York: Random House, 1966.

Dewey, J. (1899b). *The School and Society.* Chicago: University of Chicago Press.

Dewey, J. (1900). The aim of history in elementary education. *The Elementary School Record*, 1, 199–203.

Dewey, J. (1901). The situation as regards the course of study. *Journal of Proceedings and Addresses of the Fortieth Annual Meeting of the National Education Association*, 332–48.

Dewey, J. (1902a). *The Child and the Curriculum.* Chicago: University of Chicago Press.

Dewey, J. (1902b). Interpretation of the savage mind. *The Psychological Review*, 9, 217–30.

Dewey, J. (1909). *Moral Principles in Education.* Boston: Houghton Mifflin.

Dewey, J. (1910). *How We Think.* Boston: D. C. Heath.

Dewey, J. (1914). A policy of industrial education. *The New Republic*, 1(7), 11–12.

Dewey, J. (1915a). Education vs. Trade-training – Dr. Dewey's reply. *The New Republic*, 3, 42–3.

Dewey, J. (1915b). Industrial education – A wrong kind. *The New Republic*, 2, 71–3.

Dewey, J. (1916a). *Democracy and Education: An Introduction to the Philosophy of Education.* New York: Macmillan.

Dewey, J. (1916b). Method in science teaching. *General Science Quarterly*, 1, 3–9.

Dewey, J. (1917). Learning to earn: The place of vocational education in a comprehensive scheme of public education. *School and Society*, 5, 331–5.

Dewey, J. (1928a). Progressive education and the science of education. *Progressive Education*, 5, 197–204.

Dewey, J. (1928b). Why I am for Smith. *The New Republic*, 56, 320–1.

Dewey, J. (1931). *The Way Out of Educational Confusion*. Cambridge, MA: Harvard University Press.

Dewey, J. (1936). The Theory of the Chicago experiment. In K. C. Mayhew and A. C. Edwards, *The Dewey School: The Laboratory School of the University of Chicago, 1896–1903*, (pp. 463–77). New York: D. Appleton-Century.

Dewey, J. (1938). *Experience and Education*. New York: Macmillan.

Dewey, J. M. (ed.) (1939). Biography of John Dewey. In P. A. Schilpp (ed.), *The Philosophy of John Dewey* (pp. 1–45). Evanston: Northwestern University.

Dewey, J. (1966). *Lectures in the Philosophy of Education [1899]*. R. D. Archambault (ed.). New York : Random House.

Dilling, E. (1934). *The Red Network: A "Who's Who" and Handbook of Radicalism for Patriots*. Kenilworth, IL: The Author.

Discussion of [the] report of Dr. Harris. (1895). *The Journal of Education*, 41, 165–7.

Discussion [on work and play in youth] (1901). *Journal of Proceedings and Addresses of the Fortieth Annual Meeting of the National Education Association*, 518–23.

Douglass, H. R. (1949). Education of all youth for life adjustment. *The Annals of the American Academy of Political and Social Science*, 265, 108–14.

Drost, W. H. (1967). That immortal day in Cleveland – the report of the Committee of Fifteen. *Educational Theory*, 17, 178–91.

Du Bois, W. E. B. (1902). *The Negro Artisan*. Atlanta, GA: Atlanta University Press.

Dunkel, H. B. (1970). *Herbart and the Herbartians: An Educational Ghost Story*. Chicago: University of Chicago Press.

Educational Policies Commission. (1943). *What the Schools Should Teach in Wartime*. Washington, DC: Educational Policies Commission, National Education Association and the American Association of School Administrators.

Educational Policies Commission. (1944). *Education of ALL American youth*. Washington, DC: Educational Policies Commission, National Education Association and the American Association of School Administrators.

Eliot, C. W. (1892a). Shortening and enriching the grammar school course. *Journal of Proceedings and Addresses of the National Education Association, Session of the Year 1892*, 617–25.

Eliot, C. W. (1892b). Wherein popular education has failed. *The Forum*, 14, 411–28.

Eliot, C. W. (1905). The fundamental assumptions in the report of the Committee of Ten (1893). *Educational Review*, 30, 325–43.

Eliot, C. W. (1908). Industrial education as an essential factor in our national prosperity. In *Bulletin No. 5 of the National Society for the Promotion of Industrial Education* (pp. 9–14). New York: The Society.

Ellwood, C. A. (1914). Our compulsory education laws, and re-tardation and elimination in our public schools. *Education*. 34, 572–6.

Engelhart, M. D. and Thomas, M. (1966). Rice as the inventor of the comparative test. *Journal of Educational Measurement*. 3, 141–5.

Evans, H. R. (1908). A list of the writings of William Torrey Harris, chronologically arranged, with subject index. In Bureau of Education, *Report of the Commissioner of Education for the year ended June 30, 1907, Vol. 1*. Washington, DC: US Government Printing Office.

Finney, R. L. (1928). *A Sociological Philosophy of Education*. New York: Macmillan.

Fisher, B. M. (1967). *Industrial Education: American Ideals and Institutions*. Madison, WI: University of Wisconsin Press.

Forbes, B. C. (1939, August 15). Treacherous teachings. *Forbes*, p. 8.

Fuller, H. J. (1951). The emperor's new clothes, or prius dementat. *The Scientific Monthly*, 72, 32–41.

Get adjusted. (1947, December 15). *Time*, p. 64.

Goebel, E. J. (1948). The total experience of the school child for life adjustment. *Bulletin of the National Catholic Educational Association*, 45(1), 376–81.

Gompers, S. (1910). President Gompers' report. *Report of Proceedings of the Thirteenth Annual Convention of the American Federation of Labor*, 14–53.

Gould, S. J. (1981). *The Mismeasure of Man*. New York: Norton.

Graham, P. A. (1967). *Progressive Education, from Arcady to Academe: A History of the Progressive Education Association, 1919–1955*. New York: Columbia University, Teachers College.

Gray, W. S. (1925). *Summary of Investigations Relating to Reading*. Chicago: University of Chicago.

Group IV. (1900). Unpublished material. Columbia University, Teachers College Collection, February 3, 1900.

Group V. (1900). Unpublished material. Columbia University, Teachers College Collection, 405-01.

Hall, G. S. (1883). The contents of children's minds. *Princeton Review*, 11, 249–72.

Hall, G. S. (1888, June). The story of a sand-pile. *Scribner's Magazine*, 690–6.

Hall, G. S. (1892). Editorial. *The Pedagogical Seminary*, 2, 3–8.

Hall, G. S. (1895). Child study. *Journal of Proceedings and Addresses of the National Education Association, Session of the Year 1894*, 173–9.

Hall, G. S. (1901a). How far is the present high-school and early college training adapted to the nature and needs of adolescents? *The School Review*, 9, 649–65.

Hall, G. S. (1901b). Ideal school as based on child study. *Journal of Proceedings and Addresses of the Fortieth Annual Meeting of the National Education Association*, 474–88.

Hall, G. S. (1902). The high school as the people's college. *Journal of Proceedings and Addresses of the Forty-First Annual Meeting of the National Education Association*, 260–8.

Hall, G. S. (1903). Coeducation in the high school. *Journal of Proceedings and Addresses of the Forty-Second Annual Meeting of the National Education Association*, 446–51.

Hall, G. S. (1904a). *Adolescence: Its Psychology and its Relations to Physiology, Anthropology, Sociology, Sex, Crime, Religion and Education*, Vol. 1. New York: D. Appleton.

Hall, G. S. (1904b). *Adolescence: Its Psychology and its Relations to Physiology, Anthropology, Sociology, Sex, Crime, Religion and Education*, Vol. 2. New York: D. Appleton.

Hall, G. S. (1904c). The natural activities of children as determining the industries in early education, II. *Journal of Proceedings and Addresses of the Forty-Third Annual Meeting of the National Education Association*. 443–7.

Hall, G. S. (1911). *Educational Problems*, Vol. 2. New York: D. Appleton.

Hall, G. S. (1923). *Life and Confessions of a Psychologist*. New York: D. Appleton.

Hall, S. B. (1933). Cooperation in Virginia. *The Educational*

Record, 14, 338–45.

Hand, H. C. and French, W. (1937). Analysis of the present status in curriculum thinking. In H. Harap, et al., *The Changing Curriculum* (pp. 1–31). New York: D. Appleton-Century.

Hand, H. C. and Sanford, C. W. (1953). A scholar's documents. *Bulletin of the National Association of Secondary-School Principals*, 37(194), 460–504.

Hanna, L. (1939). The plan of the core curriculum in Tulsa. *Curriculum Journal*, 10, 350–2.

Hanna, L. (1940). The operation of the core curriculum in Tulsa. *Curriculum Journal*, 11, 66–8.

Harris, W. T. (1880). Equivalents in a liberal course of study: Formal and substantial studies. *Journal of Proceedings and Addresses of the National Education Association, Session of the Year 1880*, 167–75.

Harris, W. T. (1886). Psychological inquiry. *Journal of Proceedings and Addresses of the National Education Association, Session of the Year 1885*, 91–101.

Harris, W. T. (1888). What shall the public schools teach? *The Forum*, 4, 573–81.

Harris, W. T. (1889). The intellectual value of tool-work. *Journal of Proceedings and Addresses of the National Education Association, Session of the Year 1889*, 92–8.

Harris, W. T. (1896a). How the will combines with the intellect in the higher orders of knowing. *Journal of Proceedings and Addresses of the Thirty-Fifth Annual Meeting of the National Eduation Association*, 440–6.

Harris, W. T. (1896b). Professor John Dewey's doctrine of interest as related to will. *Educational Review*, 11, 486–93.

Harris, W. T. (1898a). The pedagogical creed of William T. Harris, U.S. Commissioner of Education. In O. H. Lang (ed.), *Educational Creeds of the Nineteenth Century* (pp. 36–46). New York: E. L. Kellogg.

Harris, W. T. (1898b). *Psychologic Foundations of Education: An Attempt to Show the Genesis of the Higher Faculties of the Mind*. New York: D. Appleton.

Hartman, A. L. (1934). Comments by leaders in the field. In G. M. Whipple (ed.), *The Activity Movement. The Thirty-Third Yearbook of the National Society for the Study of Education, Part II* (pp. 110–12). Bloomington, IL: Public School Publishing.

Harvard University, Committee on the Objectives of General

Education in a Free Society. (1945). *General Education in a Free Society: Report of the Harvard Committee.* Cambridge, MA: Harvard University Press.

Hatfield, W. W. (1935). *An Experience Curriculum in English: A Report of the Curriculum Commission of the National Council of Teachers of English.* New York: D. Appleton-Century.

Heald, F. E. (1917). "The project" in agricultural education. *General Science Quarterly,* 1, 166–9.

Heald, F. E. (1918). *The Home Project as a Phase of Vocational Agricultural Education. Issued by the Federal Board for Vocational Education.* Washington, DC: US Government Printing Office.

High-school overhaul. (1947, December 15). *Newsweek,* p. 86.

Hockett, J. A. (1927). *A Determination of the Major Social Problems of American Life.* New York: Columbia University, Teachers College.

Hoodless, A. (1910). The education of girls. In *Bulletin No. 10 of the National Society for the Promotion of Industrial Education* (pp. 179–84). New York: The Society.

Hopkins, L. T. (1937). A correlated curriculum evaluated [Book review]. *The English Journal,* 26, 417–18.

Horn, E. (1918). Economy in learning in relation to economy of time. *Journal of Proceedings and Addresses of the Fifty-Sixth Annual Meeting of the National Education Association,* 526–8.

Hosic, J. F. (1921a). Editorially speaking. *Journal of Educational Method,* 1(1), 1–2.

Hosic, J. F. (1921b). Editorially speaking. *Journal of Educational Method,* 1(2), 1.

Hosic, J. F. and Chase, S. E. (1926). *Brief Guide to the Project Method.* Yonkers-on-Hudson, NY: World Book.

Hotchkiss, E. A. (1924). *The Project Method in Classroom Work.* Boston: Ginn.

Houston, V. M., Sanford, C. W. and Trump, J. L. (1948). *Guide to the Study of the Curriculum in the Secondary Schools of Illinois.* Springfield, IL: Illinois Secondary School Curriculum Program.

Hulburd, D. (1951). *This Happened in Pasadena.* New York: Macmillan.

Hutchins, R. M. (1936). *The Higher Learning in America.* New Haven: Yale University Press.

Individualizing instruction. (1925). *School Life,* 10, 177.

Industrial education. (1907). *Proceedings of the Twelfth Annual*

Convention of the National Association of Manufacturers, 109–38.

Industrial education. (1912). *Proceedings of the Seventh Annual Convention of the National Association of Manufacturers*, 149–77.

Jackman, E. D. (1920). The Dalton plan. *The School Review*, 28, 688–96.

James, W. (1890). *The Principles of Psychology*, Vol. 1. New York: H. Holt.

James, W. (1899). *Talks to Teachers on Psychology, and to Students on Some of Life's Ideals*. New York: H. Holt.

Johnson, M. (1926). The educational principles of the school of organic education, Fairhope, Alabama. In G. M. Whipple (ed.), *The Foundations and Technique of Curriculum-Construction, Part I. Curriculum-Making: Past and Present. The Twenty-Sixth Yearbook of the National Society for the Study of Education* (pp. 349–51). Bloomington, IL: Public School Publishing.

Jones, T. J. (1908). *Social Studies in the Hampton Curriculum*. Hampton, VA: Hampton Institute Press.

Kaestle, C. F. (ed.). (1973). *Joseph Lancaster and the Monitorial School Movement: A Documentary History*. New York: Teachers College Press.

Kaestle, C. F. (in press). Review. *Chicago History*.

Kandel, I. L. (1947). Adjustment to life. *School and Society*, 65, 372.

Kean, C. J. (1983). The origins of vocational education in the Milwaukee Public Schools, 1870–1917: A case study in curricular change. Unpublished doctoral dissertation, University of Wisconsin, Madison.

Keppel, A. M. (1960). Country schools for country children: Backgrounds of the reform movement in rural elementary education, 1890–1914. Unpublished doctoral dissertation, University of Wisconsin, Madison.

Kilpatrick, W. H. (1917). Project teaching. *General Science Quarterly*, 1, 67–72.

Kilpatrick, W. H. (1918a). The problem-project attack in organization, subject-matter, and teaching. *Journal of Proceedings and Addresses of the Fifty-Sixth Annual Meeting of the National Education Association*, 528–31.

Kilpatrick, W. H. (1918b). The project method. *Teachers College Record*, 19, 319–35.

Kilpatrick, W. H. (1922). Subject matter and the educative process – I. *Journal of Educational Method*, 2, 95-101.

Kilpatrick, W. H. (1923). Subject matter and the educative process – II, III. *Journal of Educational Method*, 2, 230–7, 367–76.

Kilpatrick, W. H. (1924). How shall we select the subject matter of the elementary school curriculum. *Journal of Educational Method*, 4, 3–10.

Kilpatrick, W. H. (1925). *Foundations of Method: Informal Talks on Teaching*. New York: Macmillan.

Kilpatrick, W. H. (1926). Statement of position. In G. M. Whipple (ed.), *The Foundations and Technique of Curriculum-Construction, Part II. The Foundations of Curriculum-Making. The Twenty-Sixth Yearbook of the National Society for the Study of Education* (pp. 119–46). Bloomington, IL: Public School Publishing.

Kilpatrick, W. H. (1928). Curriculum-making in an elementary school [Book review]. *Progressive Education*, 5, 86–8.

Krug, E. A. (1962). Graduates of secondary schools in and around 1900: Did most of them go to college? *School Review*, 70, 266–72.

Krug, E. A. (1972). *The Shaping of the American High School*, Vol. 2. 1920–1941 Madison, WI: University of Wisconsin Press.

Lancelot, W. H. (1943). A close-up of the eight-year study. *School and Society*, 58, 449–51.

Lauchner, A. H. (1951). How can the junior high school curriculum be improved? *Bulletin of the National Association of Secondary-School Principals*, 35(177), 296–304.

Leonard, J. P. (1937). Is the Virginia curriculum working? *Harvard Educational Review*, 7, 66-71.

Lewis, M. H. (1928). *An Adventure with Children*. New York: Macmillan. *Life adjustment curriculum*. (1949). Billings, MT: Billings Senior High School.

Life adjustment education for youth – "statesmanship of a very high order . . . in operation." (1949). *School Life*, 32, 40–2.

Lybarger, M. B. (1981). Origins of the Social Studies Curriculum: 1865–1916. Unpublished doctoral dissertation, University of Wisconsin, Madison.

Lynd, R. S. and Lynd, H. M. (1929). *Middletown: A Study in Contemporary American Culture*. New York: Harcourt, Brace.

McCaul, R. L. (1959). Dewey's Chicago. *School Review*, 67, 258–80.

McLellan, J. A. and Dewey, J. (1889). *Applied Psychology: An*

Introduction to the Principles and Practice of Education. Boston: Educational Publishing.

McMurry, C. A. (1893). *The Elements of General Method Based on the Principles of Herbart*. Bloomington, IL: Public-school Publishing.

Maritian, J. (1943). *Education at the Crossroads*. New Haven : Yale University Press.

Marshall, F. M. (1907). Industrial training for women: A preliminary study. *Bulletin No. 4 of the National Society for the Promotion of Industrial Education* (pp. 5–59). New York: The Society.

Massachusetts Commission on Industrial and Technical Education. (1906). *Report of the Commission on Industrial and Technical Education*. Boston: Wright & Potter Printing.

Mathews C. O. (1926). *The Grade Placement of Curriculum Materials in the Social Studies*. New York: Columbia University, Teachers College.

Mayhew, K. C. and Edwards, A. C. (1936). *The Dewey School: The Laboratory School of the University of Chicago, 1896–1903*. New York: D. Appleton-Century.

Meltzer, H. (1925). *Children's Social Concepts: A Study of Their Nature and Development*. New York: Columbia University, Teachers College.

Meriam, J. L. (1920). *Child Life and the Curriculum*. Yonkers-on-Hudson, NY: World Book.

The model school. (1896, January 16). *University of Chicago Weekly*, 707.

Moore, J. C. (1916). Projects. *General Science Quarterly*, 1, 14–16.

Moseley, N. (1936). Content and conduct of teachers' conventions. *Progressive Education*, 13, 337–9.

Mott, F. L. (1941). *American Journalism: A History of Newspapers in the United States through 250 years, 1690–1940*, New York: Macmillan.

Munsterberg, H. (1899). *Psychology and Life*. Boston: Houghton, Mifflin.

National Defense Education Act. (1958). Public Law 85–864, 85th Congress, September 2, 1958.

National Education Association. (1893). *Report of the Committee on Secondary School Studies*. Washington, DC: US Government Printing Office.

National Education Association. (1895). *Report of the Committee of Fifteen on Elementary Education, with the Reports of the*

Sub-committees: On the Training of Teachers; On the Correlation of Studies in Elementary Education; On the Organization of City School Systems. New York: American Book.

National Education Association. (1913). Preliminary Statements by Chairmen of Committees of the Commission of the National Education Association on the Reorganization of Secondary Education. Washington, DC: US Government Printing Office.

National Education Association. (1915). The Teaching of Community Civics, Prepared by a Special Committee of the Commission on the Reorganization of Secondary Education. Washington, DC: US Government Printing Office.

National Education Association. (1916). Social Studies in Secondary Education: A Six-year Program Adapted to the 6-3-3 and the 8-4 plans of Organization. Report of the Committee on Social Studies of the Commission on the Reorganization of Secondary Education. Washington, DC: US Government Printing Office.

National Education Association. (1918). Cardinal Principles of Secondary Education: A Report of the Commission on the Reorganization of Secondary Education. Washington, DC: US Government Printing Office.

National Education Association. (1936). The Development of a Modern Program in English. Ninth Yearbook of the Department of Supervisors and Directors of Instruction. Washington, DC: The Association.

National Education Association. (1943). Wartime Handbook for Education. Washington, DC: The Association.

Newlon, J. H. and Threlkeld, A. L. (1926). The Denver curriculum-revision program. In G. M. Whipple (ed.), The Foundations and Technique of Curriculum-Construction, Part I. Curriculum-Making: Past and Present. The Twenty-Sixth Yearbook of the National Society for the Study of Education (pp. 229–240). Bloomington, IL: Public School Publishing.

Nickell, V. L. (1949). How can we develop an effective program of education for life adjustment? Bulletin of the National Association of Secondary-School Principals, 33(162), 153–6.

Oberholtzer, E. E. (1934). Comments by leaders in the field. In G. M. Whipple (ed.), The Activity Movement. The Thirty-Third Yearbook of the National Society for the Study of Education, Part II (pp. 136–42). Bloomington, IL: Public School Publishing.

Original papers in relation to a course of liberal education. (1829). American Journal of Science and Arts, 15, 297–351.

O'Shea, M. V. (1927). *A State Education System at Work. Report of an Investigation of the Intellectual Status and Educational Progress of Pupils in the Elementary and High Schools and Freshmen in the Colleges, Public and Private, of Mississippi, together with Recommendations Relating to the Modifications of Educational Procedure in the State.* Washington (?), DC: The Bernard B. Jones Fund.

Page, C. S. (1912). Federal aid for vocational education from the standpoint of a United States Senator. In *Bulletin No. 16 of the National Society for the Promotion of Industrial Education* (pp. 116–21). Peoria, IL: Manual Arts Press.

Peabody, F. G. (1918). *Education for Life: The Story of Hampton Institute, Told in Connection with the Fiftieth Anniversary of the Foundation of the School.* Garden City, NY: Doubleday, Page.

Progressive Education Association, Commission on the Relation of School and College. (1942–1943). *Adventure in American Education* (vols 1–5). New York: Harper & Brothers.

Redefer, F. L. (1949). Resolutions, reactions and reminiscences. *Progressive Education*, 26, 187–91.

Report on industrial education. (1905). *Proceedings of the Tenth Annual Convention of the National Association of Manufacturers*, 141–51.

Resolutions regarding technical education. (1897). *Proceedings of the Second Annual Convention of the National Association of Manufacturers*, 92–3.

Rice, J. M. (1893a). *The Public School System of the United States.* New York: Century.

Rice, J. M. (1893b). The public schools of Chicago and St Paul. *The Forum*, 15, 200–15.

Rice, J. M. (1912). *Scientific Management in Education.* New York: Hinds, Noble & Elredge.

Rice, T. D. (1938). A high school core program. *Curriculum Journal*, 9, 201–3.

Rickover, H. G. (1959). *Education and Freedom.* New York: E. P. Dutton.

Ringel, P. J. (1980). The introduction and development of manual training and industrial education in the public schools of Fitchburg, Massachusetts, 1893–1928. Unpublished doctoral dissertation. Columbia University, Teachers College, New York.

Robins, R. (1910). Industrial education for women. In *Bulletin No. 10 of the National Society for the Promotion of Industrial*

Education (pp. 77–81). New York: The Society.

Roosevelt, T. (1907). [Letter to Henry S. Pritchett.] In *Bulletin No. 3 of the National Society for the Promotion of Industrial Education* (pp. 6–9). New York: The Society.

Ross, D. (1972). *G. Stanley Hall: The Psychologist as Prophet*. Chicago: University of Chicago Press.

Ross, E. A. (1901). *Social Control: A Survey of the Foundations of Order*. New York: Macmillan.

Rugg, H. O. (1916). *The Experimental Determination of Mental Discipline in School Studies*. Baltimore: Warwick & York.

Rugg, H. O. (1921a). How shall we reconstruct the social studies curriculum? An open letter to Professor Henry Johnson commenting on committee procedure as illustrated by the report of the joint committee on history and education for citizenship. *Historical Outlook*, 12, 184–9.

Rugg, H. O. (1921b). Needed changes in the committee procedure of reconstructing the social studies. *Elementary School Journal*, 21, 688–702.

Rugg, H. O. (1925). *A Primer of Graphics and Statistics for Teachers*. Boston: Houghton Mifflin.

Rugg, H, O. (1929–1932). *Man and his Changing Society. The Rugg Social Science Series of the Elementary School Course* (vols 1–6). Boston: Ginn.

Rugg, H. O. (1931). *An Introduction to Problems of American Culture*. Boston: Ginn.

Rugg, H. O. (1932). Social reconstruction through education. *Progressive Education*, 9(8), 11–18.

Rugg, H. O. (1938). *Our Country and Our People: An Introduction to American Civilization*. Boston: Ginn.

Rugg, H. P. (1941). *That Men May Understand: An American in the Long Armistice*. New York: Doubleday, Doran.

Rugg, H. O. (1947). *Foundations for American Education*. Yonkers-on-Hudson, NY: World Book.

Rugg, H. O. and Shumaker, A. (1928). *The Child-Centred School: An Appraisal of the New Education*. Yonkers-on-Hudson, NY: World Book.

Ryan, H. H. (1933). The teaching and learning situation in junior high-school classrooms. *Bulletin of the Department of Secondary-School Principals*, 17(45), 139–47.

Ryan, H. H. (1935). Experimental college entrance units: A committee report. I. Introductory statement. *North Central Associa-*

tion Quarterly, 9, 345–50.

Ryan, H. H. (1937). Some principles behind the core-curriculum. *California Journal of Secondary Education*, 12, 14–16.

Sanford, C. W., Hand, H. C. and Spalding, W. B. (eds). (1951). *The Schools and National Security: Recommendations for Elementary and Secondary Schools*. Springfield, IL: Department of Public Instruction.

Saunders, F. H. and Hall, G. S. (1900). Pity. *American Journal of Psychology*, 534–91.

Schneider, H. G. (1893). Dr. Rice and American public schools. *Education*, 13, 354–7.

Scrapbook IX. (1900). Unpublished material. Columbia University, Teachers College Collection, September 1899–June 1900.

Search, T. C. (1898). [President's annual report.] *Proceedings of the Third Annual Convention of the National Association of Manufacturers*, 3–32.

Sears, J. B. (1925). *The School Survey: A Textbook on the Use of School Surveying in the Administration of Public Schools*. Boston: Houghton Mifflin.

Shaffer, L. F. (1930). *Children's Interpretations of Cartoons: A Study of the Nature and Development of the Ability to Interpret Symbolic Drawings*. New York: Columbia University, Teachers College.

Shaw, A. (1900, June). "Learning by doing" at Hampton. *American Monthly Review of Reviews*, 417–32.

Sister Mary Janet, SC. (1952). The Catholic schools and life adjustment education. *Bulletin of the National Catholic Education Association*, 49(1), 341–5.

Sivertson, S. C. (1972). Community civics: Education for social efficiency. Unpublished doctoral dissertation, University of Wisconsin, Madison.

Sizer, T. R. (ed.). (1964). *The Age of the Academies*. New York: Columbia University, Teachers College, Bureau of Publications.

Small, A. W. (1896). Demands of sociology upon pedagogy. *Journal of Proceedings and Addresses of the Thirty-Fifth Annual Meeting of the National Education Association*, 174–84.

Smith, B. O. (1942). The war and the educational program. *Curriculum Journal*, 13, 113–16.

Smith, M. B. (1949). *And Madly Teach: A Layman Looks at Public School Education*. Chicago: Henry Regnery.

Smith, E. R. and Tyler, R. W. (1942). *Appraising and Recording*

Student Progress. New York: Harper & Brothers.

Snedden, D. (1912). Report of Committee on National Legislation. In *Bulletin No. 15 of the National Society for the Promotion of Industrial Education* (pp. 126–34). New York: The Society.

Snedden, D. (1915). Vocational education. *New Republic*, 3, 40–2.

Snedden, D. (1916). The "project" as teaching unit. *School and Society*, 4, 419–23.

Snedden, D. (1919). Cardinal principles of secondary education. *School and Society*, 9, 517–27.

Snedden, D. (1921). *Sociological Determination of Objectives in Education*. Philadelphia: J. B. Lippincott.

Snedden, D. (1923). "Case group" methods of determining flexibility of general curricula in high schools. *School and Society*, 17, 287–92.

Snedden, D. (1924). Junior high school offerings. *School and Society*, 20, 740–4.

Snedden, D. (1925). Planning curriculum research. *School and Society*, 22, 259–65, 287–93, 319–28.

Snedden, D. (1935, April 3–6). Social reconstruction: A challenge to the secondary school. *Pennsylvania Schoolmen's Week*, 48–54.

Spring, E. (1936, March 25–28). An adventure in Latin teaching. *Pennsylvania Schoolmen's Week*, 503–7.

Stevenson, J. A. (1921). *The Project Method of Teaching*. New York: Macmillan.

Stimson, R. W. (1914). *The Massachusetts Home-Project Plan of Vocational Agricultural Education*. Washington, DC: US Government Printing Office.

Stockton, J. L. (1920). *Project Work in Education*. Boston: Houghton Mifflin.

Taylor, F. W. (1895). A piece-rate system, being a step toward partial solution of the labor problem. *Transactions of the American Society of Mechanical Engineers*, 16, 856–903.

Taylor, F. W. (1903). Shop management. *Transactions of the American Society of Mechanical Engineers*, 24, 1337–1480.

Taylor, F. W. (1911). *The Principles of Scientific Management*. New York: Harper & Brothers.

Taylor's testimony before the Special House Committee. (1912). In F. W. Taylor, *Scientific Management*. New York: Harper & Row, 1947.

Thirty Schools Tell Their Story. (1943). New York: Harper & Brothers.

Thorndike, E. L. (1901). *Notes on Child Study*. New York: Macmillan.

Thorndike, E. L. (1906, October). The opportunity of the high schools. *The Bookman*, 180–4.

Thorndike, E. L. (1913). *Educational Psychology, Vol. 2. The Psychology of Learning*. New York: Columbia University, Teachers College.

Thorndike, E. L. (1921). *The Teacher's Word Book*. New York: Columbia University, Teachers College.

Thorndike, E. L. (1924). Mental discipline in high school studies. *Journal of Educational Psychology*, 15, 1–22, 83–98.

Thorndike, E. L. and Woodworth, R. S. (1901). The influence of improvement in one mental function upon the efficiency of other functions. *Psychological Review*, 8, 247–61, 384–95, 553–64.

Todd, H. M. (1913, April). Why the children work: the children's answer. *McClure's Magazine*, 68–79.

Tonne, H. A. (1941). Is essentialism synonymous with traditionalism? *School and Society*, 53, 311–12.

Townsend, A. M., OP (1948). Implications contained in the life adjustment program concerning the tools of learning. *Bulletin of the National Catholic Educational Association*, 45(1), 363–75.

Troen, S. K. (1976). The discovery of the adolescent by American educational reformers, 1900–1920: An economic perspective. In L. Stone (ed.), *Schooling and Society: Studies in the History of Education* (pp. 239–51). Baltimore: Johns Hopkins University Press.

Turbayne, C. M. (1962). *The Myth of Metaphor*. New Haven: Yale University Press.

Tyack, D. B. (1974). *The One Best System: A History of American Urban Education*. Cambridge, MA: Harvard University Press.

Tyler, R. W. (1930). Evaluating the importance of teachers' activities. *Educational Administration and Supervision*, 16, 287–92.

Tyler, R. W. (1931). More valid measurements of college work. *Journal of the National Education Association*, 20, 327–8.

US Office of Education. (1945). *Vocational Education in the Years Ahead: A Report of a Committee to Study Postwar Problems in Vocational Education*. Washington, DC: US Government Printing Office.

US Office of Education. (1948). *Life Adjustment Education for Every Youth*. Washington, DC: US Government Printing Office.

US Office of Education. (1951). *Vitalizing Secondary Education:*

Education for Life Adjustment. Washington, DC: US Government Printing Office.

University Primary School. (1896). Unpublished material. Columbia University, Teachers College Collection, March 6, 1896.

Van Liew, C. C. (1895). The educational theory of the culture epochs viewed historically and critically. In *The First Year Book of the National Herbart Society for the Scientific Study of Teaching* (pp. 70–121). Bloomington, IL: The Society.

Virginia State Board of Education. (1934). *Tentative Course of Study for Virginia Elementary Schools, Grades I–VII*. Richmond, VA: Division of purchase and printing.

Ward, L. F. (1883). *Dynamic Sociology, or Applied Social Science as Based upon Statistical Sociology and the Less Complex Sciences*, Vol. 2. New York: D. Appleton.

Ward, L. F. (1893). *The Psychic Factors of Civilization*. Boston: Ginn.

Washburne, C. W. (1924). Merits of the individual plan of instruction. *School Life*, 9, 179.

Washburne, C. W. (1926). The philosophy of the Winnetka curriculum. In G. M. Whipple (ed.), *The Foundations and Technique of Curriculum-Construction, Part I, Curriculum-Making: Past and Present. The Twenty-Sixth Yearbook of the National Society for the Study of Education* (pp. 219–28). Bloomington, IL: Public School Publishing.

Washburne, C. W. (1928). The limitations of the project method. In National Education Association, *Official Report of the Department of Superintendence, February 26 to March 1, 1928* (pp. 187–8). Washington, DC: The Department.

Washington, B. T. (ed.). (1905). *Tuskegee and Its People: Their Ideals and Achievements*. New York: D. Appleton.

Wells, M. E. (1921). *A Project Curriculum, Dealing with the Project as a Means of Organizing the Curriculum of the Elementary School*. Philadelphia: J. B. Lippincott.

Wesley, E. B. (1957). *NEA, the First Hundred Years: The Building of the Teaching Profession*. New York: Harper.

Whipple, G. M. (ed.). (1926a). *The Foundations and Technique of Curriculum-Construction, Part I. Curriculum-Making: Past and Present. The Twenty-Sixth Yearbook of the National Society for the Study of Education*. Bloomington, IL: Public School Publishing.

Whipple, G. M. (ed.). (1926b). *The Foundations and Technique of*

Curriculum-Construction, Part II. The Foundations of Curriculum-Making. The Twenty-Sixth Yearbook of the National Society for the Study of Education, Bloomington, IL: Public School Publishing.

Whipple, G. M. (ed.). (1934). *The Activity Movement. The Thirty-Third Yearbook of the National Society for the Study of Education, Part II*. Bloomington, IL: Public School Publishing.

Wiebe, R. H. (1967). *The Search for Order, 1877–1920*. New York: Hill & Wang.

Winters, E. A. (1968). Harold Rugg and education for social reconstruction. Unpublished doctoral dissertation, University of Wisconsin, Madison.

Wolff, C. F. (1740). *Psychologia rationalis: methodo scientifica pertractata . . . cognitionem profutura proponuntur*. Francofurti: Lipsiae.

Woodward, C. M. (1885). Manual training in general education. *Education*, 5, 614–26.

Woodward, C. M. (1887). *The Manual Training School, Comprising a Full Statement of its Aims, Methods, and Results, with Figured Drawings of Shop Exercises in Woods and Metals*. Boston: D. C. Heath.

Woodward, C. M. (1890). *Manual Training in Education*. New York: Scribner & Welford.

INDEX

- Curriculum pendulum
- what is role of teachers
  in response to
  curricula shifts?

- 237, 238
  doesn't democracy
  and intelligent
  thoughts apply to
  teachers as
  well as

  Both
  Dewey

  - stability amongst
    change?
    ability to reflect,
    lead, change...